ADVANCE PRAISE FOR

spatializing literacy research and practice

"How do literacy practices turn spaces into places? How do the spaces we make and resist both contain us and also let us slip outside and in-between? This timely book takes the 'spatial turn' in social theory for a spin around our emerging social views of literacy and identity, to unsettle them and us. It projects lines of flight through the lived literacy spaces of schools, neighborhoods, prison cells, and online sites along which researchers are learning as much from the placemakers as about them. This is not just 'spatialized' literacy research, it is challenging and insightful literacy research."

Jay L. Lemke, Professor of Education, University of Michigan

spatializing
literacy research
and practice

new
literacies
q

AND DIGITAL EPISTEMOLOGIES

Colin Lankshear, Michele Knobel,
Chris Bigum, and Michael Peters
General Editors

Vol. 15

PETER LANG
New York • Washington, D.C./Baltimore • Bern
Frankfurt am Main • Berlin • Brussels • Vienna • Oxford

spatializing literacy research and practice

kevin m. leander

and margaret sheehy,

editors

PETER LANG
New York • Washington, D.C./Baltimore • Bern
Frankfurt am Main • Berlin • Brussels • Vienna • Oxford

Library of Congress Cataloging-in-Publication Data

Spatializing literacy research and practice /
edited by Kevin M. Leander, Margaret Sheehy.
p. cm. — (New literacies and digital epistemologies; v. 15)
Includes bibliographical references and index.
1. Literacy—Social aspects—United States.
2. Spatial behavior—United States. 3. Human geography—United States.
4. Postmodernism and education—United States.
I. Leander, Kevin M. II. Sheehy, Margaret. III. Series.
LC151.S67 302.2'244—dc22 2003016261
ISBN 0-8204-6749-9
ISSN 1523-9543

Bibliographic information published by **Die Deutsche Bibliothek**.
Die Deutsche Bibliothek lists this publication in the "Deutsche
Nationalbibliografie"; detailed bibliographic data is available
on the Internet at http://dnb.ddb.de/.

Cover design by Joni Holst
Cover art, *Silos at Indiana*, by Anderson Kenny

The paper in this book meets the guidelines for permanence and durability
of the Committee on Production Guidelines for Book Longevity
of the Council of Library Resources.

© 2004 Peter Lang Publishing, Inc., New York
275 Seventh Avenue, 28th Floor, New York, NY 10001
www.peterlangusa.com

Printed in the United States of America

This book is dedicated to people who continue to create
new spaces for thinking, relating, and learning—to the people of everyday life
who inspire imagination and hope.

CONTENTS

PREFACE

Edward W. Soja

In the last decade of the twentieth century, attention to the spatial aspects of human life and social relations spread in unprecedented ways into nearly every academic discourse. Disciplines as varied as art, archeology, anthropology, and accounting began not only to accept the geographer's assertion that "space matters" but also to discover that exploring their subject matter from a critical spatial perspective often opened up significant new empirical insights and challenged long-established frameworks of disciplinary theory and practice. This transdisciplinary *spatial turn* as it has affected the specific fields of education and critical pedagogy is the formative context and stimulus for this innovative collection of essays.

On the surface, each chapter is an experimental exercise aimed at adding a significant spatial dimension to literacy research and practice. But there is much more happening on these pages than addition. In the words and worlds of its authors, there begins to emerge a more transformative and edgy retheorization that goes well beyond what might be called a spatialization by "adjacency," by which I mean the now-fashionable attachment of geographical facts and spatial metaphors to conventional forms of analysis and interpretation. In spatializing literacies, as with the spatial turn in other fields, traditional approaches and taken-for-granted ideas are opened to new forms of critical rethinking. The editors aptly describe the results of their spatializing as "unsettling," and while not all its contributors are equally aware of the disruptive effects of *putting space first* as a critical interpretive perspective, there is a serendipitous resonance running through the chapters, a string of insightful moments of realizing that foregrounding a critical spatial perspective, rather than merely adding it on, can ignite a radical reconfiguration of literacy studies and education theory.

The unsettling effects of such spatial heuristics arise from several sources, the most fundamental being the adoption of a dynamic and processual conceptualization of space and human spatiality to match the similar approach the authors take to literacy and learning. In every essay, implicitly or explicitly, space and the more concretely defined spatiality of human life are seen not just as built forms or materialized and mappable geographies, but also as active and formative processes developing over time—what Henri Lefebvre, perhaps the leading spatial theorist and philosopher of the twentieth century and a presence in nearly all the essays, defined as the (social) production of (social) space. Seen through this dynamic spatial perspective, all the spaces and places in which we live, from the home and the schoolroom to the city and the global economy, are socially constructed; and as real and imagined geographies they shape our lives in various ways, at times enabling and enhancing, at other times constraining and oppressing. This recognition alone opens up new ways of looking at literacy and learning, building on the interplay of spatial and literary practices as social constructs, real and imagined forms, and dynamic processes.

The opportunities and insights that arise from spatializing literacy research and practice are expanded by another related realization. If our spaces and places, our human geographies, are socially constructed, it logically follows that they are not immutable or naturally given. This means that they can be socially changed, made into something better than they were through collective action. It is precisely this possibility of meaningful spatial transformation that gives to the production of space a significant practical and political dimension. Every essay in this book attempts to explore these generative and transformative possibilities not just by adopting a spatial language and terminology, or simply displaying an awareness of the new spatial theory literature, but by taking a particular interpretive stance, one that consciously and intentionally prioritizes a critical spatial perspective in understanding literacy theory and practice.

Something remarkable happens when literacies and spatialities are conjoined in a process of mutual construction, a dialectic if you will. For literacy scholars and educators, the traditional confines of the classroom explode with new possibilities of interpretation, as this preeminent learning space is opened up to a wider, real and imagined world of ethnic, gender, and class consciousness, conflicting identity formations, creative cultural hybridities, new political positionings, an extensive microcosm of everyday life at multiple geographical scales, from the local to the global. In her expanded reading, Elizabeth Hirst (chapter 3) traces student identity formation in an Indonesian second-language classroom using Bakhtin's spatiotemporal notion of the chronotope. Margaret Sheehy (chapter 5) decodes a seventh-grade classroom via thick description and Lefebvre's trialectics of perceived, conceived, and lived spaces. Kevin Leander (chapter 6) also uses Lefebvre's work to investigate identity formation in school as a geohistorical process of positioning.

When seen as a *heterotopia* or as fully *lived space*, to use the evocative concepts provided by Michel Foucault and Henri Lefebvre, the classroom becomes an encapsulation of everything and everywhere, a kind of hieroglyphic site that opens up a potentially endless realm of insightful reading and learning. At the same time as the heterotopological classroom in itself becomes an expanded world of learning and literacy practice, the roles also become reversed, as every space and place in the world becomes readable or interpretable as a classroom. This provides a rather special pathway for literacy scholars to contribute their particular skills to interpreting the spatiality of human life. Moving beyond the conventional classroom, Elizabeth Birr Moje (chapter 2) uses the city and the suburban shopping mall to explore the out-of-school literacy spaces of Latina/o youth. Anita Wilson (chapter 4) does time in prison to show the insides/outsides of carceral literacy spaces. Margaret Hagood (chapter 7) presents a "rhizomatic cartography" of adolescent literacy, drawing on Deleuze and Guattari, while George Kamberelis (chapter 8) continues the rhizomatic exploration, focusing in on the literacy space of a postcolonial, feminist, Asian-American Internet site.

What unites this diversity of approaches is an open-minded attempt to explore the spatiality of literacy and learning by starting with a decidedly spatial perspective, by putting space first as I have described it earlier. This interpretive privileging of a spatial perspective may be the most significant product of the spatial turn, as I see it, but it is an approach that remains highly controversial and not widely practiced. To understand why this is so requires some further comments on the origins and development of the spatial turn itself. In what follows, I draw on the particular version of this geohistory of spatial thought that I have discussed in *Postmodern Geographies* (1989), *Thirdspace* (1996), and *Postmetropolis* (2000).

In many ways, the spatial turn paralleled—and was made necessary by—a similar transdisciplinary diffusion that affected intellectual thought in the late nineteenth century. During this period and for the next hundred years various modes of *historical thinking* and analysis became central to the formation and development of the social sciences and their radical alternative, scientific socialism or Marxism. This locked together the study of history and society, the historical and sociological imaginations, and this history-society dynamic or dialectic entered the mainstreams of nearly every disciplinary tradition. The discipline of history was accepted as part of both the social sciences and the humanities, and historians were welcomed as vital members of all fields, including the physical and biological sciences. At the same time, Western Marxism, stripped of alternative forms of socialist thought such as the geographically rich tradition of anarchism, riveted its attention on a materialist interpretation of history, on primordially historical materialism.

Throughout nearly all of the twentieth century, this epistemological and intellectual privileging of history became almost taken for granted. It was assumed that everything that exists or ever has existed has a significant historical dimension and that whatever happens or has happened can be best understood, first of all, through a critical historical perspective. History in this sense was process, cause, explanation, the groundwork for societal development, change, transformation, and liberation. What about human geography, the spatial dimension? For the most part, it too was taken for granted, but mainly as an external stage or container-cum-environment for the making of history and the historical development of society. Geography complicated history, to be sure, and needed to be addressed to help understand societal development, but history and society were driven by social processes, by social consciousness and social will, and these social forces worked best when freed from external or environmental constraints. Moreover, it was thought that these social forces could, or perhaps should, be theorized as aspatial, unconstrained by their specific location and context.

There were many individual scholars who attempted to break through this privileging of the historical and social to explore a more causal, explanatory, and potentially transformative critical spatial perspective, but very few addressed this privileging directly or questioned its intellectual and theoretical hegemony. The first to do so explicitly and with lasting impact was probably Michel Foucault. In an observation that has been cited repeatedly over the past ten years, Foucault (1980, *Power/knowledge: Selected interviews and other writings*, 1972–77, p. 70) asked the key question of why and how time and space, and hence historicality and spatiality, had come to be seen so differently in Western thought. Space, he noted, tended to be treated as "the dead, the fixed, the immobile, the undialectical," as an extrasocial background or decidedly physical or natural environment. In contrast, time was "richness, fecundity, life, dialectic," the primary carrier of societal development and change.

Foucault's question implied that something happened in the late nineteenth century that distorted the inherent ontological and epistemological equivalence of space and time, attributing dynamic force to time and history while deadening the social forces arising from space and geography. Also implied was that there was no inherent logic to this imbalancing act. Although he would continue to write about the "great obsession" with history in the nineteenth century and would argue that we have, in the late twentieth century, moved beyond its distortions to enter an "epoch of space," few would follow up on his ideas or accept his spatial critique of the privileging of time and history. Even among Foucaultian scholars, the assertive triad of space, knowledge, and power often lost its spatiality, being reduced to the binary knowledge-power alone. That space could be so central was almost inconceivable.

It was primarily with the writings of Henri Lefebvre that there developed an elaborated critical spatial perspective that could convince scholars of the equivalent importance of the historical and geographical imaginations, or, as I would argue in *Thirdspace* (1996), of spatiality, historicality, and sociality. Without this expansive critical spatial perspective, most forcefully developed in Lefebvre's *The Production of Space*, published in French in 1974 and in English translation in 1991, there were very few scholars who would be willing and able to open up their critical historico-social perspective to the equivalent powers of critical spatial thinking and the possibility that society and spatiality, history and geography, were mutually constructed, with no a priori privileging whatsoever.

Tracing the origins of the reassertion of a critical spatial perspective in social theory and philosophy, and hence the spatial turn, thus takes us back to the urban crises of the 1960s, and especially to Paris just before and after the uprising in May 1968. Looking back from the present, particular importance can be given, first, to a lecture prepared by Foucault in 1967 and published only after his death in 1986 as "Of Other Spaces" (*Des Espaces Autres*); and then to the series of major books published by Lefebvre between 1968 (*Le Droit à la Ville*) and 1974 (*La Production de l'Espace*). Although there were many others writing about space and, in particular, urban spatiality, only Foucault and Lefebvre, in remarkably similar ways, explicitly criticized all prevailing forms of spatial thinking and analysis, both brilliant (as in Bachelard) and banal, and insisted on expanding the scope of the geographical imagination in radically new ways, encapsuled in Foucault's heterotopology (literally a different mode of interpreting space) and Lefebvre's expansive notion of lived space and his revolutionary reconceptualization of urbanism and the rights to the city.

For two decades, this call for a radically new way of thinking about space had relatively little impact, at least in the Anglophonic academic world, where it was either ignored or misunderstood by most scholars. Spatial thinking in France continued to be enriched by such figures as Deleuze and Guattari, de Certeau, Bourdieu, Derrida, Lyotard, and others, as well as by Lefebvre and Foucault, but their impact on the English-speaking world was significantly blunted or sidetracked. Many simply interpreted the spatial critique as reinforcing traditional modes of spatial thought, unable to see the challenges it represented. Others saw the forceful assertion of a more critically central spatial perspective as challenging and insightful, but excessively deterministic and potentially depoliticizing. This was especially prevalent among Marxist spatial thinkers such as the early David Harvey and Manuel

Castells, who saw Lefebvre's privileging of space and his notion of urban revolution as moving too far away from specifically social relations and the traditions of historical materialism. Particularly unacceptable was the suggestion of putting space first as an interpretive perspective, before the historical and the social, before one's privileged favorites, be it Marxism, feminism, structuralism, discourse analysis, psychoanalysis, hermeneutics, etc.

But the powerful core of the argument would not disappear. There developed vigorous debates among Anglophonic geographers, architects, and urbanists through the 1980s and into the 1990s, drawing on the full panoply of primarily French spatial thinkers. These debates would attract the attention of scholars outside these so-called spatial disciplines—in feminism, cultural studies, film theory, art history, literary criticism, anthropology, postcolonial studies, law, economics, psychology, philosophy, political science, and, of special relevance here, education and critical pedagogy. Around 1995, a certain threshold had been reached. More scholars from a wider variety of disciplinary backgrounds than ever before had become engaged in one form or another with thinking spatially about their fields of interest. In almost every branch of the human sciences, there was some recognition of the growing interest in space, even if the full force of the transformative spatial critiques was not being felt. In many ways, those outside the traditionally spatial disciplines of geography, architecture, and urban studies were less constrained by older frameworks of thought, and hence could be freer in their spatial investigations, pushing the developing spatial turn in potentially innovative new directions, while the spatial disciplines continued to argue vigorously amongst themselves about the dangers and opportunities of the new spatial theory and epistemology.

What has been emerging from this transdisciplinary diffusion is a growing awareness that space is more than an attribute or simple outcome of social processes but is also a causal force with as yet relatively unexplored explanatory power. This brings to life—and gives new meaning to—an assertion made by Henri Lefebvre almost thirty years ago, that all social relations remain abstractions until they are concretized in space. In other words, sociality and spatiality are mutually constitutive, and this socio-spatial dialectic, as I have called it, develops in space and time as intertwined geographies and histories, as geohistory. Putting space first is thus not a rejection of historical and social analysis but a reincorporation of them in a balanced three-sided relation of the social, the historical, and the spatial.

But in this sense, the spatial turn has not yet gone far enough, for the triad still remains biased toward the historical and the sociological imaginations. Spatializing all fields of knowledge thus obtains a special, if temporary, privileging for contemporary scholarship. Such privileging is also backed by extraordinary promise, for if the knowledge accumulated in every field is weakest and least understood in its spatial dimensions, then the spatializing project has the potential for uncovering radically new and different ways of looking at the world. Here my prefatory remarks come full circle to invite you to read *Spatializing Literacy Research and Practice* as an enthusiastic and revealing voyage of exploration.

ACKNOWLEDGMENTS

We are thankful to a number of people for the various types of kindness and smartness they have given to this project. First, our heartfelt thanks to Barb Leander and Ralph Johnson for putting up with all the phone calls and for their support in too many ways to count. Colin Lankshear and Michele Knobel have guided us in the editing process and offered appreciated wisdom and humor along the way. We are thankful for the scholarship and response of a group of scholars that have inspired and critically challenged us in our pursuits of spatial theory, including Donna Alvermann, Chip Bruce, Kris Gutiérrez, Jay Lemke, Alan and Carmen Luke, Jan Nespor, and Edward Soja. Of course, we are also thankful for the work and inspiration of all the authors represented in this collection as well as others not represented here who are also working with spatial theory. Finally, we are especially grateful to Carrie Hong, for her careful and diligent text editing work and Nancy Middleton and Sun Hwa Lee for painstaking labor on the index and administrative support.

1

Introduction

Margaret Sheehy and Kevin M. Leander

Educators and researchers of culture are increasingly turning to space to understand and explain socio-cultural practices and processes. Comparative educational theorists are creating cartographic methodologies that visually communicate the distribution of social changes in education discourses (Paulston, 1996). Spatial metaphors such as boundaries (Phelan, Davidson, & Yu, 1993), borders (Anzaldúa, 1987), margins, centers, and peripheries (hooks, 1984; Lave & Wenger, 1991) are similarly visual means of addressing physical experiences and effects of social life. Whereas space was once thought of as empty, available, and waiting to be filled up, recent theorizing about space has brought to light that space is a product and process of socially dynamic relations. Space is not static—as in metaphorical images of borders, centers, and margins—it is dynamically relational. Space, as a noun, must be reconceived as an active, relational verb, which is our intent in invoking "spatializing" in the title of this collection. As Foucault wrote,

> We do not live in a kind of void, inside of which we could place individuals, and things. We do not live inside a void that could be colored over with diverse shades of light, we live inside a set of relations that delineates sites which are irreducible to one another and absolutely not superimposable on one another. (quoted in Soja, 1989, p. 17)

The chapters in this book have been compiled in order to begin, within literacy studies, theorizing space as a social product and process. The chapters draw out, through investigations of literacy practices, what space is made of, how space constructs its makers, and how political formations capable of discomfiting any singular ideology or social order are created as space is made.

The Near and the Far

Rather than introduce the book as one that exemplifies space as "settled and settling," we feel it is more appropriate to introduce the chapters in the book as exemplars of "unsettling" research. Indeed, the purpose of spatial analysis is not to reduce space to a stability, but to show that it is always changing and to question, "how, when and into what" (Harvey, 1996, p. 55). Because change necessarily involves power, spatial research requires that the researcher make choices about how to examine and explain power. Like other perspectives on social life (e.g., anthropological, sociological, psychological, economic), spatial research confronts the problem of how to explain political struggle in people's daily lives. Does one explain literacy life as that which can be immediately observed? Or would a reading of literacy life be more encompassing of complexities if one moved away from an observable situation and considered how that life was produced outside what is visible? In either case, what do people make of their place and stake in a struggle?

Feminists and critical race theorists have leveled a critique against studies that move away from observable social life, because of the risk of privileging theory over people's idiosyncratic means of engaging in their lives. Arguing that cultural studies requires both close description as well as abstracted views of what is seen, Soja relies upon Lefebvre (1991) to examine issues of "the near and the far order" (Soja, 1996, p. 312). Lefebvre worried over "macro" (far) analyses because of the tendency to erase contradictions in social life in favor of an orderly master narrative. According to Lefebvre, everyday life is less orderly than appearances may convey, and it engages politics. What is visible to a researcher is shot through with political struggle. Soja (1996) contends,

> We must realize that both views from above [far] and from below [near] can be restrictive and revealing, deceptive and determinitive, indulgent and insightful, necessary but wholly insufficient.... To set them in antagonistic opposition only constrains critical interpretation and severely limits the possibilities for strategic intervention and radical spatial praxis. (p. 314)

So, what does strategic intervention literacy research look like? We have examples in this volume, examples that index a rich variety of complexity in a field only beginning to reckon with space. In each case, explanation of data is to some degree restrictive and revealing, deceptive and determinitive, indulgent and insightful.

Words and the World

Because discursive practices are located in space, and because discursive practices actively produce space, this volume purposes to disrupt folk notions of how literacies are "situated." Implicitly and explicitly, these studies engage a critique of situation as "material place." Considering classrooms, prison cells, bedrooms, and suburban malls as readily apparent material settings, within which some focal literacy practice happens, drops away an entire series of interpretations regarding how material settings come to be realized as social spaces. Authors in this volume work to recover the interpretive loss experienced when a context of literacy practice is considered to be background to the situated practices happening "within" it. Here, context is brought to the fore as an ongoing process and practice deeply tied up with the word. When we use words, we are always situating ourselves; when we read contexts, we are always reading words and discursive relations extending into other space-times. Classrooms are realized not only with brick and mortar, but also with institutional documents, student sketches, curriculum plans, and the ways in which persons and the state are co-constructed in teacher discourse, among others. Similarly, prison cells are constructed in the mental representations of prisoners and the ways in which these representations circulate in spoken jokes and printed correspondence.

Thus, these studies complicate how context, in literacy research, has been over-determined in its meaning by a seemingly natural interpretation of material setting or place. Space has been over-materialized. These studies also engage the opposite critique: that literacy research, in its focus upon discursive practices, dispenses with the material world through a Cartesian separation of mind or word from matter. While the immediate material tools of literacy (e.g., pencils, computer screens, document designs) have received some research attention, little work has been done on the circulation of paper in classrooms and media practices, on the boundaries for literacy shaped by walls, desks, and neighborhoods, and on the ways in which material participants in the world—such as the bodies—become sites for the writing of myriad texts. In sum, literacy spaces have been produced as metaphors without material substance. Our metaphorical spatial lexis matters, and tracing how it matters inevitably leads us to "matter" in the world, to the material stuff of our home lives and cityscapes, which absorbs us and which we continually interpret through the word.

Studies in this collection push us beyond the thin perspectives offered by either words or the world and are variously engaged in interpreting spatializing processes across multiple material and semiotic means. These studies draw upon various theoretical and interpretive means to move beyond dualisms of objectivism-idealism and subjectivism-idealism in theorizing the production of space. One body of theory that some of the work draws upon, directly or indirectly, is Lefebvre's (1991) trialectic of perceived, conceived, and lived space. Perceived space, produced in social practices, is associated with daily routine. An excessive interpretive focus upon perceived space—mapping space from readily visible practices alone—is termed the "illusion of opaqueness" (Lefebvre, 1991) or the "realistic illusion" (Soja, 1989). Conceived space (also called representations of space) is planned space—much like a science curriculum (see chapter 5) or a school within a school (see chapter 6). Conceived space is dominated by ideology. In this space, representations and everyday practice seem true, right, and natural. To avoid the illusion of opaqueness, or its contrary, the "illusion of transparency" (e.g., space as symbolic mental construct alone), Lefebvre formulates "lived space" in trialectical relation to perceived and conceived space. Lived space is passively experienced but is space that imagination seeks to change. Representations of conceived space are experienced—and changed—in lived space. Social practice is always dominated by particular representations that seem "natural," but people's bodily experiences of social life differ, and contradictions to dominant, conceived space enable the impossibility of the production of a fixed, stable space.

In the following, we continue our consideration of broad issues and tensions in the collection by shifting to a thematic synopsis of the contributing authors' chapters. Several themes emerge across these studies, and we feel it will be helpful to the reader if we draw them out as a means of introducing both the chapters and some of the spatial issues the chapters address. This thematic overview, however, should not be seen as encapsulating all the issues of space. It scratches the surface.

Scratching Surfaces: Themes of Space

Those picking up this collection as a guidebook to spatial literacy research will not find a formula. Instead, we have research utilizing a number of social theories and frameworks for understanding and explaining literacy practice as spatial practice. The spatial lens in this book is wide. It's wide enough to reveal people's agency in their daily lives as well as the docility that daily life can enact, the play between identity and place and between identity and subjectivity, tensions between mass structures and loosely organized factions, and tensions between real and imagined literacy life. While the chapters traverse a broad thematic terrain, we consider in the following how literacy is spatialized by the construct of hybridity, by researching and living out identities, and by complicating the real.

Hybridity

The hybridity of social space through literacy practice is a central argument of two chapters: Wilson's "Four Days and a Breakfast" and Hirst's "Diverse Social Contexts of a Second-Language Classroom and the Construction of Identity." Wilson's chapter examines literacies in prisons, whereas Hirst examines literacies practiced in a second-language (Indonesian) classroom. The notion of hybridity is necessary for these works and is "the radical thirding," or the Other view so stressed by Soja (1996). Yet, the researchers accomplish this view in different ways. Wilson's hybridity is a third space materiality—a space of practice made from both institutional and individuals' practices and artifacts. Hirst's hybrid space is demonstrated discursively.

In "Four Days and a Breakfast," Wilson outlines "outside" and "inside" prison spaces that construct prison life, then situates third-space literacies within that framing. Outside spaces and outside literacies reflect official spaces of welfare, justice, and job-seeking along with their attendant bureaucratic texts—letters, claims, and applications, to name a few. In the outside public world, prisoners tended not to engage in school-type literacy of reading, but inside prison, the prisoners negotiate bureaucratic texts and school-type literacy, constructing hybrid third spaces.

Inside spaces and inside literacies reflect incarcerated space. Even though prison spaces are intended to be controlled spaces, the prisoners re-appropriated them to reflect rules of the streets. Literacies in inside space might include reading a newspaper or book, literacies which might be characterized as outside prison life. Wilson draws on Bhabha's (1994) third space to theorize the hybridity between outside and inside prison literacies and provides a number of examples of these hybridized literacies. In one example of hybidity, a prisoner reappropriated an institutional form, and as it circulated, a third space for prisoner-officials relations was also created. Through reappropriation of an institutional literacy practice, outside and inside prison cultures merged and prison space was recolonized.

Wilson also demonstrates the materiality of time. Prisoners' lives occur in numbers of time frames and they measure their days by them, hence the title of Wilson's chapter, "Four Days and a Breakfast." Everyday life in the prison was regulated by timetables, and certain activities occurred at certain times; yet, Wilson shows that prisoners translated judicial and incarcerative time into manageable chunks. During dead time, when prisoners were alone in their cells, time was appropriated for personal use when some prisoners used literacy to maintain ties to the outside world. Wilson's research is a strategic intervention. She seeks contradictions and finds how prisoners reconstituted prison life in their own terms.

Hirst's hybridity is demonstrated through her use of Bakhtin's chronotope. The chronotope (literally, time-space) is a construct developed by Bakhtin (1981) to analyze how authors create time-spaces in their narratives, and how these time-spaces index different ideological possibilities for characters and readers. The chronotopes Hirst reveals in a Language Other Than English (LOTE) classroom are discursive and ideological classroom activities that interface social identities and global relations. This interface of chronotopes—the LOTE classroom—is "an arena of conflict," where student and teacher relationships are shaped not only by practices in the LOTE classroom but by the relations of other school personnel.

Hirst demonstrates how space and time are made through the clashing of chronotopes. Time management and nationalism chronotopes, for instance, are discursive forces that influence practice. LOTE education is conceived as efficient and has been calculated: 420 hours are needed for students to acquire linguistic competency. The LOTE teachers' 420 hours are squeezed by traditional courses and at least one teacher of such a course lets the LOTE teacher know that his work is marginal work. Her interactions with the LOTE teacher are about time, the time his marginal work is taking from her central work. The LOTE classroom always operates in relation to other school subjects and is also situated within the politics of Australian nationalism. The nationalist chronotope is tied to the market. In an effort to reduce racial tensions between Australia and Asia, so as to facilitate the flow of capital, the Indonesian language was given a place in Australian curricula.

Hirst argues that second-language learning is a process of appropriating the cultural resources and voices of a range of discursive practices. It is in this sense that her use of chronotopes utilizes hybridity; discursive practices construct different spaces and times as chronotopes. In addition to nationalist and time-management chronotopes, Hirst reveals other classroom chronotopes such as "meetings and partings." The position of LOTE in the school curriculum is marginal, and the LOTE teacher is seen by his students, also, as Other. Traditional subjects are privileged: the teachers of these courses have their own classrooms. It is the LOTE teacher who travels, the LOTE teacher whose "meetings and partings" with his students seem to produce an "other space"—a heterotopia. Identities of both students and teachers are constructed in the play of chronotopes, the crossing and clashing of discourses and practices that enable specific possibilities for specific teachers and students. The LOTE classroom is a heterotopia, an other place, constructed in relation to privileged spaces.

Identity

Explaining identity and space construction are central to five authors' goals: Wilson and Hirst (already noted), as well as Moje, Leander, and Hagood. In their chapters, social space enables performance of particular identities; yet, each chapter demonstrates identity-space relations differently.

In "Powerful Spaces," Moje takes the reader around a city, borrowing de Certeau's (1993) method of reading New York City from the street level. For de Certeau, subjects have will and power (Harvey, 1996), and Moje demonstrates such agency in her examination of seven youth in the everyday life spaces they inhabit. She does this by drawing relationships between spaces the youth inhabit and their identity enactments.

Moje examines identity constructions across seven spaces, which she asks us to imagine in concentric relation: national space, city space, community space, neighborhood space, home space, suburban space, and virtual space. From Gee (2000/2001), Moje takes four analytic categories for identity analysis (nature, institutional, discursive, and affinity group) and adds a spatial and temporal category. Then Moje, with her participants, walks and drives the aforementioned spaces frequented by seven of the thirty adolescents in her larger study. In these spaces, and drawing from her interviews, Moje discusses identity. Moje notes that "actual physical arrangements—work together powerfully with institutional, discursive, affinity and nature relations and identities to shape how people use language and literacy in practice." One can see that the youth have resources, in their various lived spaces, from which to choose. Moje illustrates some of them, across the seven spaces, arguing that literate, textual, and technological practices provide resources for the youth's identity constructions. The youth experienced spaces as (1) othering and being othered, (2) novelty and familiarity, (3) danger and comfort, and (4) hybridity and Mexicanness. These themes were evident when, for instance, the youth raised questions in their classroom about teacher lay-offs. One youth, Ramiro, questioned why teachers were being laid off in city schools but not in the suburbs. Moje contends that the youth, as this example illustrates, recognized privileged spaces and themselves in relation to them. Examples of other-othering relations abound in Moje's data: youth construct their racial identities within and against "Arab guys" in their own neighborhood; and as they walk a suburban mall, they feel "othered" as they are scrutinized by passersby.

Moje's argument that space and identity shape one another is made further as she walks through the youth's own neighborhood space. On Virnot Street, the youth engage in different conversations than the ones they'll have over lunch, at their friend's family's restaurant on another, less public street.

The distribution of bodies on Virnot Street is one of excitement, danger, comfort, and familiarity. The youth are at home on Virnot Street. But home is not only what is seen. The familiarity of home is also clearly revealed in virtual space, where the youth seek sites about race, ethnicity, lowriders, and sexuality. For Moje, space matters because it affords so much possibility for racial, ethnic, sexual, and gender identity enactments.

Drawing upon Lefebvre's (1991) trialectic of perceived, conceived, and lived spaces, Leander provides an interpretation of identity positioning that considers how positions are stretched out over space and time. Identities are developed historically (as in narratives of development) but also geographically. This interpretation of positioning is directed at unsettling the identity relations readily evident in a literacy event by reading these relations in relation to diverse space-times. Without reducing spatial processes to historical ones, Leander writes a history of a literacy event. A brief segment of discussion in a U.S. high school American Studies classroom is analyzed as an opening or window through which spatialization processes may be considered. Within this segment, the "sediment" of ongoing spatial histories saturates the words, bodies, texts, practices, and classroom of the participants and their positioning practices.

In order to interpret the spatial histories of positioning, Leander posits that we need to raise new questions that cut across micro- and macro-level analyses. These questions resist the impulse to associate material, perceived space with micro-level analysis and discursive, conceived space with macro-level analysis. Rather, conceptions and perceptions traverse micro- and macro-levels in the lived spaces of the moment as well as in the (lived) spatial histories coordinated and newly produced by the moment. Three key questions organize the analysis of the focal interaction.

First, who gets in the door? This reading of spatial history is focused upon institutional positioning. Interpreting how the focal interaction recruits and organizes particular participants involves tracing how this American Studies classroom participates as part of the Kempton Technological Academy (KTA), a school-within-a-school, that involves the conception of a bounded space for a conceived identity of the "middle-level student." The analysis begins to suggest some of the conflicts and tensions between conceptions of the KTA indexed within the interaction, including how the KTA recruited students across class and race barriers that were typically more bounded in the regular school program.

Secondly, what pedagogy is taking place? Pedagogy is asserted as a form of identity work—a positioning practice. The term "taking place" is used to suggest that the particular curriculum enacted in this instance was part of a larger stream of positionings that were working to establish their place and shape the KTA as a social space. The history of the KTA is interpreted ideologically, and the way in which competing ideologies conflicted within the KTA is also traced through the divisions of meeting (classroom) spaces. As lived spaces, different classrooms came to signify different teachers, types of activities, and associated ideologies.

Third, how are certain social identities enacted and recognized during the course of classroom discussion? Leander interprets the focal interaction in relation to a racial-spatial history of positioning among the group. In particular, he follows how the construction of a "black community" becomes associated, by some white European-American students, with a sense of shrinking space in the KTA. The notion of shrinking space is traced as a discursive construct within the event and beyond it in interview data, and is also articulated with the material shift of the junior class to an alternate classroom space. Thus, the racialization of space within the interaction is read as a historical construct that coordinates diverse processes of spatialization even as it is instantiated in a given moment.

Hagood's construction of identity takes a twist; the twist is strategic, a chiasmic aspect of Deleuze and Guattari's (1987) rhizomatic cartography. Rhizomatics is a methodology based on rhizomes, not rooted trees: one looks for contradictions and discontinuities within social life rather than for a cohesive, rooted logic. Kamberelis (chapter 8) explains that rhizomes are examined as lines of articulation and lines of flight. Lines of articulation demonstrate the logic of organizations, which territorialize. Lines of flight reveal multiplicities, which are more loosely organized to deterritorialize and reterritorialize. Rhizomatics does not whisk away structured territory and replace it with unstructured multiplicities, however. Rather, one examines the construction of territory, according to its logic, but pays particular attention to its lines of flight. In this way, cartography does not merely represent structures, it reinvents them.

In "A Rhizomatic Cartography of Adolescents, Popular Culture, and Constructions of Self," Hagood shows the tension between rhizomes and structures as two youth work out tensions between identity formations. Hagood uses tensions between identity and subjectivity as connected points of her rhizome. The points of tensions include different forces for the girls, Tee and Rosa. For both the girls, Christianity acts as an organized structure of logic. It shapes their identities in ways that seem rooted. Yet, upon closer examination, Hagood reveals the rhizomes of the girls' lives. Hagood suggests that rhizomes enable an agency that the arborescent expectations of Christianity do not.

To demonstrate the complexity of Tee and Rosa's living realities, Hagood uses relational images. The relational image (of a T-shirt or a song, for instance) brings into view a tension within the arborescence and the rhizome. In Christianity, an identity is created for both Tee and Rosa, and expectations of that identity structure the girls' relationships both to Christianity and to their fellow Christian friends and families. Yet, Hagood points out, there are fissures to the structure of Christianity; it is not merely arborescent; the girls bring other interests to the structure, thereby deterritorializing Christianity and reterritorializing it, as a reinvention. They reterritorialize with music, clothing, dance, and other representations.

Christianity acts as a structural category for both Tee and Rosa, but rhizomatics reveals that the girls are not bound by the tree, not rooted in a singular identity. Both girls reterritorialize their Christian identities, using relational images to reinvent both themselves as Christians and Christianity as a category.

Complicating the Real

In Sheehy's and Kamberelis's chapters, attention is paid to the real. Sheehy holds up a discourse pattern common to middle and high schools in order to question why this pattern, which was not a positive means of learning in the seventh-grade classroom she researched, gets reproduced, especially in low-income schools. Kamberelis, on the other hand, pays attention to the real in order to demonstrate its instability.

Sheehy's "Between a Thick and a Thin Place" makes use of Lefebvre's (1991) trialectic of perceived, conceived, and lived spaces in a different way than Leander does (chapter 6). Sheehy examined the social processes involved in the production of space in a classroom where a teacher was trying to change daily routines. Sheehy contended that if space produces space, a classroom (literacy practice, planned arrangements, lived space) also produces space. The trialectic can inform literacy research and practice, which has never fully explained why certain schools consistently fail their youth.

Sheehy first describes the typical daily literacy routine (the spatial practice) of a seventh-grade classroom. She ties social practice to representation and lived experience, noting that the lived (and often passive) experience of the typical literacy practices of the classroom are soaked in ideology, an ideology that stays afloat via representations, social practice, and people's experience of the practice. Sheehy argues that classroom exchanges of information, mediated by representations such as worksheets, created a boundary around the classroom. The classroom became an instrument of power through the social processes that produced it as a place. While space and place are not coterminous, Sheehy demonstrates a dialectic relationship between space and place. The classroom becomes a decipherable place through the production of space—this space and not that. Sheehy calls the typical classroom practices she observed in her study "a thick place" because the ideas traded there seemed to travel a well-trod path between the teacher and students. The thick place of trade was a narrow channel; the seventh graders experienced the space passively, and the place became alienating. Alienation stifled students. While, in the thick place, other practices contradicted dominant ones, contradictions, at most, interrupted the dominant flow of information; they didn't permanently disrupt dominant practices.

When the seventh graders eventually made a thin place, the thick channel of trade thinned out and ideas were distributed in multiple routes. Literacy practices were not centered on worksheets, and the flow of ideas traded was not predominantly a teacher-controlled conversation. Instead, students chose content from a number of previously visited sources, and they rearticulated these ideas into new relations, such as between them and their school board. As students wrote and talked about their ideas, the flow of information enabled more ideas into and out of the classroom. Whereas, in the thick place, relationships made between teacher, students, and content followed one main channel, in the thin place, relationships made between students, teacher, and content moved out of the classroom, into the youth's neighborhoods, the city, the state, and even across the nation. The thick place classroom was an instrument of power. Its predictability enabled passivity and alienation. The thin place classroom was also an instrument of power. It was empowering, but short-lived. Sheehy argues that the thin place did not reproduce itself for long because such a place was not supported by the political organization of educational space, which is tied up in an ideological arrangement with single disciplinary knowledge/power. Thus, while space was transformed, the spatial saturation of single disciplinary study exerted force on transformed space and de-formed it quickly and without effort once the teachers' line of flight from typical curriculum ended.

In "The Rhizome and the Pack," Kamberelis demonstrates the transformative effects of two literacy formations: historical African-American slave literacies and a contemporary postcolonial feminist Internet site. Kamberelis argues that formations organized as rhizomes and pack multiplicities are useful to examine because their histories can help us reconceptualize collective affiliation and action.

Accordingly, African-American slave literacies are shown to be historically resistant practices whereby African Americans intervened in reality. Slave literacies involved aural, visual, and print literacies. These and other literacy artifacts contained hidden messages, through double-coding. For instance, whites would hear a song that sounded innocent enough; yet, the songs contained hidden information about how to escape to the North. Kamberelis argues that double-coding allowed subversive communicative activities to be both visible and invisible. These communications were, for African-American slaves, lines of flight. The slaves were tactical in their use of language, appearing to serve the master while actually undermining the master's authority.

Print literacies were also double-coded and were more powerful than oral literacies because of their connection to European-American literacies and ideologies. In the 1800s, Kamberelis explains, European societies tied literacy to reason, and those who were not literate were seen as inferior. When southern states made it illegal for slaves to read and write, hidden passages—in churches and in some masters' households—became the lines of flight for education opportunity for slaves. Churches were viewed by whites as safe places, since religious instruction was occurring; yet, in churches, African Americans deterritorialized oppressive religious instruction and reterritorialized it as a place of resistance toward slavery.

Kamberelis also shows how a postcolonial, feminist, Asian-American Internet site works as a rhizome and a pack. The site resists categories by being, like other Internet sites, seemingly endless. Yet, Kamberelis points out, the site has no misogynist, antigay, or right-to-life links. It is heterogeneous but also includes 18 specific buttons, all pertaining to women's issues, organizations, grants, and academic discussions. The site is a pack, of sorts, because it is a line of flight from typical Asian sites, where porn proliferates, as well as from other feminist and Asian sites. The site intends to decenter rather than territorialize. It is off-putting and enticing at once. While the site's owner, Mimi Nguyen, is out in front of the pack, on the site's home page, her leadership recedes on other links and others step forward. The site links with other sites that have political force, and Kamberelis points out that Internet communication reconfigures space and movement.

While we have presented these chapters thematically, in order to draw out important issues in spatial studies of literacy practices, we undo this logic in the pages that follow and let each chapter stand on its own. The chapters lend their own take on literacy's spatialities that have, generally, been taken for granted. Each chapter asks researchers or teachers of literacy to look more closely at what we presume to be real and consider, also, a view from an Other side. We believe that spatial insertions into literacy research and practice can be transformative, but not generically so. Rather, literacy spaces will be reworked and reinterpreted through the particularities of their production.

References

Anzaldúa, G. (1987). *Borderlands/La Fontera*. San Francisco: Spinsters/Aunt Lute Press.

Bakhtin, M. M. (1981). Forms of time and the chronotope in the novel (C. Emerson & M. Holquist, Trans.). In M. Holquist (Ed.), *The dialogic imagination: Four essays* (pp. 84–258). Austin: University of Texas Press.

Bhabha, H. K. (1994). *The location of culture*. London: Routledge.

de Certeau, M. (1993). Walking in the city. In S. During (Ed.), *The cultural studies reader* (pp. 151–160). London: Routledge.

Deleuze, G., & Guattari, F. (1987). *A thousand plateaus: Capitalism and schizophrenia* (B. Massumi, Trans.). Minneapolis: University of Minnesota Press.

Gee, J. P. (2000/2001). Identity as an analytic lens for research in education. In W. G. Secada (Ed.), *Review of research in education* (Vol. 25, pp. 99–126). Washington, DC: American Educational Research Association.

Harvey, D. (1996). *Justice, nature, and the geography of difference*. Cambridge, MA: Blackwell.

hooks, b. (1984). *Feminist theory: From margin to center*. Boston: South End Press.

Lave, J., & Wenger, E. (1991). *Situated learning: Legitimate peripheral participation*. Cambridge: Cambridge University Press.

Lefebvre, H. (1991). *The production of space*. Cambridge, MA: Blackwell.

Paulston, R. G. (1996). Preface: Four principles for a non-innocent social cartography. In R. G. Paulston (Ed.), *Social cartography: Mapping ways of seeing social and educational change*. New York: Garland.

Phelan, P. K., Davidson, A. A., & Yu, H. C. (1993). Students' multiple worlds: Navigating the borders of family, peer, and school cultures. In P. Phelan & A. L. Davidson, (Eds.), *Renegotiating cultural diversity in American schools* (pp. 52–88). New York: Teachers College Press.

Soja, E. W. (1989). *Postmodern geographies: The reassertion of space in critical social theory*. New York: Verso.

Soja, E. W. (1996). *Thirdspace: Journeys to Los Angeles and other real-and-imagined places*. Cambridge, MA: Blackwell.

2

Powerful Spaces: Tracing the Out-of-School Literacy Spaces of Latino/a Youth

Elizabeth Birr Moje

You should write a book, and you should call your book, *On the Streets of [the City]*...no, *Underneath the Streets of [the City]*. You should write about what we, what the people who live here, think of the city, not the police or the high society, but the people who really live here.

(Ramiro, informal interview, 2003)

What's in a space? For that matter, what *is* a space? Is it constituted by material conditions? Or is a space what it is because of the people who occupy the space? Ramiro, the 14-year-old young man quoted at the beginning of this chapter, suggests that how a space is seen, experienced, and understood depends on the positionality of people relative to the space. Ramiro's words further suggest that he expects different perceptions of a given space depending on people's identities, their cultural backgrounds, and their positioning in society:

When people go to Hale Plaza for the Mexican festival or to Cinco de Mayo, the tourists only come and see the parade or go to the food booths, but they don't see the real meanings underneath it, they don't understand it. (Ramiro, interview, 2003)

In this chapter, I want to take up Ramiro's charge to me, to reveal the different ways that youth see the spaces of their everyday lives, all spaces within a major urban area in the United States. I intend for my representation of seven youth's experiences with and perspectives on their everyday space to illustrate how these material spaces and places shaped and reflected the social, ethnic, identity, and literate practices of the youth who moved through them. I demonstrate that these spaces are defined by simultaneous experiences of danger and comfort, familiarity and excitement, othering and being othered, and hybridity and Mexicanness, and that these experiences mediate youth's literacy and language practices and their uses of text.

Theoretical Perspectives: Bringing Literacy Spatiality to Youth Literacy Studies

My research with young people (ages 12–16) over the last eight years has pushed me toward a study of the spaces youth have access to and the ways they use literacy to claim, reclaim, or construct new spaces and particular identities. Specifically, the youth with whom I worked in multiple urban spaces have led me to examine space and time as an aspect of how they use literacy and of how they identify and are identified. The different youth's comments about space, and their unique tactics and practices in particular spaces, have compelled me to confront the common assumption that youth literacy and identity practices can be abstracted from particular spaces. In fact, the words "literacy spaces" in the title of the chapter represent something of a misnomer, in the sense that all spaces are in some sense "literate" spaces. As part of their everyday practices, people use a variety of written texts and other forms of representation (i.e., oral language, dress, gestures and movements, icons, etc.) to navigate within and across physical spaces. In the same sense, all spaces are spaces of identity enactment, and these enactments shape and are shaped by literate practices (McCarthey & Moje, 2002).

Identity can be considered an enactment of self made within particular activities and relationships that occur within particular spaces (geographic, social, electronic, mental, cultural) at particular points in time (see Anzaldúa, 1999 and Moje et al., 2002). To enact these versions of self, people draw upon "histories of participation" (Rogers, 2002) in other activities, relationships, and spaces; and they use different kinds of texts, languages, and literacies, all of which are shaped by various Discourses—or ways of knowing, doing, believing, and acting (Gee, 1996)—to position themselves in particular ways. Simultaneously, people are positioned by others within these activities, spaces, times, and relations. These relationships and positionings occur within relations of power (which are produced within particular spaces), and the Discourses people draw on in positioning self and others are situated in and mediated by institutions. Consequently, our enactments of self via language and literacy always produce power and are always produced in relations of power (see Foucault, 1980).

Following this definition, I draw to some extent on James Gee's (2000/2001) analytic categories for thinking about identity. Gee's notion suggests that we examine any enactment of self from four perspectives: nature identities (e.g., physical markers), institutional identities (the identities assigned to people or "recognized" by institutions of power), discursive identities (identities constructed in relationships), and affinity group identities (ways of knowing and doing we engage in to build relationships around a particular interest or goal). According to Gee, these categories represent aspects of identities that get performed and recognized in various ways.

To Gee's four categories, I add "spatial and temporal identities," or versions of self that are enacted according to understanding of and relations in different spaces and time periods. While Gee might argue that space and time are captured in institutions, discourses, and affinity groups, theorists such as Lefebvre (1996) would suggest that reducing space and time only to the social or contextual diminishes one's ability to examine how actual physical spaces and material conditions can, at particular points in time, call up or constrain various enactments of self.

An example of the impact of time and space is reflected in my own identity enactments and discourse practices in professional meetings, all held within the same institution and discourse groups. In large-group meetings I tend to sit silently, listening to the conversation swirl about me. At most, I might whisper—or mutter, as a colleague recently stated—*sotto voce* comments to someone sitting nearby. In small-group meetings, however, I am typically a vocal participant, and at times have to restrain myself from dominating the conversation. Time factors into these different institutional and discursive identities as well; even my small-group practices were muted when I first arrived at my current institution. As I came to know my colleagues better, was tenured and promoted, and served in a leadership role (changes in time, relationships, and activities), I became more dominant and vocal in my participation, but only in small-group settings. I continue to sit quietly in large-group meetings, a practice that suggests that space—actual physical arrangements—works together powerfully *with* institutional, discursive, affinity, and nature relations and identities to shape how people use language and literacy in practice.

I bring these theoretical and personal musings about space, time, and identity to my work with youth, especially as I move with them throughout the multiple spaces of their lives. In addition to forcing me to think about space and place as important to their everyday practices, the youth with whom I have worked have also pushed me to think beyond singular notions of ethnicity, gender, race, and class. That is not to say that these constructs do not matter in the lives, literacies, and identities of these youth. However, their lives take them through multiple spaces and their identities are consequently articulated at borderlands (Anzaldúa, 1999) or in multiple spaces that make their identities a complex hybrid of many different qualities of difference (Bhabha, 1994). Thus, rather than identifying youth as having a strong Latino/a identity simply because they are a particular generation of Mexican immigrants, for example, my research team colleagues and I trace how different ethnic identities can be tied to the ways that spatial positionings allow youth to develop relationships that support or contest those identifications. One participant, Pilar, for example, has claimed,

> At my old school, it was mostly black people, and I didn't speak Spanish much or talk about being Hispanic. I would never deny my heritage, but I just didn't talk about it very much.... At the [current school] it's, like, all Mexicans, so I speak Spanish more and, it's just more Mexicans and Chicanos.

To recognize that Pilar's comment is about *space* and not just about the difference between predominantly Latino/a and predominantly African-Americans' *contexts* requires that one know, for example, that these youth live in a city in which groups of people were, in the city's history, assigned—or "distributed," in Foucault's (1980) terminology—to live in certain physical spaces, certain geographies (Vargas, 1993). These distributions were not neutral—they were articulated to and reproductive of gendered, classed, raced, and religious positionings within the larger community. Foucault (1980) argues that certain strategies and tactics are employed to distribute different kinds of bodies to different kinds of spaces and that it is no coincidence that those who are marginalized are distributed to spaces with minimal or problematic resources.

These distributions of certain bodies into certain spaces, furthermore, help us understand why other Latino/a youth, 3,000 miles away or 30 miles away, living in different material and social spaces, read and write different texts and identify differently, despite the ethnic roots, social class, generational status, and gendered positions they share with the youth represented in the study described here. In other words, my examination of the relationship between urban space and youth's practices assumes that social, racial, gender, and other differences are articulated in particular ways in particular material and social settings, places, and spaces (Foucault, 1980, 1993; Lefebvre, 1996; Soja, 1993, 1996).

Just as interesting as how youth are positioned and read in different spaces is an analysis of how youth read and position themselves (enact identities) in different spaces. Theories of spatiality are not merely concerned with how larger structures act on people to assign them to spaces or to deny them resources within spaces, but with how people make sense of and act in spaces.

De Certeau's (1993) essay, "Walking in the City," provides an example of an analysis—or more aptly, an experience—of being in and in touch with a city space. De Certeau's interest in his walk was in how he and other people engage with space as they move through. What strategies do people use to control spaces and the other people in them? What tactics do people engage, unconsciously, as they experience a city (or any space)? Orellana and Hernandez's (1999) study of young children walking in and reading the city provides a particularly useful example of the importance of the relationship between literacy practices and space in all its material and physical glory. Their walk with first graders through an urban space yielded few signs of the children reading and engaging with the print of the city until they happened past an area where the print was written at just three to four feet off the ground. Orellana and Hernandez realized, with a jolt, that the children's physical size shaped their access to space and to literate interactions within the space.

My data suggest that the youth with whom I work have many resources from which to choose as they walk, drive, or just live in various urban spaces. The data also demonstrate that regardless of their construction of space and of the ways their bodies are positioned in spaces, different urban spaces offer both possibilities and problems to youth as they try to navigate and make spaces of power for themselves. In the chapter, I illustrate some of the ways that this one small group of youth accessed a variety of spaces—national, discursive, local, and virtual—via a variety of literate, textual, and techno-logical practices that afforded them resources for constructing hybrid identities, while also maintaining ethnic, community, and family affiliations.

About the Larger Study

This paper draws from data collected as part of a seven-year community ethnography and school study (currently in its fourth year) of an urban, predominantly Latino/a community nestled within a large Midwestern city. We draw from theoretical perspectives offered by work in critical cultural studies (Bhabha, 1994; Fiske, 1994), sociocultural theory (Vygotsky, 1978), and symbolic interactionism (Blumer, 1969). We start by defining *community* as a geographic area, but we also ask our participants to define what they count as their communities. Thus, our notion of community includes the intersection of physical, geographic space with qualities of difference such as ethnicity, age, and social class, as well as the young people's cross-national, transnational, popular cultural, youth cultural, and cyberspace relationships.

For the purposes of this chapter, I propose that a *space* can be constituted by an ethnic community; by the city surrounding the community; by a set of

streets, stores, and homes where one lives; by a school building, park, or
some other landmark important to the youth; by a country, a home, or a
room. Each of these constitutes a space, but each may also be redefined as a
place within a space. Places may be considered spaces to which people—in
this case, the youth of the study—ascribe particular meanings and importance. But places are also spaces.

Spaces exist in both hierarchical and dialogical relations with other
spaces. For example, a home can be considered a space within a set of other
spaces (imagine a set of concentric circles), such as a neighborhood, ethnic
community, city, metropolitan area (a city, together with its surrounding
suburbs), a country, and so on. But a home can also be a space unto itself, a
space that produces or constrains, opens into or shuts out other spaces. A
home can double as an ethnic community space, for example, even within a
neighborhood that is physically constituted by people of differing ethnic
backgrounds. A virtual space can likewise constitute a national space or an
affinity group (Gee, 2000/2001) space.

Most relevant to this study are the labels of national space, city space,
community space, neighborhood space, home space, bedroom space, suburban space, and virtual space. In the chapter, the *national space* refers to the
United States and Mexico (although youth in the larger study claimed affiliation with other Spanish-speaking countries as well). My references to the *city
space* include the city limits of a large Midwestern city in which these youth
lived. The *community space* in this study is both a geographic and social (ethnic)
designation. The community is described as being on particular "side" of the
city and is typically referred to as Mexican Town. The community is home to
the largest cluster of people of Latino/a origins in the entire urban area (city
and surrounding suburbs). The *neighborhood spaces* of the chapter vary depending on the youth and our travels throughout the community space.
Typically, however, youth refer to one section of the community as the ethnic
center of the community. This area includes their former middle school and
two of their current high schools; a third high school is in a nearby neighborhood, but not in what is commonly regarded as the center of their Mexican
Town community. *Home spaces* are important because the youth spend a great
deal of time in such spaces. The *suburban spaces* are particularly important to
this study and include areas outside of the city limits. These suburban spaces
are typically racially and ethnically defined as well. And the *virtual space* of this
study is, predominantly, the telephone and the Internet. Each provides access
to other people, languages, and practices throughout the city and in other
countries. Virtual space is, thus, connected in important ways to national
and/or ethnic spaces and to affinity group spaces.

Participants

Primary participants in the larger study are seven youth drawn from a larger sample of thirty youth (twenty females and ten males), ages 12–14, who live in different neighborhoods within the community. Their self-identified pseudonyms in the study are Ramiro, Pilar, Viviana, Alexandra, Yolanda, Mario, and James. The youth all live in low-income or working-class homes. I use the words and experiences of these seven youth because I have worked directly with them throughout the study.

Although all thirty youth from the larger sample could identify as Latino/a, they claim different countries as their countries of origin, and they identify in more complex ways than a single term could represent. All but three in the full sample claim some aspect of Mexican ancestry; the others are Puerto Rican and Dominican (the representation in the community is more diverse, however). Among those whose ancestry is Mexican, the youth identify variably as Mexican, Chicano/a, Tejano/a, Mexicano/a, and Mexican American, depending on when and where they were born, and when and where I ask them about their ethnic identities.

Each of the seven youth represented in this chapter identifies as being of Mexican ancestry. Ramiro and Yolanda were born in Mexico and identify as Mexican. Ramiro, however, often comments as he did in a recent interview, "I was born in [a state of Mexico], but then I lived in Mexico City, so I can't say that I'm from [state of Mexico], and now I've lived half of my life in America, so it's hard to say what I am." In fact, on one outing at a Mexican restaurant, Ramiro admired a baseball cap worn by a member of the wait staff. The cap sported the city's baseball team logo (the first letter of the city name), embroidered in the colors of the Mexican flag. "It's cool," said Ramiro, "because it's [city name], but it's Mexico, too," thus revealing that space and the texts that represent different spaces mattered, at least in Ramiro's identity representations.

Three other youth, Pilar, Alexandra, and Viviana were born in the United States to parents who were born in Mexico. Pilar and Alexandra represent themselves most frequently as Chicanas or Tejanas (residents of Texas of Mexican ancestry), citing their origins in Texas whenever they name themselves as Chicanas. They also call themselves Mexican, Latina, and Hispanic. Viviana describes herself simply as Mexican, perhaps because she has lived in her current community for most of her life.

Mario and James, who were both born in the United States to second-generation Mexican immigrants, typically speak of themselves as Mexican Americans, Hispanic, or Latino. Thus, the sample is representative in terms of generational status and identity enactments of the larger sample of youth who identify as being of Mexican ancestry in this urban area. Latino/as from other Spanish-speaking countries are not represented in this small sample.

As assessed by language of media representations and storefronts, the community identifies using the words *Hispanic, Latino, Mexican,* and *Spanish* (with the last word used primarily in reference to language). In individual conversations, however, community members (including the youth) are careful to specify their particular Latino/a roots (e.g., Ecuadoran, Mexican, Dominican, Tejano/a). When I write and speak about the community, I most often use the term *Latino/a*, but I also make every attempt to be true to the language of the participants. In this chapter, although I focus on only the participants of Mexican ancestry, readers may see that use different ethnic identifiers as I attempt to be true to the language of the participants.

Participants in the larger study include teachers, parents, and community members. Data drawn from the larger study inform this work in important ways because it is through the entire team's participant observation of the community space and the surrounding city spaces that I have come to understand how people make sense of and are recognized in different spaces. These data include participant observation and interviews at festivals and community events, at an after-school program sponsored by a Latino organization in the community, with prominent Latinas in the community; and at other middle and high schools throughout the community.

All youth participants are bilingual in Spanish and English, although some of the researchers, teachers, and parents are not bilingual in those two languages. Most community leaders are also bilingual in Spanish and English. The research team represents a mix of ethnicities, but only one gender: female. Three Latinas and five European-American women (including me) have routinely collected data across the four-and-a-half-year period. A Latina, a European-American, and an African-American researcher also participate in data analysis. All of the researchers have some facility with more than one language; however, only the five of the researchers are fluent in Spanish and English. I am not fluent in Spanish, although I can follow general streams of conversations and can read the gist of relatively simple texts. The seven young people represented in this paper are patient with my fumbling attempts to speak Spanish and are helping me learn new aspects of Spanish with every interaction.

All participants and place names, except the names of research team members, are represented with pseudonyms.

Data Sources

Data collection methods include (a) participant observation of community and school-classroom interactions recorded in field notes; (b) surveys; (c) interviews (informal and formal semi-structured, individual and focus group) conducted in various settings around the community and school; (d) the collection of documents, artifacts, and photographs; and (e) walking and driving the city, sometimes to construct maps, other times just to feel or experience the space. Although I have to drive a fair distance to the community from my home and office, I often park a significant distance from my designated target space and walk the space as much as possible. And whenever I can, I (and the other researchers on the team) walk the space with the youth of the study.

Six different researchers observed classrooms for a total of two to three times per week each year, for four years (year four is in progress). We have interviewed all primary participants at least once (interviews are ongoing over the entire course of the study), and seven of the youth have been formally interviewed five or more times each. Ten other youth have been interviewed at least three times outside of the classroom. These interviews and accompanying participant observations are the primary source of data for the chapter.

I typically engage in formal interviews with the youth in settings outside of school (restaurants, shopping malls, movie theaters, homes) and spend between 90 and 150 minutes in each interview. Interview protocols include questions about what the youth do in their free time, how they prepare for and interact in school, and their goals for the future (e.g., "What kind of music do you listen to?" "What kinds of after-school activities do you engage in?" "What do you want to do when you graduate from high school?"). The interviews generally provide occasions for participant observation as well as formal interviewing, and I write field notes to accompany verbatim transcription. I have also asked youth to describe themselves in writing to someone who has never met them. For example, I have asked youth to create identification (ID) necklaces, bumper stickers, and notebook sticker logos that they feel would represent them to others. Finally, the team has surveyed—in a structured response format—the focus participants on their language practices and on how they identify ethnically. We gave the surveys in a focus group interview format, however, so that we could record youth's interactions as they completed the survey. These data sources provide contextual data for the analyses I present in this chapter.

Data Analysis

The research team uses a variety of analytic methods to interpret the data, including constant comparative, narrative, semiotic, and discourse analyses. In this spatial analysis, I relied most heavily on constant comparative analysis (Glaser & Strauss, 1967) and narrative analysis (Patton, 1990; van Manen,

1990). I read and reread observations, interview transcripts, interview field notes, and artifacts, searching for codes that related to the youth's language, literacy, and identity practices in particular spaces. To examine the interview data more deeply, I drew on discourse analytic methods (e.g., Fairclough, 1992) to look closely at what youth said about themselves and the material spaces they inhabit. I was especially interested in the level of *modality*—that is, how they claimed spaces through "I" statements about themselves and others—in their talk and writing and in whether their modality changed from space to space. I also examined what the youth *foregrounded* and *backgrounded* in their talk and writing, and I looked for evidence of how their embodied practices changed from one space to another.

I also reviewed the narrative analyses (Patton, 1990) that several team members and I had constructed of the youth's interactions, looking for aspects of their identities that were linked to particular space. Then, following van Manen (1990), I constructed narratives of both my individual experiences with walking and driving in the community and my experiences with a small group of youth as we maneuvered various spaces together. I then searched the narratives, which were constructed from field note and interview data, for themes, ultimately turning the themes of the narratives back on the data, searching for further evidence of the themes or for new themes. The themes I analyzed as evident in the narratives of our experiences in the community, city, and neighborhood spaces include (a) othering and being othered, (b) novelty and familiarity, (c) danger and comfort, (d) hybridity and Mexicanness. In my analysis, I fought the temptation to ascribe these seeming binaries to one or another space. Instead, as I generated each theme in my analysis of data and my writing of narratives, I tried to find evidence of these themes in both of the kinds of spaces I examined. I also tried to see how these oppositional experiences lived side by side within each enactment of space. To provide a sense of the larger urban space, I begin with a description of the city and community constructed primarily from the youth's words.

This city, community, and neighborhood is a space on an edge and with an edge. The community is a space that is literally on the edge of river (a major waterway used by heavy industry), an edge of a state, and edge of a country. It is edged by an extensive and predominantly African-American population throughout the rest of the city limits, all which are edged by affluent suburbs inhabited predominantly by people of European-American heritage. One suburb that boasts a significant Arab-American population sits to the immediate west of the youth's community.

The city is a space that is on the edge of transition, with the city's (within city limits) population declining from 1,027,974 in 1990 to approximately

950,000 in the 2000 census (http://factfinder.census.gov/servlet/, January 2003). If considered as an urban area (metropolitan area, including surrounding suburbs), however, the population remains relatively stable at approximately 4,000,000, suggesting that the city proper continues to diminish as dwellers within the city limits move "out" into surrounding suburbs.

The city also has an edge for the youth who live there. In interviews with all the youth of the larger sample about the concept of community, we heard responses similar to Pilar's and Mario's in the following interview exemplar (P = Pilar; M = Mario; E = Elizabeth):

> E: If I said what community do you live in, what would you say?
> P: ...[the city name] community?
> E: Is that what you say, too, Mario?
> M: Yeah, it's true—
> P: [The city], where you live....
> M: Or Latin community or something
> P: Yeah, Latin community. On my street it's like all kinds of Hispanic people. There's only one house with white people.

In the same interview, Pilar later went on to talk about her view of [the city] as a particular kind of space, with Mario challenging her view:

> P: I know, we live in [the city].... I like [the city], it's just like, *ghetto*. But ghetto in a good way.... I don't mean that.... I don't know—I like [the city]; it's cool. It's one of the worst cities...in the United States.
> E: Really?
> P: They mention [the city] a lot.
> E: In what way would you hear the mention of [the city]?
> P: A lot of people dying.
> M: The ---- city that doesn't sleep... [---- represents a descriptive term that would identify the city and therefore cannot be used]
> E: When you say "they," what do you mean?
> P: I don't know, like the news—they say a lot of people died in [the city].... On the Spanish channel.... It's in Miami... but they mention [the city], like there's a big fire or house burned down or somebody died.... And I don't know.

Pilar and Mario's conversation, which was actually more extensive than this excerpt illustrates, was filled with tensions around the label of their community as "good," "bad," or "Latino," supporting the notion of a city and community on the edge and with an edge.

In contrast to the image offered by Pilar of the city as a "good ghetto" because it offered excitement and notoriety, other youth talked about the city and their surrounding neighborhoods in disparaging terms, citing the same qualities that Pilar cited, but expressing their disgust with or fear of those qualities of the city and community space. Some of the young women in the larger study, for example, mentioned the abundance of large—and seemingly vicious—dogs that would bark at them from behind chain-link fences as they walked in their neighborhoods. Some noted that men seemed to hang out on street corners. Others mentioned the burned-out houses they would pass on their walks. Similarly, Jaime discussed the community space in les-than-glowing terms when discussing the national census that had recently been conducted (J = Jaime; I = Interviewer):

> I: Are there other things that you could see, Jaime, that money, if there was money
>   that came into the community, that it could be used for?
> J: Uh-huh, like cleaning up [the city] because you know, you go to [the neighboring
>   suburb], you know you go to other places that are all clean and stuff, but over
>   here it's like, I don't know, more crappy and stuff.

Jaime's comment about the city and its relation to a nearby suburb, which he named specifically, makes visible another edge of the city and community, an edge on the opposite side from the river and nearby nation. The suburbs that edged their community space were ever-present in the talk of these youth, as demonstrated by another a comment Ramiro made during a classroom discussion of school funding. Like Jaime, Ramiro indicated his sense of the community and of the city's positioning vis-à-vis the rest of the state, when he raised questions about local school district policies in regard to state budget cuts.

> "How come," Ramiro asked in a classroom discussion about teacher layoffs,
> "There's no problems in the suburbs? Why is it only happening in the public
> schools? Why is it only happening in [the city]?"

Ramiro's question about the city, posed in contrast to the suburbs, illustrates his awareness of the geopolitical nature of the space in which he lived. He recognized that the suburbs were somehow privileged in relation to his community, his city. In each case, the youth in the study demonstrated their awareness of the space, their sense of it as a Latino/a or Hispanic community space, their varying judgments about the spaces, and their sense of place within the different spaces to which they had access.

Analyzing Spaces, Literacies, and Identities

To document the youth's sense of the various spaces of the city and the places that they constructed for themselves within those spaces, I spent a great deal of time walking and driving with youth. In this next section, I use some of those interactions in a variety of spaces to analyze how spaces, identity enactments, and literacy practices co-construct one another.

Other than Viviana, who seemed to be engaged on a regular basis in work-related activity, library trips, or special learning experiences (she took drama, art, and dancing classes at the local Hispanic Catholic church program), many of the other youth I worked with directly spent time in different spaces with less structured and adult-mediated activity. On our outings, we typically went to restaurants or to the mall to "mess around," and on some occasions, we went to movies. On one trip to a movie with Pilar and Mario, I had the opportunity to observe how the youth thought about areas outside of their immediate communities and neighborhoods, which they defined both geographically and ethnically (see their earlier comments).

Neighborhood and Suburban Spaces

We drove from their neighborhood, which does not support any kind of mainstream shopping mall or movie theater, to a neighboring suburb wherein a major shopping mall and multiplex theater can be found. As we moved across what appeared to be invisible boundaries, the two youth talked about the people they saw on the streets, the stores and restaurants they encountered, and the changes in the neighborhoods. On our trips to the mall, when asked about where their community stopped and started, the different youth always marked the two spaces in ethnic terms, usually naming Mexicans in their community and the "Arabs" who lived in the neighboring suburb.

Note this conversation, for example, which occurred while we were moving from their neighborhood to a neighboring suburb:

> P: Over by here is like Rainbow, you go into like.... Yeah right there—
> M: No.
> P: Yeah, it's in the back, it's like on the other side.
> E: What are you talking about?
> P: A Rainbow store, Rainbow junior, Rainbow kids—
> M: And Radio Shack, a dollar store, I think—
> P: Radio Shack. There's a good Chinese store where you can buy a whole lot of nice Chinese stuff—
> M: And isn't there a Kroger's—
> P: No....
> M: I thought there was.
> E: You guys come down here a lot?
> M: No, I just memorized it.
> P: That's where I shop.... I used to come here and go to Montgomery Wards. They were cheaper and really nice clothes. It closed down.
> E: I know....

P: That's bad—I like Montgomery Wards.
E: I used to go there when I was little. So even though you would, would you count
     this as part of your community?
P: I don't think so. Are we in [suburb name] yet? Yeah, 'cuz there's like [suburb
     name] City Hall.
E: Right—
P: I know, we live in [city name].

Pilar's and Mario's familiarity with the retail stores (and restaurants) of
this neighboring suburban space underscores an important point about their
own neighborhood space. Although they had access to Mexican music,
fashion, and groceries in their neighborhood, they did not have access to
mainstream fashions (such as were available at Rainbow) and technology and
telecommunication supplies (Radio Shack). Nor did they have access to the
mainstream music or movies they enjoyed; hence, our trip to another community space.

These youth also talked about their immediate neighborhoods and
community spaces in ethnic and racial terms. In this exchange, Pilar, Mario,
and I talked about her immediate neighborhood (which was about three
miles from the ethnic center as marked by Virnot Street and Mexican Town):

P: My neighbor used to ask me do you know if I can come over there and buy some
     cigarettes. She smokes and would like call me to tell me to go buy some more
     cigarettes. I'm like OK. But I don't come no more to [store name].
E: You don't.
P: No, I don't.
E: Why?
P: I don't know, I don't like that store. Too many Arabs....
M: Arabs always own party stores or dollar stores.
P: I know right. Now the Arabic guys are, like you are like, really cute. Brianna used
     to hang around with Arabs, and she started like going out with white guys, and
     then Mexican guys, and I was like, what, changing race every year or some-
     thing? Say yeah.
M: I don't know any Arab guys....
P: You don't—you sure? On this street, oh my god, here, if I could name all the
     Arab guys, there'd be like at least hundred.

This marking of neighborhoods in ethnic and racial terms was a regular
occurrence among the youth. However, what is particularly notable about
Pilar's comment is how her access to resources and to relationships in her
neighborhood space was constrained by her identification and positioning of
non-Mexicans as others. Prior to this comment, Pilar had noted that her
neighborhood school was not one at which many Hispanics attended. When
in company of other Latino/as, however, Pilar was among the most vocal

youth in terms of self-identification as Mexican and Chicana. She was also most often quoted as stating an explicit preference for Mexican boys. Thus, Pilar's experience of othering and being othered in her home space was strong; her home space put her at the margins of Mexican identity, and she seemed to seek out opportunities to spend time in spaces she defined as Mexican, Latin, or Hispanic.

Suburban Spaces (Malls and Movie Theaters)

On three other occasions, which included Pilar, Alexandra, Yolanda, Mario, Ramiro, and James (all of whom identified as Mexican, Mexican American, and/or Chicano), we went to a large shopping mall in the same neighboring suburb. On these outings, we would shop (or just walk around), take in a movie, or eat at a mall restaurant, depending on how much time we had on each outing. On one occasion, we headed first to buy batteries and bandages (I needed the batteries, and James needed a bandage for a chin wound he had suffered while riding his bicycle around his neighborhood). Our mission completed, we engaged in a more aimless wandering, stopping to look at the Guess clothing store, at a shop that sold Tommy Hilfiger and other popular brands, at a music shop where the youth looked for CDs by the rapper Tupac, and we skittered by a woman's lingerie shop with much snickering, whispering, and shoving.

As we wandered, I could not help but notice the responses of other mall patrons. Several people gave us a wide berth, often looking back over their shoulders as we passed by. Others—usually middle-aged women—would catch my eye and shake their heads with amused smiles, as if to express sympathy for my plight of having to shepherd four teens around the mall. Others looked at us curiously, wondering, perhaps, what a white woman was doing with four dark-skinned youth, all about the same age, some of them dressed in the popular baggy pants and oversized shirts often associated with street gangs and skaters (skateboarders). It is worth noting that I did not observe similar responses from passersby when I was walking the city (or mall) with just one youth. Viviana and I, for example, made two different trips to the same shopping mall, and I did not observe people looking askance at us as we roamed, rather aimlessly, from store to store. In other words, the number of young people in the group appeared to make a difference in how others positioned the youth and me in the mall space (in contrast to walks with the same number of youth on a Mexican Town street). Perhaps the number suggested a "pack"; perhaps our leisurely pace (a stroll) throughout the particular space (a mall) suggested idle—and therefore suspect—behavior. The youth, meanwhile, were making their own judgments about passersby, commenting on people's clothing and physical appearance.

On one of our visits, Ramiro, James, Mario, Pilar, and I had lunch at an Italian restaurant in the mall. The youth were dismayed (and disgusted?) at my willingness to slather bread with the roasted garlic the restaurant served, and they each opted for a "normal" meal of pizza. Most noteworthy, however, was the waitress's reward to us at the end of the lunch. Commenting that the youth were "the nicest kids she had waited on in a long time," she brought them each a complimentary dish of ice cream. I found myself wondering what was the behavior of other youth who frequented the restaurant, as well as wondering what she had been thinking when we had initially been seated in her section.

The mall thus seemed to be a space for othering and being othered, a space in which identities and behaviors were subject to scrutiny, but also a place in which multiple performances of identity were possible, and "nice" ones were rewarded. The mall's selection of goods and services, however, constrained the enactment of Mexicanness and seemed to promote the youth's attention to broader popular cultural texts, such as the Tupac albums they sought in the mall, compared to the Intocables (a Mexican music group) albums they sought whenever we went walking in their local community. At the risk of seeming to reduce the youth's ethnic identity enactments to particular spaces, I will argue that the mainstream space of the mall evoked more hybrid and sometimes mainstream identity enactments; I heard less Spanish spoken while we were in the mall, and I saw less attention to Mexican or Latino/a texts (i.e., music, books, T-shirts with Mexican slogans), although they often wore such texts on their bodies (Atzlán [borderlands], Brown Pride, and lowrider T-shirts, for example).

It might be argued that it is not surprising that the youth did not look for items such as Mexican T-shirts or music when they knew none would be available. That seemingly obvious conclusion is, however, one that is often overlooked: The access the youth had to particular kinds of space—most often to their ethnic community space—shaped the texts they consumed and produced, which in turn shaped the ways they chose to identify and were identified. The multiple spaces of their lives conjured up or enabled multiple ways of being, multiple tools—identity kits, in Gee's (1996) parlance—for enacting those ways of being, and, ultimately, multiple identities to be enacted. Whereas mall walking gave lessons in how to be mainstream, walking Virnot Street—one of the central neighborhood streets—provided the youths with ways of being Latino/a, and Mexican, in particular.

Neighborhood Spaces

On one such stroll down Virnot Street, Alexandra, Pilar, and I shopped at a series of stores that sold everything from blankets to clothing to tapes and

CDs. As we stood outside one shop window, I asked the young women about several T-shirts on display, all of which represented Mexican or Chicano/a themes.

> E: Why do I always see the eagle with the snake in its talons?
> P: Oh, that's a Mexican symbol, a story about an eagle.... I don't know really, but it means it's Mexican.
> E: It's like a legend, or something?
> P: Yeah.
> E: What's the car for on this one?
> A: Oh, that's a lowrider, you know, those are cars that Mexicans really like.

Pilar and Alexandra spoke often of their desire to spend time in public spaces at the center of their community. The young women's sense of these spaces is illustrated in the following conversation, initiated as we were headed out of school after a half day, on our way to meet Yolanda at her aunt's restaurant in a neighborhood different from their own. We were just pulling out of the parking lot when Pilar started the conversation:

> P: The bad thing about kind of like going to Yolanda's aunt's restaurant is like, is that like, we don't get to go on Virnot—
> A: Yeah, because it would kind of be better to like go on Virnot Street.
> E: Why would it be better to go here?
> P: Because it's like Friday afternoon and everyone's there—
> A: All the guys... But Pablo works at Yolanda's restaurant—
> P: I don't even know if he was in there last time, but there wasn't very much guys there.
> E: Ah, right—
> P: It's just like we're like at a family place [at Yolanda's].
> E: Well, you know—
> P: I mean, it's cool....
> E: Maybe we can go to Virnot next time.

As Pilar and Alexandra demonstrate in their talk about different spaces of their everyday lives, space matters, not just for the physical environment it provides (although that is part of the excitement and possibility of Virnot Street), but also in terms of the meanings, relationships, and identities to be made in these spaces. What is particularly important about the sense of the "Virnot Street space" experienced by these young people is not only their interest in seeing and perhaps meeting other people, but also the knowledge that these spaces provide them with opportunities to build, maintain, or reconstruct ethnic identities. Virnot Street, for example, runs through the center of the community which the youth in our study have identified as "the Latin community" (among other labels). The ethnic relations available in the space of Virnot Street are important because the space could give these young women access to the kind of men—Mexican men—with whom they want to build relationships, a desire expressed countless times by several of these Latina youth in interviews (e.g., "I only like Mexican boys, Elizabeth." Pilar, interview, 2003).

Although Yolanda's family's restaurant (to which we were headed on the occasion of the interview) is a Mexican restaurant, it is situated in a mixed ethnic community and located on a busy, divided highway. Virnot Street is also a busy street, but it is a two-lane street with sidewalks on which the young women could walk, could perform, and could connect with other Mexicans. The speed limit on Virnot Street is lower than it is on the other restaurant's street. The shops and stores that line Virnot Street are typically owned and patronized by Latino/as, and the items displayed in the windows have particular meaning and appeal for these young Latinas. What's more, on every occasion that we have walked Virnot Street, we have seen someone we know. On one occasion with Alexandra and Pilar, occupants of a car that passed us by turned around to come back to talk with us:

A: Hey, Ramiro! That was Ramiro!
E: It was? Where? [I turn in all directions, confused.]
P: Oh, great. [Ramiro and Pilar had recently experienced some difficulties in their friendship.]
A: Miss Elizabeth, they're coming back!
E: Oh, my gosh, they are.

The driver of the car has made a U-turn in the middle of Virnot Street, and I can see the car headed back toward us. We wait for the car to pull to the side, Pilar hanging back, reticent to engage in conversation with Ramiro. As I look—admittedly with some apprehension—into the front seat, I see, to my surprise (and relief), Mario's mother driving the car. She pulls to the side of the street, and she and I chat as Alexandra talks to Mario and Ramiro. Pilar hangs back on the sidewalk. Mrs. C. tells me that they are coming from school, where Mario has joined the school band. I talk briefly to Mario and Ramiro; Pilar says nothing. Mario and I, at his mother's urging, exchange cell phone numbers, and they drive off, making another U-turn to return to their original destination.

It was clear from this interaction, as well as from a number of other walks and drives down Virnot Street, that Virnot was a space of comfort and familiarity. On our walks and drives, the youth often recognized people passing by, including their own parents and other relatives. And, as illustrated in the above exemplar, Virnot Street was a space where people met and stopped to talk, even changing direction to interact with one another. At the same time, Virnot was an exciting space for these young women, a space to see and be seen by young men. Despite Pilar's discomfort with seeing Ramiro, both Pilar and Alexandra engaged with the space of Virnot Street with excitement and familiarity, risk and comfort, all occurring simultaneously. It was also a space to be Mexican, Chicano/a, or Latino/a.

When asked to describe herself in writing, Pilar produced a text that underscores the relationship between identity and physical and social space (spelling, punctuation, capitalization intact; emphasis mine):

> *I'm Mexican, well acutualy CHICANA I was born in Dallas Texas.* I'm *dark skined have long straight hair that's dark brown.* To me I think I'm an intelligente person I love to go out to partys The thing I most look forward to is my quincininera.. I'm funny very outgoing and express my opinions to me that importants *another thing is that I would like to go pimpin down virnot.*

In this identity artifact, Pilar explicitly linked her ethnic identity to what she labeled (through the use of the word "pimpin'") a playful and potentially sexualized space of Virnot Street. Thus, Virnot Street, like the Mexican festival at Hale Plaza or the Cinco de Mayo festival in Clare Park, is a physical and social space wherein Pilar's Chicana-ness (both a gendered and politicized identity, one that is rendered visible in this writing through her reference to another space, her Texas birthplace) is read as valuable and desirable, as are the color of her skin, the shape of her body, and the language she speaks. In these physical spaces in which identities are made, reproduced, and enacted from the physical and social resources provided in the space.

It is important to note, however, that these spaces (from Virnot to the suburban mall, from homes in the city to homes in Mexico or the suburbs) were never discrete or isolated from one another, and thus, the youth's identities are not constructed or enacted as wholly separate identities. The youth is not one person in one space and a completely different person in a different space. As mentioned above, even in the mainstream mall space, where Mexicanness was not highlighted, the youth wore clothing such as Atzlán T-shirts that signaled their borderlands identities, and they brought physical markers (or nature identities [Gee, 2000/2001]) that required an integration of Mexicanness with mainstream identities. Each space was, then, a space in which hybridity was built, a space that offered a variety of texts (including conventional written texts such as magazines, menus, and newspapers, the texts of T-shirts and hats, and the texts of CDs, posters, and movies) in which the youth engaged with comfort and risk, familiarity and novelty, and became simultaneously more Mexican, more mainstream, and more hybrid.

These physical neighborhood and community spaces within the city space provided resources for the development of both rich ethnic identities (see Moje et al., 2002; Young, Dillon, & Moje, 2002) and strategic and hybrid identities (Moje et al., 2002). Strong ethnic identities were enhanced by the youth's everyday interactions with many other Mexicans, with written and oral texts produced in Spanish, and with Mexican and other Latino/a customs, traditions, and practices. Hybrid identities were simultaneously constructed as youth accessed texts in a variety of languages, as they crossed community spaces and encountered people of ethnic groups other than their own, as they purchased mainstream "American" texts and clothing, and as they engaged with television, radio, and other media that presented a variety of customs, traditions, and cultural practices. Virtual spaces enabled the development of both ethnic and hybrid identities.

Virtual (Internet) Spaces

One virtual space site, for example, titled "[city name]raza.com," (*raza* is the Spanish word for *race*) is dedicated to providing community resources to Latino/as (bringing Latino/as who were physically distributed across the city space together into a virtual Latino/a community) and to maintaining an awareness of and pride in their Mexican *race* (despite the fact that "race" is not a term used to define Mexicans or Latino/as, in general, on the U.S. census or in other mainstream texts). Other uses of the Internet involved connecting to chat rooms to practice Spanish or searching for sites that illustrated Aztec art and drawing techniques (see Moje et al., 2002) and searching the Internet for information about Latino/a street gangs, as Alexandra described during one interview:

> A: Oh, I went to... member directory, right?
> E: Of what, what member directory?
> A: AOL. And I typed in where it said key word, I typed in "Sureño." It gave me every email of every Sureño on there.
> E: Oh my gosh.
> Y: How do you do the "ñ"?
> A: Alt, Alt 164.

In what may seem to be a trivial observation and interpretation, I was immediately fascinated by Alexandra's knowledge of how to produce an "ñ," which was, for me, a laborious learning process, for which I still struggle to remember the shortcut keys. That Alexandra had learned the keyboard shortcuts signals her facility with the literacy skills necessary to navigate the electronic medium (as does her navigation of the member directory and other tools), as well as her motivation to learn those skills in order to connect with a broader space occupied by both Latino/as and street gang members worldwide.

In addition, Pilar and Alexandra developed a joint unique name that identified them as lovers of Latin men and music, a way of signaling to other Latino/as (they actually wanted Chicana in their unique name, but the combination they proposed was already taken) their identities and a way of building relationships across spaces. The fact that the unique name they desired was already taken was also an important aspect of building that space: Others who shared their interests and their ethnicities existed in virtual space.

While the young women in this sample were searching the Internet for information and conversations about music and gangs, the young men were reading texts on cars, lowriders especially. The website www.lowrider.com is a popular virtual space that reflects and shapes ethnic as well as affinity group and familial identities as young Latinos interact with their elders (fathers, brothers, and uncles) around the care and maintenance of lowriders. These young men also named virtual spaces such as www.thefastandthefurious.com (a site devoted to information on a popular movie about, among other things, cars) and www.speedlogic.com, which they described as a site devoted to imported cars.

Each of these virtual spaces provided the youth with access to other people and a wide variety of texts, and although their access of virtual spaces, texts, and people seemed weighted toward Latino/a texts, they also gained information about and engaged in communication with people and texts from a wide variety of sources. As Ramiro remarked in one interview with Pilar and me:

R: Technology is making you more lazy and stuff....

E: Really?

R: Yeah, 'cause like in the old times you used to change the TV with your hands and you'd be sitting down—

P: Next thing [you just push a remote]—

R: Or if you wanted to order a movie, just push a button.

E: Some people say, though, that because we don't have to do all that physical stuff we can think more, think faster. We have more time to do other things—

R: But still it helps you think more, you need to learn all the things you have to do with the remote.... *My grandpa and my grandmother from Mexico said they were amazed when they saw that I was on the computer with somebody in France. They were saying that when they were young they were thinking that was ever going to be possible because that was like a fantasy but now that it's coming true....*

Ramiro's linking of technology and the ability to cross space virtually to the ability to expand our access to physical space in the future exemplifies the youth's sense that, via virtual space and technological innovation, they were linking to and constructing new communities, spaces, and, potentially, texts and identities.

Does Space Matter?
Conclusions about Youth, Literacy, and Space

It seems that space does matter, especially for how people represent themselves. As in the example of my own identity enactments in the different spatial arrangements of meetings I attend, these youth enacted different identities and were differently positioned in different spaces. Perhaps more important, the youth had access to different material, textual, discursive, and human resources in different spaces. As they read menus in restaurants, for example, they encountered particular kinds of information, particular languages, and particular representations of people and cultures. As they looked through music texts of stores in different spaces, they saw particular kinds of music, certain colors of skin, and certain languages, depending on the space. The space of mainstream malls provided them with, perhaps, more possibilities for building hybrid identities, but they carried markers of their ethnic identities with them into those mainstream spaces, and they carried the globalized and hybridized identities into their ethnically constructed neighborhoods via dress, music, oral language, and print texts.

No matter the space, ethnic identity was particularly salient for this group of young people. All of their conversations, even when engaged in suburban spaces with mainstream texts, involved some sort of ethnic or racial labeling. Even the mainstream music texts they listened to were inscribed with race and ethnicity. Although they chose mainstream gangster rap when at the mall (as opposed to the Mexican CDs they perused in shops on Virnot Street), the youth identified the music with an explicit eye toward the race and ethnicity of the performers. Their choices were shaped by the spaces they inhabited, but the ethnic community space of their lives remained dominant in their textual choices and literacy practices. The books I saw the youth read outside of school were books about Latino/as, the newspapers that dominated their reading were papers produced within and for their ethnic community space, and the Internet sites they frequented were ones that foregrounded Latino/as.

Thus, space did matter to these youth and to their literacy and identity practices. The historical distribution of Latino/a bodies into their neighborhood or community space contributed to their strong Mexican identification. Their neighborhood-community edging of a predominantly African-American city population, a predominantly Arab-American suburban community, and several, more distant and predominantly European-American suburban communities contributed to their deeply ethnic identification. Finally, their lack of mobility, due in part to their age and in part to the poor mass transit of the city space, shaped the material, human, and textual resources to which they had access (Moje et al., 2002). Their turn to virtual spaces mitigates some of the physical or geographic segregation they experience, but, again, their access to virtual spaces is constrained by their access to computer hardware and to adequate telecommunications systems for using their hardware to obtain Internet access.

That said, although these youth are relatively isolated beings, limited for now to accessing particular physical spaces and, on some occasion, virtual spaces, they are also constructing strong, but hybrid, ethnic identities that draw increasingly from multiple texts of multiple spaces. As they grow older and more mobile, they will continue to consume and produce texts of different spaces. They will use the texts—whether websites or ball caps, music lyrics or written essays—to build identities and relationships that maintain strong ethnic, cultural, and familial relationships and claim new spaces. And this is where schools can come in. Rather than attempting to restrict the space to which youth have access, educators and schools should provide young people with opportunities to learn to navigate these spaces both strategically and tactically (see Lankshear and Knobel, 2002) and to help them build portfolios that allow them to access other spaces (Gee, 2002). The more we know about the literacies and identities of the multiple spaces of youth's lives, the better chance we have to develop curricula and pedagogy that work within their life spaces, rather than against them.

References

Anzaldúa, G. (1999). *Borderlands/La frontera* (2nd ed.). San Francisco: Aunt Lute Books.

Bhabha, H. K. (1994). *The location of culture.* London: Routledge.

Blumer, H. (1969). *Symbolic interactionism: Perspective and method.* Englewood Cliffs, NJ: Prentice-Hall.

de Certeau, M. (1993). Walking in the city. In S. During (Ed.), *The cultural studies reader* (pp. 151–160). London: Routledge.

Fairclough, N. (1992). *Discourse and social change.* Cambridge, MA: Polity Press.

Fiske, J. (1994). Audiencing: Cultural practice and cultural studies. In N. K. Denzin & Y. S. Lincoln (Eds.), *The handbook of qualitative research* (pp. 189–198). Thousand Oaks, CA: Sage.

Foucault, M. (1980). *Power/knowledge: Selected interviews and other writings, 1972–77.* Brighton, UK: Harvester Press.

Foucault, M. (1986). Of other spaces. (J. Miskowiec, Trans.). *Diacritics, 16,* 22–27.

Foucault, M. (1993). Space, power and knowledge. In S. During (Ed.), *The cultural studies reader* (pp. 161–169). London: Routledge.

Gee, J. P. (1996). *Social linguistics and literacies: Ideology in discourses* (2nd ed.). London: Falmer.

Gee, J. P. (2000/2001). Identity as an analytic lens for research in education. In W. G. Secada (Ed.), *Review of research in education* (Vol. 25, pp. 99–126). Washington, DC: American Educational Research Association.

Gee, J. P. (2002). Millennials and bobos, *Blue's Clues* and *Sesame Street*: A story for our times. In D. E. Alvermann (Ed.), *Adolescents' multiliteracies in a digital world* (pp. 51–67). New York: Peter Lang.

Glaser, B., & Strauss, A. (1967). *The discovery of grounded theory: Strategies for qualitative research.* New York: Aldine.

Lankshear, C., & Knobel, M. (2002). Do we have your attention? New literacies, digital technologies, and the education of adolescents. In D. E. Alvermann (Ed.), *Youth's multiliteracies in a digital world* (pp. 19–39). New York: Peter Lang.

Lefebvre, H. (1996). *Writings on cities* (E. Kofman & E. Lebas, Trans.). Oxford, UK: Blackwell.

McCarthey, S. J., & Moje, E. B. (2002). Identity matters. *Reading Research Quarterly, 37*, 228–237.

Moje, E. B., & Ciechanowski, K. M. (2002, April). *Literacy, language, and life in the millennial world: A study of Latino/a youth literacy in one urban community.* Paper presented at the American Educational Research Association, New Orleans, LA.

Moje, E. B., McIntosh Ciechanowski, K., Carrillo, R., Ellis, L. M., & Kramer, K. E. (2002, April). *"I'm not white:" Racial and ethnic identity representations among Latino/a youth in urban spaces.* Paper presented at the Society for Research on Adolescence, New Orleans, LA.

Orellana, M. F., & Hernandez, A. (1999). Talking the walk: Children reading urban environmental print. *The Reading Teacher, 52*, 612–619.

Patton, M. Q. (1990). *Qualitative evaluation and research methods.* Newbury Park, CA: Sage.

Rogers, R. (2002). Between contexts: A critical analysis of family literacy, discursive practices, and literate subjectivities. *Reading Research Quarterly, 37*(3), 248–277.

Soja, E. (1993). History: geography: modernity. In S. During (Ed.), *The cultural studies reader* (pp. 135–150). London: Routledge.

Soja, E. W. (1996). *Thirdspace: Journeys to Los Angeles and other real-and-imagined places.* Malden, MA: Blackwell.

van Manen, M. (1990). *Researching lived experience.* Albany: State University of New York Press.

Vargas, Z. (1993). *Proletarians of the north: A history of Mexican industrial workers in Detroit and the Midwest, 1917–1933.* Berkeley: University of California Press.

Vygotsky, L. S. (1978). *Mind in society.* Cambridge, MA: Harvard University Press.

Young, J. P., Dillon, D. R., & Moje, E. B. (2002). Shape-shifting portfolio youth: Millennials, literacies, and the game of life. In D. E. Alvermann (Ed.), *Adolescents' multiliteracies in a digital world* (pp. 114–131). New York: Peter Lang.

3

Diverse Social Contexts of a Second-Language Classroom and the Construction of Identity

Elizabeth Hirst

Literacy education sits at the interface between the construction of social identities and the construction of the national, corporate, and global social relations. Theories of literacy need to contend with this interface—both at the micro classroom level and the macro level of social and institutional planes of activity. Developing a repertoire of literacy practices involves the appropriation and mastery of the technologies of representation, of mediational means; it is a set of mediated actions or social practices, constructed in political economies. Literacy practices cannot be quarantined from the "real world" and considered as a set of asocial, amoral skills to be mastered; they are always shaped, produced, and consumed in relation to broader social and cultural conditions and inevitably involve issues of identity. Similarly, second-language literacy education can never stand alone. It is always used and produced within particular social and cultural contexts. In this chapter I argue that these contexts are not sites, locations, or containers for the learning of literacy—where the classroom context starts at the classroom door—but are active and constitutive in the appropriation and mastery of literate practices and the construction of identity.

The second-language classroom, like any other classroom, is a meeting place of a range of discursive practices, sites of "heteroglossic articulations of various historical, class, and cultural interests contending for social power and capital" (Luke, 1998, p. 52). Learning another language, or another set of discursive practices, is the process of appropriating the cultural resources or voices of these communities (Wertsch, 1991); it is a semiotic apprenticeship (Gee, 1992; Wells, 1999). In this process the individual and social are always mutually reconstituting, and the fundamental unit of communication, the utterance, is not only a site where the personal and the social meet, it is a site where the person and the society alike are produced. Identity is thus conceived as "mediated action" (Wertsch, 1998), a point of articulation and suture between discourses and practices which produce subjectivities and the agency of the individual to take up these practices.

This chapter is premised on the assumption that Language Other Than English (LOTE) classes are key sites for the contestation and construction of identity in what theorists such as Stuart Hall refer to as "New Times," times of rapid political transitions, of the new socioeconomic order of "new capitalism" (Fairclough, 2000), characterized by changed and uneven patterns of flow of capital and bodies, resulting in the emergence of "underclasses," of new poor and geographically marginalized communities, along with various forms of fundamentalism (Castells, 1996). These changes impact on school practices, including issues of work intensification, the introduction of contracts, and the commodification of education, which reflect the emergent new capitalist economy with "a strong emphasis on bringing about change in schools and thereby changing the values and attitudes of tomorrow's workers" (Gee, Hull, & Lankshear, 1996, p. 31). The new workers that are interpellated by these neoliberal discourses and the language of new capitalism have major implications for the nature of schools and schooling.

Discursive practices are generally analyzed in terms of conversations or dialogical encounters and rarely conceived spatially or temporally, not only as meaningful texts or actions, but also in relation to the reproduction and production of different spaces and times (Leander, 2001). However, the dialogical nature of utterance, as Bakhtin (1981b) insists, is a constant struggle over meaning which, he argues, obliges us to examine the conditions of "dialogised heteroglossia" (p. 276). This term describes the living interaction of the word within the "elastic environment" of other "alien" (not one's own) words, that gives import not only to its linguistic character but also to the significance of the associated socially constructed temporal and spatial conditions. These conditions are not just environments or backdrops or places, although the construction of space involves each of these elements, but are significant as a result of how they come to be engaged and changed by social practices. Not only are the social contexts of LOTE classes constituted through these discursive practices, but also different groups often construct them differently, and some constructions are more privileged than others. An understanding of the discursive and ideological activity of the classroom and the corresponding concept of identity are contingent upon an understanding of the production of both social space and time, and their associated patterns of flow and exchange.

Therefore, mediated action, individuals operating with mediational means in a social context (Wertsch, 1998), can be considered as a "trialectical" relationship, rather than a dialectical binary relationship of individual and tool user, which tends to consign social context to "backdrop." "Trialectics" is the term that Soja (1996) coins to describe Lefebvre's (1976) principle of "thirding-as-Othering": a determination to incorporate a third element to "crack open" traditional binaries by "introducing an-Other term, a third possibility or 'moment' that partakes of the original pairing but not just a simple combination of an 'in-between' position along some all inclusive continuum" (p. 60). For example, in the traditional Marxist binary of labor and capital Lefebvre (1976) asserts the significance of land, which, he argues, enriches a Marxist analysis and makes it more complex. Similarly, Soja argues that discourse analysis is incomplete without including an analysis of space. Thus, I argue that the three elements of mediated action cannot be understood in isolation or separated for analysis; in this chapter the third element of the trialectical relationship of mediated action, social context, is conceived in terms of temporal and spatial practices and relationships.

An analysis of temporal and spatial relationships is of particular salience where the time and space LOTE populates, both real and imaginary, emerges as an arena of conflict. Not only do these struggles over meaning and privilege tell us something about the positioning of LOTE in the school curriculum and within the community, but also the ways that time is conceptualized and space is re-produced in the classroom are intrinsic elements in the production of certain kinds of minds, certain kinds of people. Thus, the classroom is reframed, Luke (in press, p. 6) suggests, "as a social field engaged in a series of flows and exchanges that enable the production of texts and literate practices (and the omission of others)."

I contend that an analysis of second-language literacy education, of the interface between the macro and micro activity, is incomplete without taking account of the temporal and spatial realities and imaginaries shape the material conditions that characterize New Times—times in which, Bhabha (1994) argues, the importance of theorizing these relations of time and space has become more critical:

> The power of historical locality becomes particularly persuasive as the problem of cultural identity is staged in discourses of geographical complexity—migration, diaspora, postcoloniality. The demand for specificity increases as the subject of cultural citizenship becomes inscribed with more and more of the striations of difference found in a multicultural, pluralist, late capitalist global society. The call for historical locality is also then a dislocation of the agency of cultural and disciplinary identity. (p. 2)

This is of particular note in the study drawn on this chapter, which considers the interactions in a second-language classroom taught by an Indonesian national in an Australian classroom—a result of policies of engagement between Asia and Australia.

Analytical Framework

Identity is often theorized in terms of its construction and manifestation in discourse, with the need to study the texts of everyday life to observe the mechanisms of these processes. The ways that discourses operate in society need sophisticated linguistic and intertextual analysis to see how this happens (Fairclough, 1992). One of the aims of this chapter is to apply that kind of analysis to the texts of a LOTE classroom, analyzing the role spatial and temporal practices play in establishing power relations that constitute and sustain identities and ideologies. Considering space and time as material conditions recognizes that diverse spatialities exist simultaneously within the same physical location, each constituted by particular economic and political relations and each with its own pattern of flow and exchange which entails the production of certain texts and literate practices (Sheehy, 1999). Foucault's (1986) description of "heterotopia" provides a useful way of considering the relationships between these spaces. The socially constructed spaces in the classroom do not stand alone but are inextricably linked; nevertheless, they can be incompatible. As Foucault posits, heterotopia has "the curious property of being in relation with all the other sites, but in such a way as to suspect, neutralize, or invert the set of relations that they happen to designate, mirror or reflect" (p. 25). The LOTE classroom is a place where the rules of the normal classroom are transgressed, where the established relationships of power are challenged as students undermine the LOTE teacher's legitimacy to take up the powerful identity of teacher. Much like Bakhtin's concept of carnival, with its parodic systems, the established order of the classroom is disrupted. Furthermore, Foucault argues that each heterotopia has "a precise and determined function" (p. 25); they are not just spontaneous or idiosyncratic, but act as microcosms both reflecting and constituting larger cultural patterns. Thus, the events that occur in the classroom are not incidental but, as Soja (1996, p. 46) reminds us, "part of the (social) production of (social) space, the construction of individual and societal spatialities."

To address this interface and the intrinsic spatial and temporal relations of discursive practices, to analyze "dialogised heteroglossia," Bakhtin (1981b) utilized the principle of chronotopicity. He contends that "every entry into the sphere of meaning is accomplished only through the gates of the chronotope" (1981b, p. 199). In his analysis of the genres of the novel, he shows how their structures reveal a patterned series of events and how these events are constituted within particular relations of time and space. Using the concept of the chronotope to express the inseparability of time and space, Bakhtin identifies the unity of texts through distinct chronotopes: ways in which temporal and spatial realities are represented. Chronotopes, he argues, function as the primary means by which time is materialized in space; they are "organizing centers" for significant narrative events presented by the text. Time and space are material conditions; they are not divorced from the text but intrinsic elements of it.

The spaces of the LOTE classroom are social constructions constituted through enactive and recognitive work (Gee, 2000), informed by and implicated in cultural understandings of time and space. It is, Leander (1999) suggests, through the production of the classroom chronotope that classroom discourse is stabilized and thus can be recognized as a generic practice. For example, the spatial and temporal organization of the classroom and patterns of flow and exchange that characterize the IRE (an Initiation, Response, and Evaluation tripartite exchange dominated by the teacher) pattern of classroom talk readily conjure up a particular kind of classroom, an "old space" (Sheehy, 1999) constituted by authoritarian social relations and recognizable teacher and student identities. Bloome and Katz (1997), drawing on Bakhtin's analysis of chronotopes, describe how different conceptions of time may operate in the classroom, with different sets of social relations and identity practices. For some participants, the chronotope of the LOTE classroom may be implicitly conceptualized as "theatre," the "public square," or "adventure-time"—a time and place for overcoming obstacles and emerging unscathed and untouched by the experience, with identities fundamentally unchanged. Thus, chronotopes provide a way of analyzing classroom genres by considering how relations of time and space are differently constituted. For example, the teacher may attempt to construct the genre of the "Indonesian lesson," drawing on cultural repertoires of "the lesson": the ways in which time and space are marked out with its characteristic patterns of flow; the ways bodies are positioned in space and time; and the ways in which time is valued and measured. Meanwhile other classroom participants may reconstitute a genre that is characterized by very different social practices and cultural identities, characterized, for example, by Bakhtin's (1981b) description of the chronotope of "adventure time." These genres frame incompatible and sometimes conflicting cultural identities and relations of power. Deploying the principle of chronotopicity enables an examination of the ways social contexts are constituted, privileged, and territorialized, a focus on how the students in these classrooms acquire and master certain literate

practices, take up particular identities, and how these practices are constituted by and constitute institutional, national and global spatial and temporal
practices.

The Classroom

This study forms part of a larger investigation at an elementary school (Hirst,
2002), which serves students from low to medium socioeconomic backgrounds across a wide geographical area of outer suburbs. Data were collected using video- and audiotapes, observational notes, and interviews over
an eight-month period from a year 7 LOTE (Indonesian) class, comprising
twenty-three students (11 to 13 years of age): twelve and eleven girls. Four of
the students are of Aboriginal background, two boys and two girls; one boy is
of Asian descent. The students have been learning Indonesian since year 5,
scheduled in three half-hour lessons each week. Pak Asheed (all names used
in this chapter are pseudonyms), the itinerant LOTE teacher, services two
schools and is employed as part of a cooperative agreement between an
Indonesian provincial administration and the Queensland State Government. His first language is a regional Indonesian language and second language is Bahasa Indonesia. He trained as a secondary English-language
teacher in Indonesia. This study was conducted from the beginning of his
second year in Australia and his first year of appointment as a LOTE
teacher. Prior to this he was employed as an assistant at two high schools in
the metropolitan area. Before his current appointment he had no experience
of primary teaching and had neither planned nor taught independently in
Australia.

LOTE's Chronotopes

"Third Space" Possibilities

The "third space" is a construct to describe how other spaces might interanimate and create the possibility of a potentially more heteroglossic authentic
interaction (Gutiérrez, Rymes, & Larson, 1995); it is a space, Homi Bhabha
(1990) argues, which entails the generation of new meanings and the emergence of hybrid identities:

> This third space displaces the histories that constitute it, and sets up new structures
> of authority, new political initiatives.... [T]he process of cultural hybridity gives rise
> to something different, something new and unrecognizable, a new area of negotia-
> tion of meaning and representation. (p. 211)

In similar vein, Bakhtin discusses hybridization not as simply a combination of chronotopes but as a process whereby they interanimate and which

"radically changes their character" (Bakhtin, 1981b, p. 165) of the new chronotope that is generated. This hybridity is envisaged by Bakhtin "as a highly productive form of dialogue between persons in past, present, and future space-times" (Leander, 2001, p. 652).

Second-language classrooms are characterized by heterogeneity, considered as an essential platform for dialogical interanimation (Ballenger, 1997; Gutiérrez, Rymes, & Larson, 1995; Haworth, 1999), and afford the potential for negotiation of diversity, the articulation of cultural differences, thus the development of third spaces (Byram, 1999; Carr, 1999; Kramsch, 1998). It is these affordances that are envisaged in the rhetoric of policies and resulted in the introduction of LOTE as a compulsory curriculum area in the middle and upper years of elementary schooling over the last decade in Queensland. These educational policies, as Luke (2003, p. 132) posits, "are bids to regulate and govern flows of discourse, fiscal capital, physical and human resources across the time/space boundaries of educational systems." They envision students as mastering or appropriating certain voices and taking up particular identities, becoming certain sorts of people. LOTE classrooms are imagined as an opportunity for two (or more) cultures to come into contact, and potentially into dialogue, enabling new forms of understanding to develop, diverse voices to interanimate, and for dialogic learning to eventuate, with the concomitant construction of hybrid cultural identities (Hirst & Renshaw, in press).

Notwithstanding the cogency of the policies and initiatives realizing these outcomes has been problematic (MacKerras, 1995). In many schools in Queensland LOTE has found itself in a marginal space in the school curriculum through challenges to its legitimacy from school administrators, classroom teachers, parents, and students (Djite, 1994; Rix, 1999). The policies themselves, although framed in terms of developing intercultural competence through the negotiation of diversity, are underpinned by other discourses, notably the discourse of the market, where diversity is commodified and conceptualized as a resource to be accumulated (Connell, 2002).

Spaces of Economic Rationality: "The Time/Management Chronotope"

The economic rationale that underpins these second language policies is most obvious in initiatives that prioritized the expansion of Asian languages programs (COAG, 1994). Building on the positive correlation between linguistic skills and export growth (Stanley, Ingram, & Chittick, 1990), these initiatives not only sought to facilitate this growth but also address "the importance of minimizing resistance to export growth due to linguistic, cultural and attitudinal resistance to Asia" (MacKerras, 1995, p. 5). The underlying assumption is that by value adding to students' linguistic capital, economic benefits accrue in the nation's capital, or, more obtusely, by valuing adding tolerance students' resistance to Asia will be reduced, facilitating the positive flow of economic capital (MacKerras, 1995).

These neoliberal discourses permeate the organization and arrangement of LOTE in schools. For the most part the institutional chronotope of LOTE is an issue of time and space management: how and where to fit it efficiently both temporally and spatially so that it provides the greatest amount of benefit to students (for LOTE learning) and classroom teachers (for non-contact time [NCT]), and the least amount of problems (behaviorally), a principle to enable the flow of goods. This evokes a spatiality of the market in which the flow and exchange of goods follows established and recognized patterns of trade. Time is conceptualized as a valued commodity to be segmented and used efficiently to facilitate productivity: a resource to be distributed. Rämö (1999) argues that the ideas found in managerial discourses are equal to chronotopes: "the common denominator among these management ideas is the creation of smooth, swift and thrifty flows" (p. 319). In this time-management chronotope, Pak Asheed represents a "container"—the epitome of efficient and effective management. The container is prepacked, transported in, unloaded, and transported out. Time is quantifiable and equated with efficiency and regarded as an important yardstick to measure the value of activities. LOTE policy documents calculate that 420 hours is required for the transfer of goods to enable students to gain a certain level of linguistic competency. The chronotope of the LOTE lesson is established institutionally as a management device.

Time and space are inherently implicated in the institution's cultural ideology, including its educational ideology. Not only issues of curriculum and pedagogy but also administrative arrangements by which the school is organized define teachers' work and thus teachers' identities. Although other chronotopes must exist at the institutional level, the time-management chronotope is privileged. School administration mirrors and reinforces the patterns of dominance and subordination found in the wider society (Troyna & Rizvi, 1997), leading to a tendency to avoid examination of cultural concerns and favor the technical. This bureaucratic rationality structures much of the discourse of schooling, making it difficult to accommodate differences, whether cultural or political, except in certain symbolic ways. These are more often contained and/or commodified, for example, in the celebration of multicultural days, National Aboriginal and Islander Day of Celebration, and, it seems, LOTE lessons.

These institutional practices seriously mitigate against the legitimacy and status of the teacher and the successful implementation and sustainability of LOTE policies (NALSAS, 1998). The itinerant nature of primary LOTE teachers' work and school management practices of time-tabling LOTE to provide NCT for classroom teachers can impair the inclusion or support of both the teacher and the LOTE in the school community (Miller, 1997; Roulston, 1998). This marginal position has in many cases been further intensified by contracting overseas born and trained teachers, native speakers of the LOTE, to counter the projected and current shortfall of LOTE teachers both in terms of numbers (Djite, 1994) and proficiency (MacKerras, 1995). These teachers, Kamler, Santoro, and Reid (1998) argue, neither count, numerically, culturally, or professionally, nor receive systemic support. This is of particular moment, "if we acknowledge that parochial attitudes and covert racism are a part of the experience of overseas born teachers" (Kamler, Santoro, & Reid, 1998, p. 509). These cultural patterns can be situated within the production and reproduction of new capitalist spatiality, and, as Berland (1992) notes, one is implicated in the production of the other. The dominance of the time-management chronotope exemplifies one way in which an educational system within the emerging postmodern state is implicated in this production, through its demand for more at the lowest cost (Lingard, Ladwig, & Luke, 1998).

"Our" Space: A National(ist) Agenda

The dilemma between, on the one hand, policy initiatives which mandate for the increase and expansion of LOTE teaching, particularly Asian languages, in order to underpin Australia's economic future through the skilling of future workers with desirable linguistic competencies and attitudes, and, on the other hand, the institutional issues, which include shortfall in teachers, itinerancy, and NCT, can be located within a broader framework of wider community attitudes. Historically, Lo Bianco (1998) argues, "Australian linguistic culture made a virtue of steadfast monolingualism.... [T]these broad patterns of background civilization have an impact on the implementability of ambitious plans for languages, for these plans can never be divorced from the society which gives them life" (p. 8). These "ambitious plans" respond to a globalization agenda, but, as Castells (1996) observes, other emergent responses include various forms of fundamentalisms, in a harkening back to the imagined security and simplicity of the way it used to be, to traditional values, when lines of authority and status were firmly established and recognized. In Australia these times were explicitly "white times," constituted by homogenizing assimilationist practices and the marginalization of difference. These practices Macedo (2000) argues, sustain the structures and mechanisms of a colonial ideology designed to devalue the cultural capital and values of the Other, they also constitute a national identity defined through exclusionary practices by its "constitutive outside" (Hall, 1996).

In Australia, Pauline Hanson's One Nation Party represents the re-emergence of nationalism in Australian political landscape. This party, according to Clyne (1998), "sanctions" racialized discursive practices by reconstituting spaces of "whiteness" and monolingualism: "we speak English here" (Hanson, cited in Clyne, 1998, p. 3). This has particular bearing for this study, located in an electorate whose One Nation candidate gained 57 percent of the primary vote (Parliament of Australia, 1998).

The Communicative Chronotope

Other chronotopes also characterize LOTE at the institutional level. Curriculum documents (QSCC, 2000) encourage LOTE teachers to facilitate "communicative tasks" in their classes by engaging "learners in using real language for real or lifelike purposes" (p. 8). Students are asked to suspend belief and participate in these communicative tasks as other "real" times and spaces are imagined. However, all too often this dialogue is used as a rehearsal so that students will appropriate preexisting ways of using language (Morgan & Cain, 2000), and the "real" is "mock," making LOTE classrooms "strange places" (Macaro, 1997, p. 55). These imaginary spaces and times are mapped onto the everyday geographies of classroom life, and students are expected to participate in and move seamlessly between these classroom chronotopes, taking up different voices, for example, an Indonesian shopkeeper or an Australian tourist.

Mimicry is a significant pedagogical practice in constructing these contexts. Macaro (1997) comments, "It is a wonder that the participants 'play the game' at all and abide by the rules" (p. 56). Abiding by the rules suggests that these utterances are "uni-directional" (Knoeller, 1998), that the intentions of the speaker are aligned with the original speaker. Mimicry is closely related to parody, a form of humor that saturates the LOTE classroom. Bakhtin (1981a) describes parody as "the borrowing by one voice of the recognizable style and timbre of another; it is 'an artistic image of another language'" (p.362). He highlights the dialogic process, arguing that the speakers may use the discourse of others for their own purposes by inserting new semantic intentions. Thus, in one utterance two semantic intentions, or two voices, are not only heard but are intentionally executed in order to be heard—it is because of their audibility as two voices that the parody works. Humor depends on difference or incongruity, on the switch from one interpretative position to another. The first speaker's utterance is distorted and undermined by the second speaker's utterance; it calls into question the first speaker's utterance, undermining it by drawing it into the humorous domain (Mulkay, 1988). In this play on language and the construction of these systems of parody at least two chronotopes can be constructed, the second being directly related though often not compatible with the first, for example, the official space and the counterspace (Gutiérrez, Rymes, & Larson, 1995).

Play Time

Play is an aspect that frames the practices in the LOTE classroom and stands in stark contrast to the time-management chronotope. Previous experience and an expectation of significant behavioral problems with students during LOTE lessons underpinned the advice I received from a school principal as a beginning LOTE teacher to just play some games, sing some songs, and ensure students enjoyed the lesson to prevent behavioral problems. It is paradoxical that LOTE is framed so heavily by the managerialist chronotope yet treated playfully, as the principal recommended. The insertion of play and other infantile activities is consistent with a particular kindergarten chronotope—where students are allowed to move around the classroom, to talk more freely, and to play with artifacts and language.

To summarize, it is evident that the LOTE classroom is differently constituted through a variety of chronotopic practices. These practices are not always conducive to students' dialogic engagement with diverse cultural resources offered by the LOTE teacher. In the following I explore how actions in this time and space, designated by the institution for LOTE teaching and learning, reconstruct, contest, or subvert the spatiality and temporality of social contexts.

Chronotopes of the LOTE Classroom

Meetings and Partings

Junctures between normal and LOTE lessons provide opportunities to examine the privileging of temporal and spatial practices. At these meetings and partings, which Bakhtin identified as significant motifs of the chronotope, the macro social material conditions constituted in everyday micro interactional encounters can be made visible as tensions become evident. In the following I comment on four excerpts from data collected at these transitions.

Juncture 1. This is Pak Asheed's second week of teaching at the school. His timetable indicates his teaching responsibilities, which include two primary schools; at this school he teaches five classes, each class is scheduled to have three thirty-minute lessons per week.

Pak Asheed concludes the LOTE lesson with a formal greeting, collects his resources from the table near the door, and departs, nodding to me as he leaves the room. There is no classroom teacher present when he leaves at 2:00 p.m. Most students remain at their desks talking quietly. Their conversations are cut short as Rae Moran, the classroom teacher, returns. She stands still at the door; news of her presence flows quietly and quickly around the class as students adjust their bodies, taking up a "student" posture. She looks for several seconds at the clock located at the front of the classroom above the blackboard and then turns to me, asking where Pak Asheed is. It is 2:05 p.m., the scheduled time for the LOTE lesson to finish. The students are quiet and this exchange can easily be overheard.

Juncture 2. Comments about time are not uncommon, one week later:

Rae returns to class after Pak Asheed has left, she looks around pointedly, then asks me, "Why has he gone already? It is not time; he's a few minutes early." I suggest that he may not realize that the lesson concludes at 2:05. "I'll have to speak to him," Rae replies. This conversation is quite loud, the students are very quiet, and they can easily overhear.

Juncture 3. Three weeks later Rae informs Pak Asheed of the finishing time of the LOTE lesson:

Pak Asheed and I continue with our conversation as we walk from the staff room over to the classroom. The students are sitting on the cement pathway just outside their classroom. As we enter the classroom Rae joins us, she does not greet Pak Asheed but tells him that the LOTE lesson finishes at 2:05, not 2:00. He looks surprised and asks if that this was just for today. "No, it's always been like that," she replies. He seems flustered and checks his timetable. His timetable wrongly indicates that the lesson begins at 1:30 rather than 1:35. He checks his schedule with me several times, checking again that this is not just a change in today's routine. Meanwhile Rae supervises the students' entry into the classroom.

The temporal order of LOTE lessons, which has been institutionally defined, is policed and regulated by the classroom teacher. Time, defined in these encounters as a commodity, a scare resource, is quantifiable and can be exchanged for goods. It needs to be used productively; thus, timekeeping is important to allow LOTE time to be exchanged for NCT time. The classroom teacher asserts her identity as one who can regulate these timekeeping practices. Not only is the chronotope of time-management privileged in these exchanges, but it is the classroom teacher who is the agent of this privileging. Likewise, she asserts her authority over spatial relations. She monitors students as they move from an outside space to an inside space of the classroom following their lunch break. This transition between physical spaces is accompanied by a transition in activity and genre. Students' behavior, both physical and verbal, is monitored differently in this space. The classroom teacher watches the students as they walk in, calling one student back and insisting he repeat the performance correctly; his bodily practices are not privileged in this space at this time. Space relationships are reinscribed on the student's body; the authority over bodily practices is reconstituted (Sheehy, 1999). This authority is evident even when she is not present in this classroom as we see in the following.

Juncture 4.

> Pak Asheed has walked into the classroom; he is sorting through his resources on a desk near the door. Rae Moran is about to leave; she turns at the door, "You don't look particularly settled year 7. Why you don't have your Indonesian books out is just a little beyond me." The students take up a "student pose"; as they sit on their chairs their upper bodies are bent forward over their desks. One student does not respond. Rae moves to the back of the class and, speaking loudly as though addressing the whole class, comments on his behavior. She warns that if his behavior is not appropriate, he will be excluded; then, just before leaving, she addresses the whole class, reminding them that if their behavior is not appropriate during the LOTE lesson the games hour she has planned for the following day may be cancelled.

Not only is the classroom teacher monitoring spatial relationships and practices, and the regulation of bodily practices, she is also bargaining with students to exchange these practices in LOTE time for a reward; if they can be good, if there are no behavioral problems, the students can participate in games time. Likewise, at the beginning of another lesson she demands, "Promise me, I will not need to come back and mop up the mess after your LOTE lesson." The social context/genre is shaped by the powerful identity she adopts. Not only does she assume the power to make these bargains but also through her actions she diminishes the power of the Indonesian teacher and the value of the lesson. Bargaining for good behavior presupposes, and suggests to students, that it is not anticipated. Although Pak Asheed is now the legitimate teacher in the physical space of this classroom, the classroom teacher's power to shape the social context/genre and student's actions is evident in the following exchange.

Transcript 1: Meeting and Greeting.

26	Lily:	Shush (to students as PA walks to front of class).
27	Pak Asheed:	Stand up for a few seconds (two claps) *Selamat siang kelas tujuh* (good afternoon Year Seven).
28	Students:	*Selamat siang* Pak Asheed (not all students are standing).
29	Pak Asheed:	Stand [up (gently clapping).
30	Mike:	[Hey, Lily, [Lily, Lily. (Lily looks briefly at Mike then to PA.)
31	Simon:	[Stand up, we gotta be good.
32	Bill:	Stand u:p Will.

Here we see two students reproduce both the classroom teacher's authority and her conception of LOTE time. Simon reminds students of the contract that has been established by the classroom teacher (line 31), and Bill reinforces this (line 32) as he targets Will's noncompliance following Pak Asheed's second request to stand up. Simon's re-revoicing of the classroom teacher's utterance does the work that students often do, that is to collaborate and cooperate with teachers to construct order in the classroom (Davies, 1997), not only a linguistic but a spatial and temporal order. In this way the classroom teacher's authority is being reconstituted, and, although not present, her presence shapes the temporal and spatial conditions of the classroom. As Nespor (1994) posits, when we act, we are acting not only with people, places, and things that are spatially and temporally present, but also those that are removed yet present in the social context—both are constitutive of the social context. These comments are representative of a broad repertoire of comments made at junctures between normal lessons and LOTE lessons, and draw on discourses that constitute LOTE time and space in the organization of school life.

The LOTE teacher does not have these bargaining privileges. He never comments on students' behavior in other classes nor starts a LOTE lesson whilst the classroom teacher is physically present unless she indicates that he can do so. Neither does he speak to the teacher about her timekeeping practices, although she has often continued teaching after the scheduled start time of the LOTE lesson and lessons have occasionally been cancelled without his prior knowledge. He never interrupts other classes, yet it is not unusual for teachers and other school staff to interrupt LOTE lessons. He is employed to facilitate the flow of linguistic and cultural goods to students in exchange for students' school time—time which students relinquish control over by giving their attention to the teacher, being prepared to be answerable and attuned to the space of another. The LOTE teacher's position has already been questioned by the identity the classroom teacher takes up as a monitor of his time management practices. In later episodes it is evident that the LOTE teacher's tenuous claim to the powerful identity of teacher is constantly under threat, even as he attempts to reconstitute the social context of the Indonesian lesson.

Barriers to Free Trade. In the time-managment chronotope, time and space are commodities to be exchanged for goods—most notably, NCT for the teacher, playtime for the students, and (it seems, of much less importance) Indonesian linguistic competence. The most frequent issue that is addressed in administrative talk about LOTE that inhibits this free flow of trade is constructed as the LOTE teacher's lack of competence in the management of student behavior. This is identified as one of the central issues for LOTE teachers, particularly LBOTE (language background other than English) teachers (Kingdon, 1995). If there are no complaints and no behavioral problems that spill out of the LOTE classroom, if difference is contained and the normal mainstream times and spaces are not invaded, the administrators generally do not become involved with what occurs in the LOTE classroom. These practices are not exclusive to this school, as reflected in a national report (NALSAS, 1998), which documents the lack of support for LOTE teachers, and comments, "They [principals] are only bothered if there is a behavior problem" (p. 42). Institutionally, then, LOTE is constituted as an obstacle in the daily life of the school, a problem, a space for the containment of difference, not a space or time for engagement with difference.

Cultural difference, rather than a resource for constructing intercultural understanding, is being constituted as a deficit and engaged in the creation of cultural borders (Erickson, 2001). The construction of these borders is not only evident through the competing and incompatible chronotopes operating in the classroom, but through other key episodes which include interruptions, or invasions of the time and space of the Indonesian lesson. Other teachers will sometimes enter the class and speak to students without acknowledging or speaking to the LOTE teacher. These incursions, which work to undermine the teacher's authority to establish the social context of the Indonesian lesson, are often framed as ways of supporting the LOTE teacher, for example, by reprimanding a student. Although, generally, these are well meaning (to avoid lengthy and difficult discussions with the LOTE teacher), these actions of the mainly middle-class teachers implicitly reconstitute some aspects of their own invisible culture (Delpit, 1995).

During the period of observations, the school administration became involved in several incidents that did spill out of the LOTE classroom. Strategies were offered to fix-up the LOTE teacher to facilitate the flow of goods from teacher to student and from teacher to teacher. In attempting to employ these strategies, insisting in one lesson that students' lunch break time become Indonesian time, Pak Asheed was ridiculed and challenged by students for his inability to perform expertly with these tools. Rather than facilitating the flow of goods, they worked to further inhibit the flow. Ironically, although his difference is commodified and valued and desirable in the time-management chronotope, it is this very difference that promotes barriers to the smooth, swift, and thrifty free trade of linguistic goods.

Marking the Indonesian Border. Policy documents do not guarantee a space for LOTE classes, thus the normal classroom space, a space teeming with Australian and English symbols, has to be reterritorialized as LOTE space. The

LOTE teacher attempts to reinscribe relations of time and space for Indonesian as he moves from classroom to classroom, drawing on his cultural expectations of classroom practices. The conceived space of the classroom includes expectations of how participants use space and time, the identities taken up, the kinds of talk, values, behavior, body orientation, and movement. One way he signals the beginning of the Indonesian lesson, marking the transition to these new spatial and temporal relations, is through ritual salutations: the "standing and greeting" performances (see transcript 1). These linguistic and bodily devices significantly shape subsequent events.

Linguistic proficiency in the ritual greeting performance involves mastery of two rhythmic and semantic pairs: *Selamat siang kelas tujuh / Selamat siang Pak Asheed; Apa kabar? / Baik-baik terima kasih* (Good day, year 7 / Good day, Pak Asheed. How are you? / Fine, thank you). The sing-song intonation pattern of this couplet is reminiscent of chorusing activities of younger children, for example, as they sing the times tables. Crucial elements in this performance are the bodily practices that accompany it. Pak Asheed attempts to reconstitute the power of the *guru* (teacher) by claiming authority over students' bodies, expecting students to stand behind their chairs as they greet him, although he does this tentatively: "Stand up for a few seconds" (line 27), "Stand up" (line 29). Bodies are crucial sites to watch for the production of power, and, from his study of Indonesia classrooms, Kuipers (1998, p. 143) posits, "one's bodily attitude (*sikap*) is seen as an expression of one's relationship to authority." It is through this ritualized performance the teacher marks out the relationships of authority in this space as he attempts to reproduce his dominance of a space and time that is controlled by another and to populate this space with other symbols. Pak Asheed embodies authority as a flow from the top down. This embodiment derives in part from the arrangement of the lines of power in classrooms in Indonesia, where the teacher is not only at the front but often also on a dais and students are addressed collectively, and even in their individual responses are still treated as a collective body.

Enacting a genre serves to reconstitute the teacher's authority, and interpellate students as a class and not individuals is a characteristic of the genre of the "Indonesian lesson." Similarly, the practice of insisting on this physical as well as a linguistic performance is a cultural convention of classroom discourse in Indonesia. Although students master some rudimentary vocabulary, this performance it is more about the assertion of relationships of power than the development of linguistic competence (Kress & Fowler, 1979, p. 69). These ritualized performances are community resources; their utility constantly negotiated through social exchange. This cultural tool is no longer a shared community resource in Australian schools, where the marking of power relations has become less overt. This is not to suggest that power relations are any more democratic, but rather more implicit. The power of the classroom teacher is evident as students' bodies and voices reconstitute the time and place of the normal classroom when she returns. Her physicality embodies the institutional power in a way that Pak Asheed's does not.

Counterspace

Indeed, the symbolic force of this ritual which serves to mark a boundary for the frontier of the Indonesian lesson, where patterns of flow and practices of privileging of identities is other to that of the normal classroom, also functions as an element of very different but related sets of generic practices—of heterotopia. Many of the students show their noncompliance, some do eventually stand, whilst others lean forward with elbows on their desks, or kneel on their chairs. Sometimes students appear too busy to stand, they are tying their shoelaces, tidying their desks, or moving around the classroom. But it is the systems of parody that serve to mark out the counterspace.

> *Pak Asheed stops after his first utterance, asking Will to stand. Will complains of sore knees, another student impatiently asks him to stand, but he ignores the requests, and PA resumes the greeting. Halfway through this second attempt, Lily turns to Mike and, smiling, shakes a finger at him, a mock warning, a parody of teacher performance, once again reminding him of the omnipresence of the classroom teacher in this space. In the final response to the greeting, Lily answers with a deep singsong voice, prolonging the final syllable of the last two words, which Mike then repeats and then another pupil mimics. Mike then appropriates the final sound of the word and repeats it, making it into a laughter sound—hee hee. After PA has requested that the students sit, Mike makes a final comment, getting the last word in the exchange, then waggles his bottom at the student behind him before sitting.*

Mike's parody of both the teacher voice and display of irreverence for the ritual meeting performance indicate the dialogical conflict of two spaces—the Indonesian space that Pak Asheed has constructed for the students, a space governed not only by the teacher but by the cultural displays of obedience to the *guru*, where the performance is a mark of respect and acknowledgment of authority, and the counterspace of irreverent resistance. This latter space is constructed in opposition to the teacher's space and draws upon it for its content. It is not an alternative space but tied to the old space. It is this binary, at the intersection of old and counterspace, which Lefebvre sought to crack open, to third, in an effort to transform its closed logic, to create a "thirdspace."

This construction of counterspaces, where time and space are differently conceived, is a common occurrence, not sanctioned in the normal classroom. These conceptualizations not only frame plot development in the counterspace but also identity. Students experience adventures, overcome various obstacles, and take up different identities. Here the flow of cultural resources is distributed in unplanned and unpredictable ways; there is no top-down structure. The motif of standing and greeting signals something akin to Bakhtin's (1981b) description of the chronotope that characterizes "adventure-time":

> Moments of adventuristic time occur at those points when the normal course of events, the normal, intended or purposeful sequences of life's events is interrupted. These points provide an opening for the intrusion of non-human forces—fate, gods, villains—and it is precisely these forces, and not the heroes, who in adventure-time take all the initiative. (p. 95)

In the following I examine one student's practices as she takes the initiative, taking up the role of the rogue or the clown, creating around herself the chronotope of theatre time.

Theatre time. Just as Pak Asheed attempts to through his enactive work (Gee, 2000) to interpellate the roles of *guru* and class, Lily also constitutes the students as audience, but, in the spatial and temporal relations she constitutes and embodies, constructs an anomalous social context.

Transcript 2: Bend Over
84 Pak Asheed: Excuse [me, <u>listen.</u> (Will walks up behind Matt's chair.)
85 Lily: [Shush.
86 Jared: I'm listening.
87 Pak Asheed: In doing this you can sit behin..er beside your partner but not
                 walk around or
88   make a noise. [Right? Choose your seats=
89 Will: [<u>Work</u> around or make a noise? (looking at Matt
90   and laughing)
91 Pak Asheed: =and go to them but do not walk around.
92 Lily: (to will) <u>Walk </u>around, you Nigel.
93   (to PA quietly) He's making fun of you.
94   (to Will) Bend over touch your toes (looks at PA) and will take
95   you out to the shed. (PA moves to stand in front of Lily.) Haha.

Pak Asheed is standing in front of the class, slightly to the left of the central aisle that divides the rows of desks arranged across the classroom. Lily occupies the third desk from the center in the front left-hand row; Matt is on her left. Sitting less than a meter from Pak Asheed, she first admonishes Will for his lack of understanding (line 92) and then quietly addresses Pak Asheed as she explicitly acknowledges the teasing genre (line 93), that Will is "taking the piss." But even more insulting and ridiculing, speaking more loudly, she smiles as she draws on a popular currency of abuse by ventriloquating a homophobic voice suggesting to Will that he might engage in homosexual activity with Pak Asheed. There have been other references in the counter-script to the teacher's sexuality, references that seem to be founded on the clothes that Pak Asheed wears—tight trousers and a patterned shirt tucked in at the waist. For example, Lily has remarked that Pak Asheed wears "gay pants," constituting a social reality where outer differences are noticed and inner differences assumed. His clothes are cultural tools, at the interface of body and other, and provide the material for Lily to take up the role of comedian. In this role she plays with meaning, constructing another place and time, the "shed"—a private male space—implying the sexual orientations and relationships of the participants.

As a comedian she plays to her audience, shocking them, ridiculing Pak Asheed. This figure, Bakhtin (1981b) argues, plays an enormous role in the consciousness: "The rogue and the clown create around themselves their own special little world, their own chronotope" (p. 159). These figures carry with them the "theatrical trappings of the public square"—they are connected to the public square, where common people congregate. For her humor to work, the audience needs to have an intimate knowledge of their cultural practices, shared access to the chronotope that Lily maps on to classroom practices, and the incongruity of the embodied chronotopes. Later in the same lesson we again hear and see Lily taking up this role.

Transcript 3: Bloody Bastard

112	Lily:	(to Jared) Can I be a partner with you?
113	Jared:	Honestly, I'm working with Matt.
114	Lily:	Please.
115	Jared:	You work (?) like a woman.
116	Lily:	Plea:se.
117	Pak Asheed:	(Claps hands) One minute excuse me (indis) walking around except
118		[(indis.)
119		[Bloody idiot... bloody bastard (cockney accent).
120	Jared:	Haha.
121	Lily:	Bloody bastard (smiling)...bloody bastard ((looking directly at PA who is standing behind Matt)=
123	Jared/Matt/Will:	Haha (looking at PA, then turn away).
124	Lily:	=bloody bastard (stands up pushes her chair under her desk flamboyantly and moves toward PA) bloody bastard (laughing, PA is blocking her pathway. As she tries to pass they stand toe to toe for a moment, she points over his shoulder to Nancy and he moves, allowing her through, and watches her progress).
129	Will:	(indis) (to Jared & Matt)
130	Matt:	Indonesian.

131 Jared:	Well what else would I write about?
132 Will:	(turns to Matt) See?
133 Lily:	Bloody bastard (into microphone).

In this episode, after being denied access to a legitimate classroom space in which she could potentially take up the identity of student, Lily swears directly at the teacher, using a thick cockney accent that she appears to have revoiced from a popular TV show. At the time the classroom episode above was recorded, an episode of *The Simpsons* was shown on local television; the episode was set in Australia and included instances of characters swearing in an "Aussie" accent—in fact, the accent was not authentically Australian but sounded like a London cockney accent. Lily appears to be drawing on both the cockney voice and the attitude of disrespect to authority figures that Bart Simpson displays on the show. The teacher does not appear to understand what Lily is saying—in fact, it is this lack of recognition that provides the impetus for her to repeat the phrase several times. This is daring and disrespectful behavior for which Lily is not held accountable because the teacher cannot understand her.

Already we have seen that the LOTE teacher is operating in a time and space that has been marginalized in the life of the school and in which he has little power; he is operating in alien territory that he attempts to claim for the Indonesian lesson. This space is already populated with conflicting chronotopes. Students challenge the space that the teacher seeks to occupy; they make forays into this territory, attempting to make it their own. Power here is about a struggle and conflict over resources and public spaces—students challenge Pak Asheed's power to claim this space. But Lily does even more than this by investing in the role of rogue, as does Bart Simpson; she is not only appropriating his speaking position in the classroom, but she also recasts Pak Asheed as the fool, and as incompetent in his performance in the Indonesian lesson. However, as Bakhtin posits, the rogue or clown cannot be understood in a direct and unmediated way but only grasped metaphorically: "their existence is a reflection of some other's mode of being—and even then, not a direct reflection—they are life maskers" (Bakhtin, 1981b, p. 159). Deploying the mask of the rogue, Lily reflects and distorts Pak Asheed's mode of being as she performs to the public gallery, self-consciously saying taboo words (bloody bastard) right into the microphone, the one that I am using to collect classroom data. This microphone becomes a tool, a prop, in the production of theater time.

Indeed, it is important to consider the audience for Lily's remarks; who are the people of the public square? Her utterances are made directly to the teacher, but she clearly does not expect him to reply to her comments. She is not talking to the teacher so much as talking for the amusement of her class-mates. I am unable to hear her clearly as I am sitting in the opposite corner of the classroom; however, her use of the microphone would indicate that I, too, am interpellated as audience. Reconstituting this space as theater time, she acts for the student audience—she is performing burlesque by making Pak Asheed appear foolish. The students can hear her and are very much aware of what she is doing. She flaunts her bravado as she performs for them. This is dangerous ground, she has ties to the real world of the normal class-room, and she has to trust that her fellow students won't inform; she also has to trust me. Though the risk she is taking is great (this behavior could get her suspended from school), so is the kudos she is earning. She builds solidarity with her audience and exposes the teacher—she is constructing an alternative reality, one in which she has a significant stake-holding.

When Lily makes these comments, she does not appear to be angry or upset but seems to be playing, almost baiting the teacher—poking a meta-phorical stick at him and seeing if he will bite. "Taking the piss" can be a game of verbal jousting if both players know the rules and are ready to play. In this instance the teacher cannot play, so Lily plays to her peers and to the camera. Sheehy (1999, p. 221) suggests that finding the barb that will silence the Other is tied to a dominant-dominated binary; the game is initiated when one authority questions another authority and there is no vision for diversity. Together the group reproduce societal violence, each mark, situated in a network of social practices, reconstitutes class, race, gender, and body norms. There is no third space imaginary with which to reposition themselves with one another.

It is through her use of "anti-language" (Halliday, 1978) that Lily con-tests the teacher's authority and displays her bravado to the other members of the class, with consequent foregrounding of interpersonal elements. Con-stituting interpersonal relations in opposition to the teacher, she looks to her audience for laughs and solidarity. In his discussion of anti-language, Halli-day (1978) draws on Podgórecki's (in Halliday, 1978) explanation of "second life," the construction of an alternative society which arises from the need to maintain inner solidarity under pressure; "at the individual level, the second life provides the means of maintaining identity in the face of its threatened destruction" (Halliday, 1978, p. 168). Paradoxically, in this instance it is the LOTE teacher's identity that is threatened; though, on the larger scale, in the face of changing demographics and globalization, it may indeed be the identity of communities like these, comprised of semiskilled low socioeco-nomic groups, that are under threat. These communities, previously secure in industrial- and agricultural-based industries, have become particularly vulnerable to the changing patterns of flow of capital and the emergence of knowledge-based economies, which may relegate them to the underclass.

Lily is not known for either her academic prowess or good behavior; she is also an Aboriginal student. Perhaps she has little investment in the role of the good school student and, as Bakhtin (1981b) suggests, employing the mask of the rogue can sustain, albeit temporarily, a powerful identity:

> In the struggle against conventions, and against the inadequacy of all available life slots to fit an authentic human being, these masks take on an extraordinary signifi-cance. They grant the right not to understand, the right to confuse, to tease, to hyperbolize life; the right to parody others while talking, the right to not be taken lit-erally, not to be oneself; the right to live a life in the chronotope of the entr'acte, the chronotope of theatrical space, the right to act life as a comedy and to treat others as actors, the right to rip off masks, the right to rage at others with a primeval (almost cultic) rage—and finally, the right to betray to the public a personal life, down to its most private and prurient little secrets. (p. 163)

At these moments, refusing to be limited by material circumstances, Lily creates a theatrical world and acts to constitute counterreality. Perhaps, less directly oriented toward success in the world than many of her classmates, Lily fulfils her short-term intentions, by being amusing and cultivating the imagination of her audience. But as she steps out of the boundaries of the social context in which she has been located as student and becomes a figure of a subaltern world, she also relinquishes her identity as student. This may have longer-term implications. At what cost does Lily take up this cultural identity, this mask, in the temporal and spatial relations of the counterscript: both for herself and for her fellow students? Is there any opportunity for dialogic interanimation of the Indonesian lesson and the counterspace, for the collapsing of their agendas and the development of a third space, for a new imaginary, for the relocation of chronotopic practices and the construc-tion of shared times and spaces, for the development of intercultural literacy practices? Or are these practices hegemonically legitimated and practiced on our behalf by some of the least powerful in our society? Is Lily, an Aboriginal student, doing the dirty work of institutional racism?

Conclusion

In the LOTE classroom teachers and students work to constitute diverse spatialities. Whilst Pak Asheed attempts to deploy resources to re-territorialize the mainstream space and mark the borders for the Indonesian lesson, some students mobilize other resources in their construction of coun-terspaces. There is conflict over the privileging of cultural resources. Who has the resources to claim authority over the public space of the classroom or restrict other's access to this space (de la Torre, 1999)? This classroom is a site of multilayered spaces, each with its own border, some more flexible than others. The counterspaces are not harmonious or entirely overlapping; their emergence reveals the inherently heterotopic nature of any classroom. The borders between these spaces are constantly being negotiated and monitored. Diversity, represented in LOTE policies as a resource to be appropriated, is fundamental in the construction of these borders, borders for the containment of difference.

One of the goals of the LOTE program is to develop students' intercultural understandings, to develop the possibility of engaging in cross-cultural and multiethnic alliances, to afford students the potential to redesign and transform identities. The Queensland LOTE syllabus (QSCC, 2000) articulates these goals, suggesting transformative possibilities, encouraging students to engage with issues of cultural identity by reflecting on the cultural self as well as of the other. But how potent is the LOTE classroom in exploiting the potential for the negotiation of diversity and the development of third spaces, for the formation of new identities"? Kramsch (1993, p. 6) argues that in these classes students can forge a new identity, one that is not established, in order "to realize a cross-cultural potential that is latent in any learner of a foreign language." In similar vein Freeman (1998, p. 81) proposes schools can actively create opportunities for students to take up alternative social identities that are not readily available in the mainstream, for example, resist or refuse an identity that is underpinned by racist ideologies. This argument implies agency; the individual not only has the possibility of investing in a social identity, resisting a social identity but also of forging a new one. It also raises the question, What other discourses are available to students and teachers to draw on other than the metanarratives of nationalism and human capital (Luke, 2002)? Although the LOTE policy is apparently a driver of the development of Australian identity, imagining a broader more inclusive identity whilst it privileges the human capital model, evident in the spatial and temporal practices that its institutional presence is realized, it is unlikely to provide these affordances and may be antithetical to the intended development of second-language literacy.

References

Bakhtin, M. M. (1981a). Discourse in the novel (C. Emerson, Trans.). In M. Holquist (Ed.), *The dialogic imagination: Four essays* (pp. 259–422). Austin: University of Texas Press.

Bakhtin, M. M. (1981b). Forms of time and the chronotope in the novel (C. Emerson & M. Holquist, Trans.). In M. Holquist (Ed.), *The dialogic imagination: Four essays* (pp. 84–258). Austin: University of Texas Press.

Ballenger, C. (1997). Social identities, moral narratives, scientific argumentation: Science talk in a bilingual classroom. *Language and Education: An International Journal, 11*(1), 1–14.

Berland, J. (1992). Angels dancing: Cultural technologies and the production of space. In L. Grossberg, C. Nelson, & P. A. Treichler (Eds.), *Cultural Studies* (pp. 38-55). London: Routledge.

Bhabha, H. K. (1990). The third space. In J. Rutherford (Ed.), *Identity, community, culture, difference* (pp. 207–221). London: Lawrence and Wishart.

Bhabha, H. K. (1994). *The location of culture.* New York and London: Routledge.

Bloome, D., & Katz, L. (1997). Literacy as social practice and classroom chronotopes. *Reading & Writing Quarterly, 13,* 205–225.

Byram, M. (1999). Questions of identity in foreign language learning. In J. Lo Bianco, A. J. Liddicoat, & C. Crozet (Eds.), *Striving for the third place: Intercultural competence through language education* (pp. 91–102). Melbourne: Language Australia.

Carr, J. (1999). From "sympathetic" to "dialogic" imagination: Cultural study in the foreign language classroom. In J. Lo Bianco, A. J. Liddicoat, & C. Crozet (Eds.), *Striving for the third place: Intercultural competence through language education* (pp. 103–112). Melbourne: Language Australia.

Castells, M. (1996). *Rise of the Network Society.* Cambridge, UK: Blackwell.

Clyne, M. (1998). The language of exclusion and inclusion. *Australian Language Matters, 6*(4), 3–10.

Council of Australian Governments (COAG). (1994). *Asian languages and Australia's economic future. A report prepared for the Council of Australian Governments on a proposed national Asian languages/studies strategy for Australian schools* (Rudd Report). Brisbane: Queensland Government Printer.

Connell, R. W. (2002, October 23). Rage against the dying of the light. *The Australian,* pp. 30–31.

Davies, B. (1997). The subject of poststructuralism: A reply to Alison Jones. *Gender and Education, 9,* 271–283.

de la Torre, C. (1999). Everyday forms of racism in contemporary Ecuador: The experiences of middle-class Indians. *Ethnic and Racial Studies, 22*(1), 92–112.

Delpit, L. (1995). *Other people's children: Cultural conflict in the classroom.* New York: New Press.

Djite, P. G. (1994). *From language policy to language planning: An overview of languages other than English in Australian education.* Canberra: National Languages and Literacy Institute of Australia.

Erickson, F. (2001). Culture in society and in educational practices. In J. Banks & C. McGee (Eds.), *Multicultural education: Issues and perspectives* (4th ed., pp. 31–58). New York: John Wiley & Sons.

Fairclough, N. (1992). Discourse and text: Linguistic and intertextual analysis within discourse analysis. *Discourse and Society, 3*(2), 193–217.

Fairclough, N. (2000). Represenciones del cambio en discurso neoliberal (Representations of change in neoliberal discourse). *Cuadernos de Relaciones Laborales, 16,* 13–36.

Foucault, M. (1986). Of other spaces. *Diacritics, 16,* 22–27.

Freeman, R. D. (1998). *Bilingual education and social change*. Clevedon, UK: Multilingual Matters.

Gee, J. P. (1992). *The social mind: Language, ideology, and social practice*. New York: Bergin & Garvey.

Gee, J. P. (2000). The new literacy studies: From "socially situated" to the work of the social. In D. Barton, M. Hamilton, & R. Ivanic (Eds.), *Situated literacies: Reading and writing in context* (pp. 180–196). London: Routledge.

Gee, J. P., Hull, G., & Lankshear, C. (1996). *The new work order: Behind the language of the new capitalism*. St. Leonards, AU: Allen & Unwin.

Gutiérrez, K., Rymes, B., & Larson, J. (1995). Script, counterscript, and underlife in the classroom: James Brown versus Brown v. Board of Education. *Harvard Educational Review, 65*(3), 445–471.

Hall, S. (1996). Introduction: Who needs "identity"? In S. Hall & P. du Gay (Eds.), *Questions of cultural identity*. London: Sage.

Halliday, M. A. K. (1978). *Language as social semiotic: The social interpretation of language and meaning*. London: Edward Arnold.

Haworth, A. (1999). Bakhtin in the classroom: What constitutes a dialogic text? Some lessons from small group interaction. *Language and Education: An International Journal, 13*(2), 99–117.

Hirst, E. W. (2002). Construction of identities in the LOTE Classroom: The interanimation of mediational means. Ph.D. diss., University of Queensland, Brisbane, Australia.

Hirst, E. W., & Renshaw, P. (In press). Diverse voices, dialogue and intercultural learning in a second language classroom. In P. Renshaw & J. van der Linden (Eds.), *Dialogical learning: Shifting perspectives to learning, instruction, and teaching*. Amsterdam: Kluwer.

Kamler, B., Santoro, N., & Reid, J. (1998). *Cultural differences in the teaching profession: How much does it count?* Paper presented at the Australian Association for Research in Education Conference, Adelaide.

Kingdon, M. (1995). Student behaviour management: Addressing the issues for teachers of languages other than English (LOTE). In R. Conway & J. Izard (Eds.), *Student behaviour outcomes: Choosing appropriate paths. Selected papers from National Conference on the Behaviour Management and Behaviour Change of Children and Youth with Emotional and/or Behavioural Problems* (pp. 86–91). Melbourne: Australian Council for Educational Research.

Knoeller, C. (1998). *Voicing ourselves: Whose words we use when we talk about books*. Albany: State University of New York Press.

Kramsch, C. J. (1993). *Context and culture in language teaching*. Oxford: Oxford University Press.

Kramsch, C. J. (1998). The privilege of the intercultural speaker. In M. Byram & M. Fleming (Eds.), *Language learning in intercultural perspective*. Cambridge, UK: Cambridge University Press.

Kress, G., & Fowler, R. (1979). Interviews. In R. Fowler, B. Hodge, G. Kress, & T. Trew (Eds.), *Language and control* (pp. 63–80). London: Routledge & Kegan Paul.

Kuipers, J. C. (1998). *Language, identity, and marginality in Indonesia: The changing nature of ritual speech on the Island of Sumba*. Cambridge, UK.: Cambridge University Press.

Leander, K. M. (1999). *Classroom community as spatialized discursive practice: Mapping the production of identities in a high school discourse-space*. Paper presented at the American Educational Research Association Annual Meeting, Montreal.

Leander, K. M. (2001). "This is our freedom bus going home right now": Producing and hydridizing space-time contexts in pedagogical discourse. *Journal of Literacy Research, 33*(4), 637–679.

Lefebvre, H. (1976). *The survival of capitalism* (F. Bryant, Trans.). London: Allison and Busby.

Lingard, B., Ladwig, J., & Luke, A. (1998). School effects in postmodern conditions. In R. Slee, G. Weiner, & S. Tomlinson (Eds.), *School effectiveness for whom? Challenges to the school effectiveness and school improvement movements* (pp. 84–100). London: Falmer.

Lo Bianco, J. (1998). The implications for languages of the emergence of the international university. *Australian Language Matters, 6*(4), 1, 8, 10.

Luke, A. (1998). Critical discourse analysis. In L. Saha (Ed.), *International Encyclopedia of Sociology of Education* (pp. 50–57). New York: Elsevier.

Luke, A. (2002). Curriculum, ethics, metanarrative: Teaching and learning beyond the nation. *Curriculum Perspectives, 22*(1), 49–55.

Luke, A. (2003). Literacy and the other: A sociological approach to literacy research and policy in multilingual societies. *Reading Research Quarterly, 38*(1), 132–141.

Luke, A. (In press). A polemical reconceptualisation of literacy as social practice. *Language and Education.*

Macaro, E. (1997). *Target language, collaborative learning and autonomy* (Vol. 5). Clevedon, UK: Multilingual Matters.

Macedo, D. (2000). The colonialism of the English only movement. *Educational Researcher, 29*(3), 15–24.

MacKerras, C. (1995). A policy initiative in Asian languages. *Australian Review of Applied Linguistics* (ARAL), Series S, *12*, 1–16.

Miller, J. (1997). Teachers who don't belong anywhere: Three themes of itinerancy. *Unicorn, 23*(1), 74–84.

Morgan, C., & Cain, A. (2000). *Foreign language and culture learning from a dialogic perspective* (Vol. 15). Clevedon, UK: Multilingual Matters.

Mulkay, M. J. (1988). *On humour: Its nature and its place in modern society.* Oxford: Polity Press in association with Blackwell.

National Asian Languages and Studies in Australian Schools (NALSAS). (1998). *Factors influencing the uptake of Modern Standard Chinese, Korean, Modern Greek & German at primary & secondary level in Australian schools.* Perth: Education Department of Western Australia and Commonwealth Department of Education, Training and Youth Affairs.

National Asian Languages and Studies in Australian Schools (NALSAS) Taskforce. (1998). *Partnership for change: The NALSAS strategy—interim progress report of the first quadrennium of the NALSAS strategy 1995-1998.* Carlton: Ministerial Council on Education, Employment, Training and Youth Affairs.

Nespor, J. (1994). *Knowledge in motion: Space, time, and curriculum in undergraduate physics and management.* London and Washington, DC: Falmer.

Parliament of Australia. (1998). *Current issues brief 2 1998–99: 1998 Queensland Election,* 2003. Retrieved January 8, 2004, http://www.aph.gov.au/library/pubs/cib/1998-1999/99cib02.htm.

Queensland School Curriculum Council (QSCC). (2000). *Languages Other Than English: Year 4 to 10 Indonesian syllabus.* Brisbane, AU: QSCC.

Rämö, H. (1999). An Aristotelian human time-space manifold: From chronochora to kairo-topos. *Time & Society, 8*(2), 309–328.

Rix, A. (1999). *Review of the languages other than English (LOTE) program implementation.* Brisbane, AU: Education Queensland.

Roulston, K. (1998). Music teachers talk about itinerancy. *Queensland Journal of Educational Research, 14*(1), 59–74.

Sheehy, M. (1999). *Un/making Place: A topological analysis of time and space representation in an urban Appalachian seventh grade civics project.* Ph.D. diss., Ohio State University.

Soja, E. W. (1996). *Thirdspace: Journeys to Los Angeles and other real-and-imagined places.* Cambridge, MA: Blackwell.

Stanley, J. D., Ingram, D., & Chittick, G. (1990). *The relationship between trade and linguistic competence.* Canberra: Australian Government Publishing Service.

Troyna, B., & Rizvi, F. (1997). Racialisation of difference and the cultural politics of teaching. In B. J. Biddle, I. Goodson, & T. L. Good (Eds.), *International handbook of teachers and teaching* (Vol. 1, pp. 237–265). Boston, MA: Kluwer Academic Publishers.

Wells, G. (1999). *Dialogic inquiry: Towards a sociocultural practice and theory of education.* New York: Cambridge University Press.

Wertsch, J. V. (1991). *Voices of the mind: A sociocultural approach to mediated action.* Cambridge, MA: Harvard University Press.

Wertsch, J. V. (1998). *Mind as action.* New York: Oxford University Press.

4

Four Days and a Breakfast: Time, Space and Literacy/ies in the Prison Community

Anita Wilson

One day I asked a young man in prison how long he still had to serve in prison. "Not long," came his reply, "just four days and a breakfast."

(Anita Wilson, 1997 ethnographic data)

Introduction

In this chapter I want to focus on the interrelation of space, time, and literacy/ies and show how they can be (re)configured in culturally appropriate and culturally specific ways. While spatial and temporal (re)configurations may be identified in many domains, arenas, and spheres of everyday life, this chapter focuses on one—the specific and somewhat marginal environment of prison. Prison remains outside the parameters of knowledge of most people, and a conventional perception of what it is like, fed by the selective reportage of the media, is often at odds with the reality of day-to-day prison life. In addition to the austere, dangerous, and total institution presented to the public, everyday prison life can, in addition, have moments of humor, exhilaration, sadness, and mind-numbing boredom—words that are more in keeping with everyday life outside the jail rather than what might be presumed to exist within. After prolonged discussion, the prisoners and I concluded that the conflict between the imposition of institutional worlds and identities and their desire to retain a social and individualized lifestyle can only be resolved by the creation and maintenance of a third space. However, while this space has a particular significance for the prison community, it would be impossible to describe or discuss it in isolation without recognizing either its interrelation with prison time or the various literacy-related activities and practices that intersect with and support the (re)configuration and melding of both. My aim here is to show that far from being the anonymous docile mass that statistics would suggest, people in prison retain a strong sense of personal agency, which they apply in culturally appropriate ways to both time and space. It is also my intention, supported by the views of prisoners and staff, to show that literacy-related activities, practices, and artifacts play a central role in this struggle to make sense of the various dimensions of the prison world.

Fundamentally, I want to show that within the third space, concepts such as "four days and a breakfast" along with "asking for a Xmas tree" and "teaching Brian to swim" are perfectly rational, logical, and appropriate prison-related activities and practices.

Chapter Outline

Separating space from time in the day-to-day reality of the prison setting is an impossible task, and yet for this discussion it is one that I am required to attempt. Therefore, I take space as the point of departure, talking in terms of the relevant space and literacy—related issues that occur both outside and inside prison, which go on to influence and impact on the creation of the third space. Having described this third space in relation to literacy-related prison activities and practices, I then move to discuss concepts of time, again aligning them to general prison issues, before (re)situating them and their attendant literacy-related activities and practices within the more appropriate space delineated by the prison community itself.

There are two issues, however, that I need to resolve as a prelude to the main discussion. One involves my methodological frame and its attendant ethical considerations and the other involves my theoretical frame and its application to prison literacy/ies.

Methodological Frame

> Research doesn't have to be another brick in the wall. It is obscene to take a researcher who actually wants to know more about people and divert them into manipulating "variables," observing "responses," and all the rest of the ways that people are falsified and fragmented. If we want to know about people we have to encourage them to be who they are, and resist all temptations to make them—or ourselves—into something we are not, but which is more observable, or countable, or manipulable. (Reason & Rowan, 1981, p. xxiii)

This chapter has a history that relies to a great extent on the voices and experiences of contributors other than the author. It is important, therefore, to touch on the collective ownership of this data, the methods by which they have been collected, and the attendant ethical considerations such as equity of representation.

Occasionally, even high quality research omits detailing the processes and approaches by which it has been undertaken, and I often find myself asking, "How did you approach this work?" "Have you permission to share this information?" or "Who was involved in this project?" It would require more space than that afforded by this chapter to answer these questions fully, but for the reader who frets over the same kinds of issues, I feel ethically bound to answer them briefly in relation to my own work described here.

As an ethnographer I find that the experiences, observations, and interactions gleaned from one project go on to inform subsequent investigation, and the information shared here is drawn from almost twelve years of sustained collaborative and cooperative qualitative inquiry in prison settings. I work from a perspective of grounded theory (Glaser and Strauss, 1967), researching alongside male and female prisoners, young and old, long term and short term. Some have stayed with me for a number of years while others have spent shorter periods of time—research time and prison time—in the spaces my projects inhabit. Without them I would have no projects and without their permission I would have nothing to say. I thankfully acknowledge the generosity with which they continue to share their prison experiences and that they allow me to share them with others. If, as Reason and Rowan (1981, p. xxiii) suggest, "we want to know about people," then we have to not only allow them to "be who they are" but ensure that they are fairly represented beyond the fieldwork. Prison ethnography would indeed be "obscene" if it denied the true voice of those upon whom the research rests. I therefore strive throughout my work to (re)place prisoners' voices in arenas where they are seldom heard, such as within policy documents (Home Office Research Study, 2000) and practical training materials, and wherever possible I choose prisoners' words over mine, hence the title of this chapter.

The second issue is that, although the central theme of this volume is literacy, we cannot assume our readings of the term to be concordant. I now outline my model for literacy/ies in order that the readers can locate their thoughts within my theoretical frame.

Theoretical Frame

Literacy is primarily something that people do; it is an activity, located in the space between thought and text. Literacy does not just reside in people's heads as a set of skills to be learned and it does not just reside on paper, captured as text to be analyzed. Like all human activity, literacy is essentially social, and it is located in the interaction between people. (Barton & Hamilton, 1998, p. 3.)

Surveys from around the world (UNESCO, 1992; Moser, 1999) make strong claims that prisoners' general standards of literacy are well below those of the outside world, with around 40 percent of prisoners identified as functionally illiterate. These claims rest on a particular view of literacy in the singular, as something to be imposed, tested, and evaluated, held within a pedagogical frame, aptly described by Street's (1984) "autonomous" model of literacy. If I or the reader were only concerned with literacy within this framework, our discussion would terminate here. But I am more concerned with locating the proliferation of multiple literacy/ies that are generated across the prison on a day-to-day basis than with confining prisoners' reading and writing activities, practices, and material artifacts within a model of literacy that operates only within the parameters of education departments and prison schools, fixed on rates of illiteracy and levels of assessment. I take a "situated" view of literacy/ies, grounded in Street's ideological model (1984) in line with proponents of New Literacy Studies and the Lancaster Literacy Research Centre, where multiplicities of reading, writing, and literacy-related activities and practice are contextualized within day-to-day life. This focus is exemplified in studies on everyday reading and writing (Barton and Hamilton, 1998), on issues of identity in academic writing (Ivanic, 1998), and in my own work on prisoners' reading and writing (Wilson, 1998). The approach is further reflected in studies from other parts of the world, such as Caniesco-Dorinila's (1996) work with island communities in the Philippines, Kapitske's (1995) work with Seventh Day Adventists, and Ahearn's (2002) study of love letters and literacy in Nepal. There is no question, of course, that prisoners do engage in aspects of autonomous literacy (hence my adherence to the complex term "literacy/ies") through various forms of institutional bureaucracy, standardized documentation, assessments, and evaluations.

But the reading and writing that I find primarily colonizing prison space resonates with the ideological model. Subsequently, this conflict of literacy/ies between the institutional (autonomous) and the situated (ideological) creates a point of tension. On the one hand, prison tries to push prisoners into an institutional space which prioritizes institutional literacy, while, on the other hand, prisoners resist by defending their personal space with contextualized literacies that carry traces of outside world practices and activities. From what appears to be a no-win situation, the tension is resolved by the selective amalgamation and colonization of institutional and situated literacy/ies which both constitute and are constitutive of a third space.

Having situated the chapter from both a methodological and a theoretical point of view, it is now possible to move forward to construct an envi-

ronment in which "four days and a breakfast" is an appropriate and understandable form of meaning-making. This first stage is to outline the relevance
of activities and practices drawn from worlds outside the prison.

Outside Space/s and Outside Literacy/ies

I put a claim in against Probation with my solicitors [lawyers] because—I got arrested, they said I'd breached my bail but I'd finished it and I finished it over a year
ago. And they said they were sending me letters, and they knew where I was living,
but I ain't got no letters or nothing. And I got picked up and arrested and put in the
cells for two nights and when I did go to court they realized they'd made a mistake.
So I've got a claim in for that now. (Young man's experience of the criminal justice
system, Home Office Research Study, 2000. p. 27).

For many people caught up in the public world of the criminal justice
system, space has already influenced their lives. A considerable number of
offenders come from backgrounds of poor housing, insecure accommodation,
or homelessness. Some are caught up in the more abstract but no-less-real
spaces of unemployment, poverty, and discrimination. From a literacy perspective many have negative experiences of schooling, few qualifications, and
a disproportionate range of learning difficulties. Ironically, they are forced to
inhabit the official spaces occupied by systems of welfare, justice, and job
seeking where they are required to negotiate complex bureaucratic paper
trails.

Engagement with literacy-related activities and practices—as noted in
the scenario above in relation to making a claim against the Probation Service—are complex and contextualized, located in a public world where people
"do" things with literacy/ies that have little to do with a school-based curriculum but a great deal to do with survival. Unemployed youth occupy their
time negotiating the bureaucracy required for benefit claims, the homeless
deal with complex applications for housing, and the addicts rely on any
number of culturally specific literacy- and numeracy-related activities and
practices for the procurement and dealing of drugs. Such skills become useful
tools for anyone who moves from the outside spaces of public life into the
bureaucratic landscape of prison spaces, and they offer the chance not only
to survive but also to disrupt and fracture the process.

Also within their parameters of knowledge but not their experience are
other regular outside world activities such as reading books, magazines,
writing poetry, or engaging in correspondence. These are not necessarily
high on the literacy-related agenda of people who are struggling to survive at
the margins of the "outside" public world, but on their entry to the "inside"
world of prisons, such activities and practices are revisited and taken up as an

appropriate rebuttal to carceral spaces. Negotiating bureaucratic texts, knowing about books, or even writing on the body become integral parts of a set of culturally designated literacy-related activities and practices that contribute to the support of a third space. This space, however, also relies on the (re)configuration of inside institutional spaces and inside literacies.

Inside Space/s and Inside Literacies

> This is the dungeon
> In which I reside
> These are the bars
> Which keep me confined
> This is the slab
> Upon which I sleep
> The same cold stone
> Where the cockroaches sleep
> This is the ceiling
> This is the floor
> This is the spyhole
> My steel studded door
> These are the walls
> All spattered with spite
> This is my world
> This is my fight
> (TC, 1987)

Space within a prison is no less complex than space in the outside world. It must be understood in both metaphorical and physical terms, as wide a concept as the entire prison estate, as individual as a cell, as personal as the mental sphere, or as minute as the palm of a hand holding a scrap of paper. Traditionally, prison is spatially constructed as a total institution (Goffman, 1961), controlled by physical and metaphorical demarcation (Cressey, 1961), where hierarchies of power rule the establishment (Sykes, 1970). Discipline—an intrinsic part of the institutional ideology—as Foucault claims (1977, p. 141), "proceeds from the distribution of individuals in space," and there is no question that the removal of bodies from outside public space to inside incarcerative space is utilized by the prison as a primary means of effecting control. From a systems perspective, the institution is bounded by concrete realities of walls and fences, its inmates confined to specific areas, corridors, and cells. In the day-to-day reality of prison life, however, prison spaces are constantly being renegotiated; described to me in the quote below, a space designed for institutional control is (re)configured as a site to resolve personal vendetta.

Now we're onto the Russian Front, which is no jest! It's the corridor which passes by all the halls that leads to the sheds as well as everywhere else. It's called the Russian Front because it's a ruthless stretch of corridor. If someone has something against you and they want to do you harm, you're more likely to get it on the Russian Front..... It doesn't happen every day but it's a war zone which is why it's aptly named. (Personal correspondence, map included, 1/10/97)

Although physical space in prison is intended to remain within the ownership and control of the establishment, in this example prison space has been colonized, renamed (using a term more in keeping with a news report or a historical document than prison terminology) and reappropriated to reflect the rules of the streets rather than the rules of the prison. Not all examples are so violent, however, and there are many occasions when ordinary day-to-day interaction blurs the distinction between inside and outside worlds and draws in both prisoners and staff.

For example, when prisons began to operate a policy of smoking only in designated areas—one of which was prisoners' cells and one of which was not staff offices—it was not uncommon to hear members of staff asking if they could enter prisoners' cells in order to have a cigarette! Transferring the activity from institutional to social space and from institutional to social spheres ruptures the demarcation lines between both personal and professional boundaries. From a literacy perspective, although staff office doors often display the official sign "No inmates beyond this point," some prisoners enter this designated official space, (re)configuring it as a social rather than as an institutional site where they borrow the newspaper, find out whether they have a visit booked, or occasionally whether they can use the phone. Prison staff themselves frequently "socialize" the same site by reading the newspaper, eating their lunch, doing the crossword, and pinning up humorous notices such as "Abandon hope all ye who enter here."

In each case, prison spaces identified by the institution are (re)configured in order to support and validate activities and practices drawn in from the outside world. Central to this (re)configuration are various activities and practices around literacy/ies. Taking place in the institution, they cannot be classed as totally outside even though many of them reflect aspects of outside public and personal worlds. Yet neither can they be said to be totally inside when many of them reflect outside as well as inside conventions. It is at this point that the third space requires a descriptive framework that would allow its transference to other sites and domains where conflicting and disparate environments and cultural demands come together.

Third Space Frame

> I was talking to my son, Brian on the phone, he's teaching himself to swim...it breaks
> my heart that he can splash a few wild strokes and thinks he can swim the ocean.I'm
> teaching him over the phone that rivers are different animals from swimming pools.
> (Thomas's personal correspondence, 7/21/96)

The normalization of activities such as leaving the prison after "four days
and a breakfast," describing a stretch of corridor as being like "the Russian
Front," or "teaching Brian to swim by telephone," as in the quote above,
suggests that these events occur in a culturally validated and culturally specific space. Attendant and equally context-dependant literacy-related activities and practices such as the nonuse of calendars, the inclusion of "moons"
into graffiti, or the importance of displaying correspondence in an iconized
way sit equally comfortably within it. I have described the third space framework in detail elsewhere and as an evolving theory the reader can follow its
progress in Wilson (1998; 2000a; 2000b; 2003; in press). However, I want to
give its broad outline here with specific attention in relation to space and
time. After considerable discussion, prisoners and I came to the conclusion
that while in prison their major concern was not to become "prisonized" or
"institutionalized." I have quoted this prisoner elsewhere but still find that his
words describe this desire so well that I include them again here in order to
stress the point.

> It is a silent battle—not with a recognizable enemy, it is a battle with our minds. To
> win we have to pamper them, cater for them, bribe them, keep them occupied or
> lose them. If we lose our minds, we lose ourselves and the battle. It is a battle that I
> will not and cannot lose. (Personal correspondence, 4/29/94)

In order to "win the battle" people in prison construct a space between
inside and outside worlds where they can "occupy their minds" while living
out their everyday prison lives. Bounded by a consensual experience—in this
case the experience of prison—such a space can accommodate a whole
community with a membership that can include both central and peripheral
players, prisoners and staff, and those who live both inside and outside the
prison walls.

The concept of the third space is not, of course, only mine, and while
concepts of liminality (Turner, 1974) and crossings (Rampton, 1995) are
appropriate for certain arenas, I find Bhabha's (1994) third space theory—mapped on to the predicament of disoriented and disenfranchised
migratory groups searching for a sense of identity—to be of particular salience. Colleagues suggest that the concept is particularly appropriate where

people find themselves operating at sites of struggle or at points of identity crisis.[1] This third space, however, regardless of where it is constructed, does not exist in a vacuum.

It is operationalized and acted upon by people taking up what Gee refers to as a Discourse, defined as:

> a sort of "identity kit" which comes with the appropriate costume and instructions on how to act, talk, and often write so as to take on a particular social role that others will recognize. (1990, p. 142)

This reading of Discourse goes beyond mere language and includes what Gee goes on to describe as:

> ways of being in the world...which integrate words, acts, values, beliefs, attitudes, social identities as well as gestures, glances, body positions and clothes. (1990, p. 142)

This concept resonates with Bourdieu's (1977) notion of habitus. In the third space of the prison world these "ways of being in the world" encompass activities such as "teaching Brian to swim by telephone" or announcing that you have only "four days and a breakfast" until release. As with the third space itself, the rules of third space discourse remain fluid and changeable. The only fundamental and concrete requirement is that the "appropriate costume" and "set of instructions" for its membership is made up from inventive and creative variations on the hybridization of outside and inside influences. Literacy-related activities, practices, and material are integrated in appropriate and salient ways. "Teaching Brian to swim by telephone" and the allocation of "Russian Front" were recounted to me in correspondence. Details of the "Russian Front" were supported by the inclusion of a hand-drawn map, which is itself is not a permissible artifact in institutional prison life.

I want to bring further life to the model of prison third space by focusing on a literacy-related aspect of everyday prison routine. For readers who do not know my work, I refer them to *Situated Literacies* (2000a, Chapter 4, p. 58) for an example involving Nike trainers. For existing readers, I offer you a fresh perspective.

Third Space Literacy/ies: A Request for a Xmas Tree

> Prisoners should receive a written reply from the prison within seven days of submitting a Request/Complaints form (F2059 (A)), either with a full answer or an indi-

---

[1] I'm indebted to Deride Prins, University of Cape Town, and Kate Pahl, Sheffield Hallam University, for their insightful comments.

cation of when they should receive a reply. Requests and complaints about certain subjects may only be handled by Headquarters. The booklet "How to Make a Request or Complaint: Information for Prisoners" is available in prison libraries (*A Working Guide—Prison Rules 1992 Requests and Complaints*, 1992, p. 42).

Within the bureaucratic institutional protocols that prisoners must attend to is an official form that allows prisoners to make a request/complaint regarding various aspects of their prison lives. Using the request/complaint procedure is a serious business. Prisoners must be able to give good reason why they feel it is necessary to implement the procedure which is only allowed after all other avenues of request or complaint have been fully explored. Records of request/complaint forms are mandated by the institution, collated, and referred on to central records. Prisoners' attitudes toward this official procedure and the powerful avenue for complaint that it affords them are somewhat ambivalent. For every request/complaint that receives a positive outcome or focused response, there are many that come back with general and somewhat anodyne replies, often deterring prisoners from activating this avenue of complaint. For example, one prisoner wrote and told me of his request for his remote control in order to set up his hi-fi equipment. The written response was this:

> The answer to your request is NO. At the present time, inmates at this establishment are not allowed to be in possession of a remote control for their own use. Things may change in the future but not at the moment.

Another prisoner wrote to me of his written request for a bed board that would alleviate a serious back problem. The written response came back:

> I have checked with the Health care centre and found you do suffer from back ache of the lower spine and there is not much they can do. Bedboards are not supplied any more as they were all withdrawn. The only alternative is to put your mattress on the floor.

However, rather than confining bureaucratic protocols within the parameters of the institution, prisoners sometimes (re)assign them to the third space. One prisoner shared his own experience of the request/complaint procedure with me, and I am permitted by him to recount it here. Approaching Christmas, he decided to use the request/complaint procedure as follows. He began at the top of the form in his own handwriting:

> *Details of Application*—Request permission to have a Xmas tree sent in; and could the works [department] build me a chimney please—cos Santa missed me last year!! Thank you!

Rather than deny the request, or attach a predictable response, the application proceeded through the official channels and was filled in thus:

Action by Landing Officer—Not authorized to order bricks—forwarded to Works. (signed [allegedly] by the landing officer)

The form continued through the system and was added to appropriately:

Action by Governor—Mr. [name of officer] has agreed to bring you in a tree from home and Mr. [name of another officer] says he'll be the fairy on the top. (signed by an officer)

Action by Wing Manager—To Works—to measure up and cost. (signed and dated by an officer)

The form ends with this instruction:

Prisoner informed of outcome of application. (signed by an officer and dated) This form should now be filed on the prisoner's wing record [personal data file].

This example brings together a number of salient points to support a claim not only that a prison third space with its own required discourse exists but that language and literacy/ies play a central part in its creation and support. Aspects of inside prison and outside prison cultures—carceral and Christmas—are brought together. The procedure is further complexified by the fracturing of roles, responsibilities, and protocols by both staff and prisoner. Each is aware of the discourse of "form filling." Each has an awareness of the official status of the request/complaint form. Each has taken hold of this knowledge and protocol and reconfigured it to fit the appropriate discourse required for the third space, where humor, complicity, and social life are essential parts of day-to-day prison existence.

This recolonization extends to any number of institutional spaces and many utilize various aspects of literacy-related activities, practices, and material artifacts. For example, the institutional space of desks, mattresses, pillows, or pinboards are recolonized by graffiti practices brought in from outside cultures and redefined according to the mores of the third spaces.

Rather than the stylized monikers and the exaggerated visual impact of graffiti in the outside world, that which is brought into the third space by young offenders carries—in conventional graphology—the real name of the writer, the date the graffiti was written, and details of the length of sentence to be served. It often alludes to people's geographical location and links to their loved ones. An example would be "Gareth Hunt o/v Lancaster...lookin' at 3 years, but I still love Louise Benson" (personal journal, 1997). In short, it is personal! Ironically, such activity continually takes place even though the author is easily identifiable by his own written admission and punishable under an offence relating to the defacement of prison property.

Interestingly, third space graffiti becomes more intense and prolific when prisoners feel the most dislocated, i.e., in the holding cells as they enter the jail, where they are most distanced from their outside worlds, or the punishment block, where they are most distanced from their fellow prisoners. It also appears that the more a person becomes separated from their outside social world, the more important it is to keep aspects of that world in existence. Prisoners in solitary confinement, for example, not only describe extreme physical spaces in graphic terms, but reiterate the importance of literacy-related activities and practices within them. The quote below was written in order to try to articulate the extreme loss felt when personal correspondence goes missing:

> A lost letter to people in sol-con is like dropping a rock down over a deep dark chasm...when there is no reciprocating echo, the chasm becomes a void, a scary pit to be avoided...you feel and grope in the darkness, lost in a box with all the universe around you in darkness—a lost letter is a severed feeler, cut off over the edge of the chasm. (Personal correspondence, 3/1/92)

These feelings tie into the emotions articulated by the prisoner quoted earlier in the chapter who described the need to occupy and nurture his mind in order to retain a sense of social being. Each instance relates to prisoners' desire to retain a sense of control over mental spaces when physical spaces are still held within the constraints of the institution. These mental spaces still hold to the culturally specific discourse and rules of the third space.

Young men, for example, against the conventional norms of gendered reading (Millard, 1994), escape into the mental and imaginative spaces of the world of fiction rather than ground themselves in inappropriate facts about the outside world. When prison poets are denied or do not have access to writing materials, many utilize the spaces in their head where they compose poetry. Many of my acquaintances can recite much of their work verbatim "because no-one can steal it if it's in your head." Again, the notion of "writing in my head" fits the model of the third space, transcending the physical space of the institution where it takes place and (re)placing it in the personal and private space of the mind.

However, while teaching Brian to swim by telephone, losing a letter in solitary confinement, or writing in your head occur not in specific spaces, they do occur at specific times. Prison time—like prison space—is complex and contradictory. Prisoners will say that time passes both quickly and slowly, that summer days are too long because of the extended daylight and that winter days, with little sunshine, pass more quickly. Time is very personal and means different things to different categories of prisoners. Like space, time is a topic that may be studied through a variety of theoretical lens; and in line with the focus of this volume, it is to the interrelation of times, spaces, and literacies that I now turn.

Times, Spaces, and Literacies

Down the punishment block on a Wed. evening spent some time speaking to Terry—we talk about his home life, his mum, dad and sister, he hasn't had a visit since March this year—during the course of the conversation I say that I must go as I have been in the jail since 10.00 a.m. this morning—so what, he says, I've been in the jail since quarter to eight on the 15th of September 1994. (personal journal 11/1/95)

Just as space and literacy cannot be conceptualized in the singular, so prisoners move to a variety of temporal rhythms. Terry's comment was a salutary methodological lesson for me and acted as a catalyst for my continued thinking on the relationship between time and the third space. His individualized view of time has been reflected in many that I have subsequently received. Taking the institutional perspective, prison times, such as time to eat, time to sleep, and time to work, are another means by which the system attempts to retain power and control over what it perceives as "docile bodies" (Foucault, 1977, part 3). Twelve years of ethnography lead me to believe, however, that the desire of members of the prison community, who in an effort to "keep their minds" are mostly anything but "docile," is to resist such control and to translate time into culturally appropriate outside-oriented parameters. In particular, (re)configuration to judicial time, incarcerative time, and calendar time have considerable relevance to the third space. I also want to touch on the notion of "dead" time (Bourdieu, 1977, p. 161), a concept appropriate for the configuration of prison as institutional and prisoners as docile, but not to the prisoners who (re)configure it as "alive" time. I now want to move to center on these four aspects of temporality.

Judicial Time

What I'm saying is that inside, ten to fifteen years
Or even more can be got through
They really can
Enough that you never let the precious stone
under your left breast grow dull
(Advice for Someone Going into Prison, Hikmet, 2002)

In the United Kingdom, judicial time initially imposes itself when sentence is passed, and fundamental and influential distinctions are made by both the system and prisoners themselves between short-term sentences (up to four years) and long-term ones (over four years). This ruling affects the cultural philosophy of the prison community not only in its perception of fellow prisoners but also in their activities and practices that involve literacies. Sentence length, for example, appears to influence prisoners' personal writing practices, and my observation, supported by prisoners comments and correspondence, is that longer-term prisoners write longer letters. A prisoner explains:

> It is due to the perception of time that long-term prisoners write longer letters than short term prisoners, the main reason for this is because people serving short sentences don't feel a real need to keep a link open with the outside world. A quick note now and then suffices as they are out very soon, they also tend to get lazy and writing a long letter is too much like work for them. Long termers will nearly always write long letters because we know we are going to spend a good few years of our life incarcerated so to keep a link open to the vast world beyond is very important. (Mick, personal correspondence, 3/3/97)

As Mick states, the need to retain links to the outside world has a special significance for those who are distanced from it the longest, and I am constantly amazed at how long-term prisoners remain aware of contemporary trends in fashion, language, or current affairs. Judicial time—as Hikmet suggests above—loses some of its power if a prisoner holds to his or her own sense of personhood and attends to matters of the heart rather than the institution. Many long-term prisoners find ways of giving an outside take on inside practices. Some tell me that transference from inside to albeit temporary outside space, such as going out to the hospital or moving to another prison, is seen as "a day out." One told me, "Court days are considered holidays" (personal correspondence, 3/20/97). In January 2003, a long-term prisoner told me that his recent day in court gave him the opportunity to meet with other long-term prisoners with whom he had had little contact over the years; he described the meeting as being like an "old boy's reunion." Graffiti, too, is (re)configured, and prisoners (re)place judicial time within third space parameters, translating their sentence into celestial time by embedding the concept of "moons" rather than "months" into the graffiti of prison vans and court cells. The reason for this, I am told, is that "moon," having a twenty-eight-day cycle, has the psychological effect of being less time than a month, which may be up to three days longer.

Judicial time is both aligned to and ruptured by the conventional calendar. The date of entry into and release from the system has obvious significance for each individual prisoner, but the halfway point in a sentence and each New Year's Eve has great significance for everyone. Prisoners' comments suggest that regardless of the length of time they are serving, the halfway point in a sentence moves their period of incarceration away from judicial time toward "getting out time," meaning that there is less time to serve than has already been served. New Year's Eve indicates the passing of another year for every prisoner—regardless of the length of sentence—and shifts judicial time into celebratory time, ritualized by lots of noise, singing, yelling, and banging on cell doors at the approach to midnight. This disruption of judicial time through the (re)configuration of inside and outside worlds is continually played out, and again the third space creates an appropriate arena for these (re)configurations.

Incarcerative Time

Rule 2. In the evening, in your cell, you are permitted to talk in a low tone until the nine o'clock bell rings, when, if you have not already previously done so, put out your light, undress, and retire....Rule 5. At the ringing of the morning bell, you must turn out, dress, make up your bed neatly, and be ready for marching out. At the signal, open the door, step out, and close the same without slamming, hold on until the bar is thrown, and remain standing with your hands upon the door until the count is made. (Rules for the Government of Convicts) (Clemmer, 1940, p. 191)

In order to effect control through disciplined activity, the prison community is programmed to move to the rhythm of incarcerative time. Time-tabling, one of the oldest means of control (Foucault, 1977, p. 149), involves the establishing of institutional rhythms, the imposition of particular occupations, and the regulation of cycles of repetition, amply illustrated in Clemmer's (1940, pp. 71–72) account above of American prisons in the 1940s and in the contemporary prison timetable outlined below.

Official Timetable

TIME

07:30	Roll Check Razor Issue
08:00	Breakfast Dine out of cell, sick, applications, collect razors
08:10 – 08:30	Sick and treatments sent to Hospital (when called for)
08:30	Works inmates collected by staff
08:30 – 09:00	Searching

(Young Offenders Institution Excerpt from Weekday Routine)

The prison is regulated by official timetables which allocate days, hours, and even minutes to work (or nonwork), exercise, eat, and sleep. Acting within the remit of prison rules, official tasks are time-tabled on a daily basis for particular times. Prisoners are "released" in the mornings to go to court or be discharged and returned in the evening; those remaining in the prison are allocated tasks (even if this includes the task of having no task). Many of these regulated activities involve aspects of literacy. Letter censoring, for example, is often undertaken in the morning, correspondence is handed out at lunchtime, and the circulation of official forms, such as official notices regarding prison regime, is usually undertaken on set evenings in the week, as noted by one of my prison diarists:

> Wednesday 1st
> wrote letter to girlfriend after I got one off her.
> Read a notice that they put under my door about inter-wing sports. It's about going out on Saturdays to watch football. The 10 cleanest cells get to watch. And kit change is on a Friday evening instead of Saturday morning.

Applications to see the doctor, dentist, or governor are scheduled only for morning unlock, while writing a symbolic signature on reception into the jail usually takes place in the evenings. Incarcerative time is imposed even more stringently upon the most recalcitrant prisoners. Those on the escape list, who are mandated at all times to document their continued and validated presence in incarcerative space during all hours of the prison day, carry a written record with them at all times which must be signed at regular intervals by an officer. Those in the punishment cells have their "time out of cell" reduced to one hour out of twenty-four. However, the disparity between constructions of official time-tabling and third space time-tabling is amply illustrated by Mick's Monday-to-Friday routine, recorded below, described to me in correspondence which shifts away from the institutional toward the social and individual.

Prisoners' Timetable

TIME
08:00	Wake up and start the day with a cup of coffee
08:20 – 09:00	circuit training down the gym
09:05 – 11:20	work
11:20	Lunch
12:00 – 13:30	writing time and listening to music
13:30	WORK
16:20	Dinner
17:00	reading time/music time
18:00 – 20:00	chill out with a few acquaintances
20:00 – 22:00	reading time or studying
22:00 – 24:00	T.V. time
24:00	SLEEP

(Mick's Monday-to-Friday routine)

While the institution sees time-tabling as a means of effecting control, Mick's timetable uses a configuration more aligned to social rather than institutional spheres, including "starting the day with a cup of coffee" and "chilling out," (re)configuring incarcerative time to fit the discoursal requirements of the third space. In another example, a prisoner described to me the signaling ritual he had taken part in as a young offender—using a form of visual literacy—in order to communicate the number of days left on a prison sentence:

> being young we clenched hands one in front of the other over the mouth, like a trumpet and blew and then raised the fingers to represent the amount of days we had left...then blew again and raised the little finger to represent a "break" which is the breakfast before leaving. This was to wind up newcomers and was a weight off the shoulders when you had ten days to go. (Personal correspondence, Zeki, 2/24/97)

The "break"—like "four days and a breakfast" cited in the title—moved the last day in prison away from incarcerative time. This practice is also found in American prison argot and illustrated most recently (Rhode Island, December 2002) in a piece of writing, given to me by a young American prisoner, entitled "Three Days and a Get Up," where he described his last day in prison as a "get up" (as in "get up and go"). Even prisoners who are not on the point of departure translate judicial and incarcerative time into more appropriate and manageable chunks. A young man described to me his strategy of "thinking in months" in order to manage his time inside:

> standing at the gate of the health care centre I was speaking to Ian and he was saying about how many months until he can apply for parole—and how many before he can be possibly released—it sounds strange for someone who was recently given a 12 year sentence to be talking about being released—he says that if he thinks in months it doesn't sound so bad i.e. that it is 52 months until he can start thinking about getting out. (Personal journal, conversation with Ian, September 1997)

At the opposite end of the carceral spectrum, a political prisoner writing in his journal used the same mechanism:

> I'm in bed at the moment, covered in breadcrumbs and skimpy British army blankets, my knees tucked up under my chin and a blue plastic mug of tea in my hand.... Only one hour, four minutes and one thousand six hundred and twenty-four days to go. (Adams, 2002, p. 20)

Given that prisoners translate days into breakfasts, months into moons, and years into minutes, hours, and days, it is hardly surprising that conventional calendar time has little currency in the third space. That which does exist is (re)configured appropriately.

Calendar Time

I don't really bother with the calendar I have, it just covers a space on the wall.

(Andy, in correspondence, 2/7/97)

Calendar time and its material representation have only selective relevance to people in prison. Terry's words, "I've been in the jail since quarter to eight on the 15th September 1994," suggest certain calendar dates are more strongly bound up with personal lives than institutional limitations. In its concrete textual form, calendar time is drawn into institutional spaces for social rather than institutional activities and practices, as illustrated when I asked Andy in correspondence whether he owned a conventional calendar.

> I've got a big sheet of paper on the wall with all the important dates like birthdays and I have a little book with other dates. The only time I'll look at a calendar is when I forget the date which is a usual occurrence for me. I'm not big on dates, just my family's birthdays for sending cards, old firm games [football matches between the Scottish teams of Rangers and Celtic] and January the 1st as it's New Year. (Andy, in personal correspondence, 2/7/97)

Although Andy states that he isn't "big on dates," having (re)configured his conventional calendar as a wall decoration, he still owns a personal record of culturally specific cyclical events to support his efforts to retain a social focus on his life. His attitude is reflected by other prisoners who also choose to mark down and remember the dates significant to their personal rather than their institutional life. John, for example:

> has a calendar made up of lines which he crosses out and also another one made of the dates of the month so that he knows when he might be getting out and also to know when the baby will be born. (Personal journal, 11/23/95)

He also confined this calendar within his personal space—placing it under the mattress of his prison bed—further colonizing institutional space with socially oriented literacy-related practices and artifacts.

Long-term prisoners, however, as already noted, think of time in temporally different but equally appropriate third space ways. One long-term prisoner distanced himself entirely from calendar time:

> [I was] speaking to someone who says that his calendar would only have years on it—not much point in having days weeks or months. He says he's thinking of getting one that only shows the decades so that the time would seem to go faster. (Personal journal, 1/24/98)

These comments further reflect the difference in the delineation and management of incarcerative time between long-term and short-term prisoners. Those incarcerated for years do not feel the need to have visual reminders of the passing of days or weeks. Young prisoners serving short sentences, however, disrupt the flow of judicial, incarcerative, and calendar time with appropriate practices. One of my prison diarists said,

> Monday 23 February I also ticked off my calendar today and counted how many weeks I had to do on my sentence. It turns out I only have nine weeks left. (Mark's diary)

I noted in my research journal that

> keeping a calendar is OK because he is absent-minded and so he forgets to cross of the days and then gets the chance to cross off 4 or 5 at one go. (Personal journal, 3/30/95)

A prison cleaner at the same establishment told me that

> he has a calendar but like everyone else forgets to mark the days off and sometimes marks off 2 weeks at one go. (Personal journal, 9/25/96)

These comments suggest that calendars are used to record the length of time a prisoner expects to remain in the jail rather than to record how much time he has already spent. The physical activity of "crossing off 4 or 5 at one go" literally makes time move quickly and (re)configures prison time, using literacy-related activities and practices in order to achieve it.

Dead Time

> I opened a box of biscuits that I bought with my canteen [commissary] yesterday, and while I was eating I read the box, mainly to see what, if any, nutritional value could be gained by eating them. I also read my prop[erty] card, to make sure I was signing for the correct things. That's all I think. God, life's boring in prison isn't it. (Mark, writing in his literacy diary)

Prisons in Britain may legally lock up prisoners for twenty-three out of every twenty-four hours, and although the numbers of people for whom this is a day-to-day reality is less than those who have greater access to time out of cell, prisoners nevertheless still experience a large proportion of what might be considered "dead" time (Bourdieu, 1977, p. 161) when they are confined within their cells.

Historically, the institution has held to a belief that dead time creates a temporal and spatial vacuum in which prisoners contemplate their misdemeanors. The ideology of the penitentiary rested on its inmates spending long periods of time becoming penitent. It might be argued that this time of "suspended animation" (Blake, 1971, p. 95) holds prisoners within the parameters of incarcerative time, but it is my belief—supported by the narratives of many prisoners—that such time is (re)configured for personal use and thus overrides any imposition of institutional temporal constraints. It is during time spent behind the door that prisoners undertake most of their nonofficial forms of literacy-related activities.

Prisoners (re)appropriate activities and practices around reading books, for example, as a way of rupturing dead time even though such activities may not have been intrinsic to their own outside world practices. Young people frequently tell me that prison offers them an opportunity to "read a book right through"; and, as referenced earlier, young men bring reading into the third space by flouting conventional outside practice (Millard, 1994), choosing to read fiction rather than fact. Reasons given are that "it lets you escape" or that "it takes you out of prison for a while" and draws attention to the phenomenon of "mental space" and the need—as noted earlier—to keep the mind as well as the body active. Prisoners use dead time to write personal letters, capitalizing on long periods of lock-down to concentrate on correspondence that may include poetry, copied text from books or newspapers, or may be decorated with artistic embellishment (Wilson, 2000b). In addition to supporting and maintaining social ties to the outside world, letter decoration and embellishment are also undertaken occupy and disrupt prison time as well as to support social ties. On asking a prisoner once how long it took him to complete a decorated envelope, his reply was a telling: "Does it matter?" During allegedly dead time, prisoners capitalize on known literacy practices, conventions, and artifacts to create temporal illusions. Celebratory time, for example, gets extended beyond conventional timescales.

Mark noted in his diary, "Wrote a Valentine's card out—Thursday 26th January," and during my years of research I have received birthday cards at the beginning of July (although my birthday is not until the end of the month) and Christmas cards at the end of November.

In prisoners' cells birthday and Christmas cards are displayed year round, (re)constructing temporal parameters to challenge the extremes of prison life and signaling to others that the prisoner has a personal as well as an institutional identity. Prisoners also spend dead time using material artifacts to (re)configure their prison cells as living accommodation rather than institutional space. When asked why he or she has displays of books, photographs, posters, and correspondence in a cell, a prisoner will reply that it is "to make it more homely" or "to make it feel like it belongs to me." It is during dead time more than in any other dimension of temporal awareness that prisoners seek to draw personal and social practice into institutional spaces.

So what does "four days and a breakfast," "teaching Brian to swim by telephone," or "reading to keep your mind" say about time, space, and literacy? I want to address these under the heading of concluding remarks. However, as I noted at the beginning of the chapter, all projects—this one included—are part of an ongoing process. Consequently, in this final section I have questions as well as points to consider.

Concluding Remarks

Firstly, let me address the questions. How can looking at the world through a spatial or temporal lens help us to understand the issues that currently face marginalized, depersonalized, or constrained groups in contemporary society? I would suggest that it provides an opportunity to challenge conventional thinking and move toward a position of ability rather than inability, of positive agency rather than negative passivity. Seeing prisoners as more than an autonomous mass, bound to an autonomous model of both prison and literacy, and constructing them instead as having the knowledge and critical ability to "keep their minds" in difficult times and constrained spaces must be a positive step towards resocialization and a sense of citizenship.

How should we construct literacy in a world of multiple spaces and identities? Is it useful to continue to constrain it to the spaces of pedagogy? Is there one literacy that exists in the spaces of the world or is it only one literacy that the world seeks to prioritize? Taking a situated view of literacies is not easy. It requires us to engage with those who use it, in the spaces in which they utilize it and at the times that it is felt to be most appropriate. For research, for policy, and for practitioners this is a difficult task and challenges us to find new ways of validating the data that is offered to us and to find equally innovative ways of disseminating it. We must resist the temptation to think about literacy as though it were, indeed, just one thing—that constructing an exam response is the same as constructing a letter home, that reading a court deposition is the same as reading a novel, that writing graffiti in the street is the same as writing your name in blood in a punishment cell. To deny the extent to which people engage with various forms of literacy-related activity and practice is to deny a sense of heterogeneity and difference.

Is the third space relevant to discussion about time and space? I can only answer "sometimes." In arenas where people are comfortable in the spatial, temporal, cultural, and personal environments that they find themselves in, there is less need to break open a third space. But at points of tension, where resistance and struggle are evident, where retaining a sense of personhood takes precedence over expected ways of being, it would seem that a third space can offer recognition to people, often constructed as powerless and ineffective, who find ways to retain and sustain a sense of relevant identity that allows them to live rather than to exist.

Looking at any area of human life through the lens of time or space can provide fresh insights into the way we construct and perceive the world. To look at the specific environment of prisons from both spatial and temporal perspectives gives us an opportunity not only to reconfigure our perceptions of the institution of prison itself but to recognize the ways in which it is acted upon by the human beings it holds. Undertaking an appraisal of these traditional and accepted concepts throws into question the docility of prisoners, their lack of agency, and their perceived lack of ability to engage literacy-related activities and practices.

However, in discussing either time or space, we cannot address one without being mindful of the other. In prison terms, judicial, incarcerative, or even dead time exists in certain spaces, and these spaces are influenced by various temporal rhythms which are constantly being renegotiated.

Prisoners create and maintain a third space drawn from the spatial and temporal influences of both outside and inside worlds, taking hold of elements of each and (re)configuring them in culturally appropriate ways that match its discourse, activities, and practices. By the same token, the temporality of investigation cannot be detached from the environment in which it takes place. As noted at the beginning of this chapter, my work is an organic process constantly in a third space, reliant on both the past and the future and governed by spatial and temporal considerations and limitations. The danger of holding to a dichotomy of either/or denies the importance of the intersection of space and time and the reality and messiness of day-to-day life. Falling into the trap of generalization is also a dangerous space to be, having the potential for elitism, discrimination, and a denial of the complexity of the human condition. The interrelation of time and space should therefore be a primary concern to all of us who are engaged with research in the field.

Also, we cannot assume that traditional indices are the only ones that count or that they can be separated from the times and/or the spaces in which they exist. To discover what really lies beneath presented statistics, variables, and abstract descriptions of various environments, groups, activities, or practices, we have to lay aside our preconceptions and put some trust in information that can only be accessed in spaces and at times that are appropriate to those environments, groups, activities, or practices we seek to understand. As I said during the early part of this discussion, talking about literacy and prisoners from a conventional perspective would have been a short conversation. In the spaces and timetables of education classes and prison schoolrooms, the literacy test would have told us that most prisoners cannot read or write. However, by looking through a contextualized lens, here we are some pages further on, having talked about prisoners' prolific literacy-related activities and practices and their interrelation with agency, resilience, (re)configuration, and resistance.

From both a methodological and an ethical point of view then, it is important to remember that neither time, space, nor literacy can be configured in the singular. Attention needs to be paid to what aspect of time, what area of space, or what form of literacy we are talking about. Again, this disrupts the notion that there is only one way of thinking about the world or that there is only one way of constructing the things that go on in it. Literacy to the institution means the autonomous model, complete with assessment and evaluation, whereas in the day-to-day existence of people in prison it means writing letters, reading books, and negotiating legal documentation at various times, in various places, and for reasons that may well transcend those of the institution. Overall then, constraining space, time, literacy, research, prison, or any other environment or concept with which we might be concerned is not only a singular impossibility but a denial of the heterogeneity of the world in which we are situated and the worlds we seek to understand.[2]

References

Adams, G. (2002). *Cage eleven.* Mount Eagle, Dingle, Ireland: Brandon Press.

Ahearn, L. M. (2002). *Invitations to love; Literacy, love letters, and social change in Nepal.* Ann Arbor: University of Michigan Press.

Barton, D., & Hamilton, M. (1998). *Local literacies: Reading and writing in one community.* London: Routledge.

Becker, H. (1996). Whose side are we one? Address to the Society for the Study of Social Problems. *Social Problems, 14,* 239–247.

Bhabha, H. K. (1994). *The location of culture.* London: Routledge.

Blake, J. (1971). *The joint.* New York: Doubleday.

Bourdieu, P. (1977). *Outline of a theory of practice.* Cambridge: Cambridge University Press.

Canieso-Dorinila, M. L. (1996). *Landscapes of literacy: An ethnographic study of functional literacy in marginal Philippine communities.* Hamburg: UNESCO.

Cannon, J. P. (1968). *Letters from prison.* New York: Merit.

Clemmer, D. (1940). *The prison community.* New York: Holt, Rinehart & Winston.

Cressey, D. R. (1961). *The prison: Studies in institutional organisation and change.* New York: Holt, Rinehart & Winston.

Foucault, M. (1977). *Discipline and punish: The birth of the prison.* London: Penguin.

Gee, J. P. (1990). *Social linguistics and literacies: Ideology in discourse.* London: Falmer Press.

Glaser, B. G., & Strauss, A. L. (1967). *The discovery of grounded theory: Strategies for qualitative research.* Chicago: Aldine.

2 I wish to express my gratitude to Rachel Hodge, Lancaster Literacy Research Centre, Lancaster University, for her insightful comments on earlier drafts of this chapter and to the Spencer Foundation, New York, for their current financial support to my work.

Goffman, E. (1961). On the characteristics of total institutions: The inmate world. In D. Cressey (Ed.), *The prison: Studies in institutional organisation and change* (pp. 15–67). New York: Holt, Rinehart & Winston.

Hikmet, H. (2002). *Beyond the walls.* London: Anvil Press.

Home Office Research Study. (2000). 'Tell them so they listen: Messages from young people in prison.' *Home Office Research Study Number 201,* J. Lyon, C. Dennison, & A. Wilson. London: Home Office.

Ivanic, R. (1998). *Writing and identity: The discoursal construction of identity in academic writing.* Amsterdam: John Benjamins.

Kapitske, C. (1995). *Literacy and religion: The textual politics of Seventh Day Adventism.* Amsterdam: John Benjamins.

Millard E. (1994). *Developing readers in the middle years.* Maidenhead, UK. Open University/McGraw Hill.

Moser, S. C. (1999). *A fresh start: Improving literacy and numeracy.* Sudbury, UK: Department for Education and Employment.

Rampton, B. (1995). *Crossing: Language and ethnicity among adolescents.* London: Longman.

Reason, P., & Rowan, J. (1981). *Human inquiry: A sourcebook of new paradigm research.* New York: John Wiley & Sons.

Street, B. V. (1984). Literacy in theory and practice. Cambridge: Cambridge University Press.

Sykes, G. (1970). *The society of captives.* Princeton, NJ: Princeton University Press.

Turner, V. (1974). Liminal to liminoid in play, flow, and ritual. *Rice University Studies, 60,* 53–90.

Wilson, A. (1998). *Reading a library—writing a book: The significance of literacy/ies for the prison community.* Ph.D. thesis, Lancaster University.

Wilson, A. (2000a). There's no escape from third-space theory: Borderland discourse and the in-between literacies of prison. D. Barton, M. Hamilton, & R. Ivanic (Eds.), *Situated literacies: Reading and writing in context.* London: Routledge.

Wilson, A. (2000b). "Absolute truly brill to see from you again": Visuality and prisoners' letters. In D. Barton & N. Hall (Eds.), *Letter writing as a social practice.* Amsterdam: John Benjamins.

Wilson, A. (2002). *Understanding and working with women in custody: Multi-disciplinary training program for custodial and non-custodial Staff.* London: Women's Policy Unit, Her Majesty's Prison Service.

Wilson, A. (2003). Researching in the third space: Locating, claiming, and valuing the research domain. In S. Goodman, T. Lillis, J. Maybin, and N. Mercer (Eds.), *Language, literacy, and education: A reader.* Stoke on Trent, UK: Open University Trentham Press.

Wilson, A. (in press). "Nike trainers, my one true love—without you I am nothing": Youth, identity, and the language of trainers for young men in prison. In J. Androutopoulos (Ed.), *Discourse constructions of youth identities.* Amsterdam: John Benjamins.

5

Between a Thick and a Thin Place:
Changing Literacy Practices

Margaret Sheehy

Data and findings in this chapter are extrapolated from a larger time/space classroom study, *Un/making Place* (Sheehy, 1999). In *Un/making Place*, I documented how a seventh grade classroom at "Sanders Middle School" (SMS) valued space and time through the social practices of science and social studies classes. My interest in that study was, in part, to explain the social processes involved when a teacher, Jade, tried to change the way students and she engaged in social studies and science. Jade, who had been unhappy teaching at SMS, taught an eight-week civics project, which veered from usual classroom practices. Jade had tried similar student-centered projects, before the civics project, and found it difficult to engage students, because the seventh graders were used to teacher-centered classroom practices. Jade continued to try, however, because she considered it a serious problem that 50 percent of the seventh graders scored poorly on their sixth grade standardized test and that, in seventh grade, many of her students were not in school. The truancy rate, in the eight months I was in Jade's classroom as an observer and participant-observer, was always at least 17 percent, usually 33 percent, and by May, 84 percent across the entire school. Jade was very vocal, with me, in her belief that schooling had to change for SMS students.

Lack of engagement in the social practices of schooling at SMS was long in the making. According to the 1990 census, 50 percent of the adults in Sanders had not finished high school. Judging by the seventh graders' truancy rate and low test scores, it appeared to me, in 1998, that they would likely reproduce this same statistic. In Ohio, students who didn't pass their statewide exam in eighth grade were held back, and students who didn't pass the twelfth grade exam could not graduate. Even though critical cultural studies have moved away from reproduction research (Giroux, 1983), in part, because that line of work (e.g., Anyon, 1980; Willis, 1977) tended to privilege structural, societal explanations of social life over explanations of people's agency in their lives (Eisenhart, 1995), there are schools like Sanders where students routinely do not get served. Poor grades, drop-out rates, and truancy do get reproduced from year to year and, in the case of Sanders, from decade to decade.

Thus, I undertook a reproduction study, to understand how the experience of school—as teacher-centered practice—becomes so seemingly sedentary. I wanted to understand why it is that teacher-centered school practices, like what Jade tried to change and what Anyon (1980) and others (Shuman, 1986; Willis, 1977) found occurring in working class schools, continues. The seventh graders' agency over their time—leaving school entirely or periodically, or just not participating in the literacy practices while in the classroom—enabled them to resist schooling, but their resistance did not change school practices. For instance, in Jade's classroom, even though students used many forms of resistance, worksheets and textbooks were still read as teacher-centered lessons in which the intent was to regurgitate the content on worksheets. When Jade resisted teacher-centered literacy practice and tried projects, students did not easily take them up; while they may have resisted worksheet and textbook practices, they also resisted alternative practices. Thus, resistance, on both Jade and her students' part, always engaged old and new practices, simultaneously.

In this chapter, I will describe the old, new, and in-between spaces of Jades' civics project, "the Building Project." I will show how the three spaces were constructed, over time, through flows of information that extended beyond the classroom in distinctly different ways. I will explain that while old and new space produced and reproduced themselves, it was when Jade and the students were between places—between old and new space—that participating in new social practices was difficult. It is the in-between space, I will argue, that requires further examination, if we hope to make long-term changes in schools that routinely fail youth.

I begin the chapter with a discussion of the exchange of information (Appadurai, 1986) as it relates to the making of space (Lefebvre, 1991). I then provide examples of old, new, and in-between spaces made in Jade's classroom. I close with a discussion of how objects play in the making of space.

Theoretical Framework

Exchange of Information

Engagement is a chief concern of literacy research because literacy involves production and consumption processes. People make and use texts. Texts, Luke and Freebody (1997) argued, are ideological, and literacy practices around them inculcate participants in relations of power. From a sociocultural perspective, engagement in literacy can be viewed as participation in networks of relations in which cultural values are formed and expressed (Rogoff, 1991). Wells (1993) has explained that exchanges of information in classroom talk are a negotiation of objects. In this research, I viewed objects as ideas, which were often mediated by actual objects-as-things: a chalkboard, a worksheet, a video, a survey, for example.

In Jade's science and social studies classroom, ideas were shared through exchanges of information—talk, writing, drawing, charting, mapping, computing. The most common type of oral exchange was the IRE pattern, in which ideas were initiated by the teacher, responded to by a student, and in turn evaluated by the teacher. This pattern often became what Gutiérrez (1995) called responsive. In these cases, Jade continued to evaluate students' responses, but students sometimes also asked questions or responded to a fellow student's response.

Appadurai (1986) argued that the base of exchange is desire. In an exchange, economic value is determined reciprocally. He means, by this, that exchange requires sacrificing one object for another. Value is established in exchange. Participation in a classroom exchange can mean that one finds value in sacrificing some kind of position—one of silence, of dreaming, of doing something else—to negotiate an object of study. However, Appadurai (1986) also noted that exchanges do not necessarily mean that one truly desires or values an object being exchanged. Sometimes, one's position in an exchange is lesser than the position of the one with whom an exchange is occurring. One can be involved in an exchange of ideas and reproduce the value of that exchange without truly valuing the object or the exchange.

Over time, exchanges on floors of classrooms create literacy economies—flows of ideas around texts. Engagement in the literacy economies of science and social studies at Sanders Middle School often produced a disembodied, lackadaisical movement of ideas. Many students slept, rested their heads on their forearms, paid no heed to the object of exchange, skipped class, or interrupted exchange by veering away from the object under negotiation. Some (often two or three students, and usually the same students) contributed the necessary responses to keep the exchange of further ideas flowing.

Giroux (1997) questioned the value of objects of study in school, arguing that "essential to this project [of critical, human-centered curricula] is a fundamental concern with the question of how we can make schooling meaningful in order to make it critical" (p. 71). Jade, in order to make school meaningful, veered away from the "ordained" objects of study in her text-books. Rather than focus on "structure and design," a category of knowledge on the Ohio standardized test, she embarked on a building project. The Building Project involved structure and design, but not as an object that focused students' attention.

The Building Project came about this way. Sanders was a neighborhood of 16,000, in the city of Crayton, a city of 1 million. The Crayton School Board, after much heated public debate around school closure, decided to close SMS. Some of the city's schools had low enrollment, and although Sanders had a high enrollment, the building itself was determined to need enough repair that the school board accepted a community-based decision, as a cost-saving measure, to close the school and renovate another school in its place.

I had been researching at Sanders for one month when this decision was made. I began my research with a language arts teacher, Audrie, but had become interested in Jade's work because she was struggling to change her students' experience of school. When the board made its decision to close SMS, I approached Jade and asked her if she would want to co-teach a building project. I knew she desired collaboration and that she liked to teach through projects. Jade agreed to embark on the Building Project because she felt it would help her teach "structure and design," a category of knowledge with which the seventh graders needed to be familiar before taking their eighth grade statewide standardized tests, the next school year.

The Building Project was an eight-week project. In the first week, students explored the school closure issue and school funding issues in Ohio. In the second and third weeks, they wrote, distributed, and analyzed a survey to learn, firstly, whether SMS students, teachers, and parents wanted a new school and, secondly, what they would want in a new school. As the students analyzed survey results, they also read and wrote about Sanders. Over several weeks, the students designed and built paper models of schools and spent the final weeks of the project writing a speech, in Audrie, the language arts teacher's classroom. Jade planned that the speech would be delivered to the school board, with all the seventh graders present, at the end of the Building Project. The speech was suppressed, however, and wasn't delivered until the end of the school year, when I, who was not in danger of losing my job, took a few of the students to the board. While the suppression of the speech was an effect of the relations of power that became evident in the exchanges of information during the Building Project, its suppression is not germane to this chapter. What I want to draw attention to in this chapter, through discussion of old, new, and in-between space, is how the flow of information around objects of study bound the classroom as a place. I examined these flows using a framework influenced by Appadurai, as I have discussed, and also by Lefebvre.

Lefebvre's Spatial Theory

Lefebvre (1991) did not want to reduce social practice to a mere transposition of the social onto a map of space. This would relegate space to the background, as mere setting for social practice. Lefebvre felt that space and social practice were of equal importance and that they could not be separated. His interest was to develop the theoretical possibility for changing hegemonic social practices by rendering them visible through the revelation of ideology at play in space. According to Lefebvre, space was not environment, not stage setting, and not place; yet it involved each of these, which came to be significant as a result of how they became engaged in and changed by social practices. Lefebvre's spatial theory includes (1) spatial practice, (2) representations of space, and (3) representational space. The three spaces work together (see also Chapter 6).

Spatial Practice. Spatial practice (or social practice) involves production and reproduction of relationships between people, people and things, and people and practice. People involved in spatial practice enjoy a range of competence at the practice. Individuals' relationship to the social space and its activity ensures a continuity of the practice and the relationships made in it. In spatial practice, reproduction of social relations is predominant. Accordingly, in a classroom such as Jade's, where the IRE was the dominant means of trading information, students became competent in their roles in that practice, and relationships developed between participants, the practice, and the objects of study—the actual ideas they produced. Since the IRE required that only one student participate at a time, one could become competent not only in participating in that exchange but in listening, sleeping, or staring at a wall, for example. The flow of information from Jade to students and back to Jade was reproduced as a spatial practice involving relationships—to the practice, to the place of practice, to the participants in the practice, and to the objects of study.

Representations of Space. Representations of space are abstract but play a part in relations between people and objects. As people engage in spatial practice, they engage in the knowledge/power at work in representations of space.

Harvey (1996) explained the power/knowledge of spatial practice around representations in school studies in this way:

> Academic disciplines constitute their distinctive objects of enquiry through a particular spatio-temporal framing of the world. This framing is political precisely because it defines a certain and restricted set of "self-other" relations for examination (if only between the investigator and the investigated): the choice of spatio-temporality is not innocent with respect to the social relations...that are highlighted or, just as significantly, rendered invisible.... (p. 266)

Power functions as people relate around objects. That one object of study exists and not another is itself indicative of power relations. For example, one of the seventh graders' objects of interest, which they discussed while also engaging in the Building Project, was sex. Sex, particularly as the seventh graders framed it, was not a curricular topic of study. The students' framing of sex defined self/other relations of gender and also homosexual and heterosexual relations. Sex, as a representation of space embroiled in power relations evident in the students' narratives, competed with the official object of study in Jade's classroom—the Building Project. The Building Project was also embroiled in power relations. Jade reported that she would not have done the project if structure and design had not been categories on the eighth grade statewide standardized test. The Building Project, as an object—a representation of space—became one because it could serve Jade in the teaching of usual curricular content. While the Building Project was embroiled in the power relations of the statewide test, because Jade tied it to the test category, the project became embroiled in other power relations, too. While structure and design figured in the project, other ideas circulated as well and distributed markedly different relationships between the seventh graders, the object of their studies, and the practices themselves.

Representational Space. Representational space is the body's experience of space. This space is dominated by ideology and power (since this is what one experiences in social practice and in living among representations of space), but it is also the space of imagination. The Building Project was an imaginative project that occurred in response to and in relation to the usual curriculum as well as in response to and in relation to Crayton city politics. It contradicted usual curricular space, providing possibility for different objects of study, different spatial practices, and different relationships to the practice. These three spaces—practice, representation, and bodily experience of space—function simultaneously.

I turn, now, to spatial explanations of old space, new space, and the in-between space. As I describe these spaces, I speak to practice, representation (objects of exchange), and bodily engagement and disengagement. Examining the three, together, enables a description of space as well as an analysis of the differences they reveal.

Old Space, New Space, and In-Between Space

Tensions occur between a known space and the making of a new space. Before explaining how these tensions play in the making of a new space, I provide two examples of space from Jade's classroom. The first, "a thick place," describes the flow of information exchanged in Jade's usual classroom. This flow was space: it was the social practice; it was tied to power/knowledge relations inside and outside the classroom; and it was bodily experienced. The second space, "a thin place," is an example of the new space made through the Building Project. The example represents typical practice among the seventh graders, in the final two weeks of the project. It is important to keep in mind that this space—where information flowed freely as students exchanged information with one another, their language arts teacher, with texts they chose to open, with imagined relations to the school board—was short lived. Not only did it not reproduce itself after the Building Project was over, its flow of information became routine only in the final weeks of the project, as students wrote speeches to their school board.

A Thick Place

Jade and her students typically exchanged information in a teacher-to-student-to-teacher flow of information, as in the following example of an IRE around first-class levers:

> Jade: First-class lever. How many remember the word "fulcrum"?
> Stu: I do.
> Jade: Okay. That word should be in your vocabulary from last year. Fulcrum.
> (Jade goes to board and draws a teeter-totter.)
> Jade: On a seesaw or teeter-totter. Looking at the sheet. The fulcrum is in the middle. This is a first-class lever. So, this is important. You will have to be able to see the difference between a first class, a second class, and third class. So, in a first-class lever system, the fulcrum is in the middle, and you have force and load. (Jade labels these on drawing.) Think about sitting on a teeter tooter, when you were younger. Think about having someone sitting, who weighs much more than you do.
> Stu: (Some chatter)
> Jade: Let's say this person is on this side. His name is Joe (labels drawing). He weighs 200 pounds.
> Stu: (Whistles)
> Jade: And this is Ann.
> Tyrone: She weighs 1.

Jade: She weighs130. Who is doing the force, who is the load? Okay.

Jennifer: Joe is the force, Ann is the load.

Jade: Okay, Joe is going to sit down here. He weighs 200 pounds. That's going to
  force the teeter-totter down. Okay. Ann's going to get on, Ann weighs 130, and
  she is going to go up in the air. She is the load. Okay?

Stu: (Can't hear, has a comment)

Jade: Okay. First-class lever system.

The IRE is a spatial practice. Relationships were made around the representation of space, first-class levers. Relationships were made not only to that object, but also between Jade and students and between Jade, students and a test. The test was implicit in Jade's comments: "So, this is important. You will have to be able to see the difference between a first class, a second class, and third class." Even though the relations made in the students' spatial practice seem to be made between just Jade and students, they are more complex. The representation—first-class levers—is embroiled in power relations: the raison d'être of the entire discussion occurs around them. These invisible relations are powerful enough to produce a category of knowledge (levers) and accompanying texts—worksheets and tests. The spatial/literacy practices in the classroom produced self/other relationships to the representation and to Jade and her students. The self/other relations involve Jade in asking her students to consider the importance of the object for purposes of a test.

The students' bodily experience of the spatial practice varied. As the example demonstrates, a few students traded information with Jade. What the example does not demonstrate is what other students were doing. Two girls were looking at photographs of boys in the youth band Hanson. Several girls and boys were slouched in their seats, some watching Jade and their worksheets and others not. Still others followed the worksheet and Jade, without slouching. The literacy practice around the object, first-class levers, cannot be viewed as embodied, engaged practice across the classroom. The two girls who stole looks at Hanson were embodied in their own practice. The students who didn't observe Jade's mediation of the object were not engaged; they marked time but did not give it value. It took only the few participating in the exchange to keep the ideas in circulation, reproducing the value of that flow. Thus, the exchanges around objects of study, which Jade put forward and which continued to circulate as an IRE, were produced and reproduced as space, even without the entire classroom's participation.

Other spatial practices and literacy economies, such as looking at photos of Hanson, could occur in old space, as long as they didn't intervene with old space exchanges. In other examples of old space, during the Building Project, if students veered from the object of study in ways that took Jade's attention off the object, that interruption was not tolerated. In those cases, students were admonished and the IRE then continued.

After Jade introduced first-class levers through this reading/writing exchange, students completed the worksheet on their own. When they finished, they brought the worksheet to Jade's desk. Later, Jade graded and returned them to students. She entered grades in her record book. The exchange of information in Jade's classroom is represented in Figure 1 as old space:

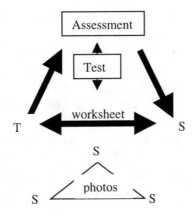

Figure 1. Old space, a thick place

The spatial practice in the example of first-class levers was the most common practice in Jade's classroom. A literacy economy was produced around it, and bodily participation in exchange varied. Old space, with its linear flow of school information, from teacher to students to the teacher, became representative of space. The underground exchanges that occurred among a few students did not disrupt the pattern, nor did the students whose engagement was not embodied. The pattern, represented in social practice, bound the classroom as a "thick place." Sack (1997) wrote:

> Places create differences. Places that are not too thick, that have complementary mixes of elements, and possess permeable boundaries, can lead to mutual dependence.... But if places are thicker and boundaries virtually impermeable, these differences can be turned inward. They can narrow membership, isolate communities, create fear and hate of others, and push us in directions of inequality and injustice. (p. 254)

Jade's classroom was a composition of difference; yet, because the objects of study set up self/other relationships between the students and the invisible gaze for whom they would, as Jade said, "have to be able to see," literacy practices produced real, geographic effects: a thick place. The thick place was made in the constant back and forth trade between Jade and students. Exchanges narrowed membership in the practice around the object of study. Rather than being invited into study that revealed possible relations of the object, students' ideas were turned inward—toward the object, as a closed system of meaning. Ann and Joe, on the teeter-totter, weren't real people to whom the students had a relationship, therefore, using them as an example did not broaden the classroom's networks of relations. When this kind of information was all that was traded on the classroom floor, a thick place was made. Bodies and ideas turned inward, most students did not engage with one another, and the object of study did not move into relations outside the classroom, other than to the relations of an invisible ideology (the students had to "be able to see" and eventually show that they could differentiate lever classes). The classroom, as a thick place, was isolated through spatial practice. Its contradictions did not change the spatial practice. Peripheral practice (Lave & Wenger, 1991), such as the girls' sneaked peaks at Hanson, had its own value, and other students' docility put no alternative object or practice forward. Docility legitimated the flow between teacher and students, and peripheral practice engaged another economy entirely. That economy did not interfere with old space.

A Thin Place

The final weeks of the Building Project were produced in different relations from the typical classroom space that Jade attempted to change. The thin place was the space that Jade imagined early on in the project, and, before that, in the other projects she attempted. It took seven weeks for the thin place to be made.

The following exchange is drawn from a writing workshop, in which three students are brainstorming ideas for the introduction to their speech to the school board. Unlike exchanges in the thick place, students in the thin place example are not focusing on the object in order to reproduce it in the invisible power relations in which it was offered them. Rather, they are claiming their own object, expressly to situate themselves in specific power relations. They do not attempt to replicate an object at all; they are negotiating its shape, taking the object from a number of relations in which it was first produced in the classroom and placing the it within yet other ones.

Rocky, Gemini, and Tyrone are writing an introduction. Rocky is writing for the group. All three students are suggesting ways to begin:

Gemini: Bonner schools. Bonner schools are better than ours and I don't think that's fair 'cause they get all kinds of computers and stuff. And you guys don't do nothin' about it.

Rocky: (writing) All kinds of computers and stuff.

Tyrone: How can they—

Rocky: How can they do something about it—

Tyrone: They're not Bonner Schools, how can they do somethin' about it?

Gemini: They can do somethin' by makin' our schools better.

Rocky: Yeah, but ya can't put it all on them 'cause it ain't their fault that Bonner Schools got better stuff than us.

Gemini: Yes, it is.

Rocky: No, it's not, because they—

Gemini: They won't raise taxes.

Rocky: Why would you want to raise taxes and—

Gemini: SO WE COULD GET better schools.

Rocky: Taxes are, were just raised not too long ago. (Rocky writes, then looks up.) Okay. Umm. I'm concerned about our children's history in this school.

Tyrone: Their FUTURE in this school.

Charting the path of the object itself—the content being exchanged—reveals a completely different literacy economy from the thick place. First, the object is not predetermined, therefore it cannot be replicated. Hence, the first thing to look at is, What is the object of the students' discussion and, secondly, where did it come from? The students were trying to address the school board. That address set up self/other relations, and the students chose an object strategically. The object Gemini chose was disparity between the school experiences of Bonner and Sanders kids. That object was retrieved from census data which the seventh graders looked at, the first week of the Building Project. At that time, most the seventh graders showed little interest in the census data, but seven weeks later, Gemini retrieved that object and situated it in new relations. In doing this, he extended knowledge—the object and his relationship to it—into new relations: he claimed the object, he resituated it in new relations, and he determined its value. The object, however, was not viewed the same by Gemini's peers, when placed in the relations Gemini imagined. Tyrone questioned Gemini's placement of the object, and Rocky completed his argument that Crayton schools could not do anything about disparity of school experiences between Bonner and Sanders: "Bonner is not a Crayton school." Gemini continued to insist that the object—disparity of experience—was a school board issue and that the board could do something about it by raising taxes. Rocky questioned this argument, too, and settled on an entirely new object, the sentence she jotted down and read to Gemini and Tyrone, "I'm concerned about our children's history in this school." Tyrone resituated that object in a different trajectory

of time, from past to future. Figure 2 is representative of the flow of exchanges in new space.

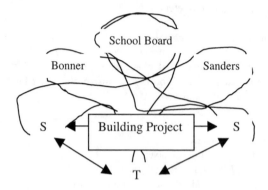

Figure 2. New space, a thin place

The difference between old and new space is this: old space turned the
seventh graders' bodies and ideas inward, inside the classroom, following a
narrow path; new space turned students' bodies and ideas outward, following
divergent paths. The path of the object matters. In old space, the path of
ideas was not directly tied to the seventh graders' everyday material lives.
New space, on the other hand, was made up of ideas that could not exist
outside real and imagined relations to the school board and Ohio school
politics. Objects in new space followed numerous paths. Students situated
objects with actual towns and an actual school board. In this thinking, the
thick boundary made in their typical classroom practices thinned out; the
membrane between their bodies and ideas became permeable, because ideas
moved into networks of relations that mattered to them. A much different
geography was made, and the classroom, bound by a permeable membrane,
became a different instrument of power than the classroom of old space. In
the thin place, the students resituated power/knowledge by virtue of deter-
mining the objects of their study as well as those objects' distribution.

   To this point, I have described two completely different literacy economies. They can be represented, as two diagrams, because the relations produced in them had become predictable: the flows of exchange in old and new
economies could be relied upon as the way the classroom did literacy practices. The in-between space, which I turn to now, cannot be represented as a
diagram. It was too frenzied a space and did not have a predictable composi-

tion. Whereas I described the composition of old and new space, I present tensions in the processes of change as my description of in-between space.

In-Between Space

Essentially, Jade and I wanted to create a new literacy economy—an exchange of ideas whereby students would introduce objects for negotiation as well as participate in channels of interaction that did not necessarily flow directly to the teacher. We had hoped that student passivity—which was one of the mechanisms by which the IRE stayed in circulation—would be replaced by exchanges which interrupted the teacher-to-student-to-teacher flow of information. Thus, we had hoped to create an entirely new literacy economy, an entirely new classroom space. While we did create such a space for a time, it was not easy. The seventh graders did not simply take up the new space imagination Jade offered because, as Soja (1996), explaining Lefebvre, wrote,

> All social relations become real and concrete, a part of our lived social existence, only when they are spatially "inscribed"—that is concretely represented—in the social production of social practice. Social reality is not just coincidentally spatial, existing "in" space, it is presuppositionally and ontologically spatial. There is no unspatialized spatial reality. There are no aspatial social processes. (p. 46)

Two factors figured strongly in in-between space. First, because students were competent participants in their classrooms, asking them to reconsider their practice disrupted some students' positions in the usual classroom space. Their relationships to old space were concrete. New space was, as yet, not inscribed. Second, as the students' bodies (always in relation to the object of study) extended beyond the teacher-student-teacher flow of information, belief and disbelief in newly distributed relationships made changing space inconsistent and, thus, difficult for students. The following examples illustrate these two factors.

New Space Confronts Old Space: Tensions at the Level of Competence in Spatial Practice. Early in the first week of the project, the seventh graders drew a master floor plan of SMS. I began the discussion and the drawing of the plan. The discussion occurred as an IRE. This was how information was traded in the classroom, and this is how it continued to be traded, even as we started the project. As the IRE ensued, however, I asked different students to come up to the master plan and draw their own ideas, rather than have me draw. The students saw SMS in different ways, and their drawing sometimes produced contention. Most students were highly engaged in this discussion. For the most part, disagreement was constructive because it prompted students to demonstrate their own views and explain why they felt someone else was wrong:

> Tyrone: (Standing at the floor plan.) The auditorium is way over here. Way in the corner.
> John: Why would it be all the way down there? (He gets up and goes to the plan.) As soon as you go downstairs, you go down here. You make a left and you go right...
> Students: (Lots of chatter in classroom; much disagreement.)
> Mariah: He's trying to fill in the whole floor.
> Margi: What are you saying?
> Mariah: He's trying to fill in the whole floor instead of like going back down the aisle. He's talking about coming in and why would you go clear down there and then go back downstairs.

Paco refused to participate in this exchange and looked angry. I approached him later in the period and asked him what was wrong. Paco perceived the talk going on in the front of the room as confusion. He did not like negotiation and said that Jade and I should have brought in the architect's rendering of SMS so there would be no question, in the first place, of what SMS looked like.

While Paco's experience was not typcial, it did cause me to consider both his position in usual classroom exchanges and how the object—the floor plans—held different power for Paco than for most of his classmates, in this instance. Paco was a good student. He didn't praise school practices, but he was good at them. He got good grades and his standardized test scores were good. The kind of exchange I promoted—opening channels of communication—threatened Paco's position as a good student in his classroom. Paco told me, earlier in the year, when his fellow students researched a country in South America and presented a lesson on the country, that his classmates couldn't teach. Later, during the Building Project, when students surveyed their parents and the SMS student body and faculty, Paco told me he did not trust his peers' survey results. Paco was a good student in the usual curricular space. That space, largely constructed through the IRE, did not put students in direct relation to each other. Their ideas flowed to the teacher.

Paco was reluctant to take on a new social practice. When he participated in the IRE exchange, his participation was commensurate with Jade's: he valued what was being exchanged and felt he was in a position to exchange ideas. He had a specific position in relation to the usual economy of literacy and a certain hierarchical position in relation to his peers, in that economy. When the exchange of information changed, Paco's usual position as a student was unstable. He did not value the exchange going on over the master floor plans. His disinterest had everything to do with the object of study. Paco knew how to read and draw an architectural floor plan. The class discussion was not valuable to Paco because it did not set up the kinds of relations in which he was interested in participating. He wanted to be engaged in relations and representations of architects. He wanted to show his competence at practice, in those relations. He had no interest in deciphering the shape of SMS with his peers. He would not engage in those relations nor that practice.

Paco did not value the kind of relational space Jade and I tried to create until the final weeks of the Building Project, when he'd made new relations to his peers, to the imagined communities of the city of Crayton, and to the objects of study. What had changed for Paco, and for his classmates, was knowledge itself: the objects of study were distributed in many relations, which were real to them. Demonstration of competence in the Building Project did not require that one know answers in order to speak. Demonstration of competence in the project required that one imagine possibilities. This change was an immense one to imagine and also to value, especially for Paco, whose position of competence in the usual classroom space afforded him ease in school.

Belief and Disbelief Influences the Movement of Ideas. While students were periodically highly engaged in the project, as most were when they drew the master floor plan, these points of engagement were more rare than frequent. Only in the final two weeks of the project did students engage with consistent desire to do so. Many students were highly experienced at engaging, passively, in school. Many students' disembodied engagement exemplified Foucault's (1984) thinking about docile bodies:

> Thus discipline produces subjected and practiced bodies, "docile" bodies. Discipline increases the forces of the body (in economic terms of utility) and diminishes these same forces (in political terms of obedience). In short, it dissociates power from the body; on the one had, it turns it into an "aptitude," a "capacity," which it seeks to increase; on the other hand, it reverses the course of the energy, the power that might result from it and turns it into a relation of strict subjection. (p. 182)

The usual classroom, as a space of relations around representations, was tied to the objects of study and the manner in which they were studied. The IRE did not involve many students in its maintenance, and as long as students didn't interrupt its flow, they could sleep, doodle, daydream, and so forth. I saw docility, and so did Jade, as strict subjection. The social practice of school had quite literally put some seventh graders to sleep. When students slept and daydreamed, I felt, as Foucault had stated, that power was dissociated from their bodies. However, the usual classroom social practices did not disappear as a result of the project. While the Building Project eventually interrupted the teacher-student-teacher flow of information around objects, this change was not developmental. Students did not daily become more and more engaged. Rather, students periodically came to life, so to speak, when the experience of representations (talk, texts, drawings, building, for example) in the classroom jolted their imaginations into relations outside the classroom. At these times, the course of energy—their own bodies, which, through classroom literacy practices, had turned inward on themselves—opened into a world of relations that had previously seemed cut off from them.

Students' imagined relations to people outside the classroom were essential to a changed space because it was when these relations were made visible, through talk and varieties of writing, that students became active. Even so, students remained students whose relations to objects of study dissociated their bodies from spatial practice. Thus, as the project progressed, engagement moved in and out of old and new relational possibilities. Students had to imagine the relations, buy into them, and trade with them. Thus, students' epistemological (who am I as a student) and ontological (what is school) worlds were being undone and remade, at once. This tension played out as belief and disbelief.

Disbelief was tied to students' imagined relations not only to the school board but to their typical work in school—new and old space intersected. Early on, one boy asked, "Why are we doing this if it isn't going to make a difference?" and a girl asked, "What if we do all this work and they don't listen to us?" Students were not used to their ideas "counting" for anything outside the economy of literacy in the classroom; in the classroom, value was made in right answers and right answers were eventually attributed value as grades on papers.

Disbelief played centrally in the inconsistent rhythms of engagement and docility that occurred from day to day. For example, when Jade conducted a whole class discussion about surveys, students were responsive. The discussion engaged students' imaginations in numbers of relational possibilities as they imagined whom their surveys would be written for and what kinds of information the surveys could gather. The day after the initial survey discussion, however, when students generated ideas to include on their own community survey, they looked bored. The imagination created in the exchanges of talk the day before did not carry over into the students' survey construction the next day. Instead, the students engaged in the survey in typical, docile ways. Yet, the day after that, when Jade brought the student-generated ideas to class, typed up as a survey, students became extremely engaged. The object (the survey) had moved through a series of imagined and real relations. In Jade's initial survey discussion, the object was, in part, a discussion of religion, of race, and students' experiences of race. When students wrote their own survey on the chalkboard, the object was rooms (student lounge) and possible activities (hanging out). When the students' ideas were represented on paper, the object incited whole-class interest in moving the survey into the community: to their parents, the SMS student body, and to the school board.

Every student participated in a whole-class interactive writing, in which they brainstormed how to write the introduction to the survey. After brainstorming, each student was just as engaged in writing his or her own introduction to the survey. Yet, students moved in and out of docile and active participation across the project, until the final two weeks, when the rhythm of participation was steadily active, as it was on the day they wrote the survey introduction.

When the project was over, and I was trying to understand these extreme rhythms of engagement and disengagement, I asked Kylene and Sarah to explain them to me. I had a photo album with pictures representing every day of the project. As we looked through it, I asked them questions:

> Margi: What did you think, were you kind of disbelieving, did you think, even then, "Survey, okay, whatever"? Did you really get the gist, that we were going to go out and conduct a survey?
>
> Kylene: First I just thought we were just doing it to see how a survey's done.
>
> Sarah: Yeah.
>
> Kylene: I didn't think we was really going to go to any classrooms and actually GIVE the surveys.
>
> Margi: Even though we were saying, "You are going to do this," you still did not believe it?
>
> Kylene: Yeah.
>
> Margi: When did it kick in, with the surveys, when did it kick in that you were going to do the surveys? Did it kick in here? (I point to a picture of ideas generated for survey on the chalkboard.)
>
> Kylene: It really kicked in when she started to say that each person is going to go into this class and this class, and then we started discussing when we was going to do it, and find a time and stuff, that's when it kicked in.

For Kylene, belief in conducting a survey kicked in after she had participated in writing it; thus, she engaged in the production of the survey docilely, just as she and other students often participated in the literacy practices of the usual classroom space. The survey, as an object, was never the same object, and bodies, in relation to the object, were never the same bodies. This was because distribution differed across time. Student relations—to the object, to peers and teachers in the classroom, and to the community whom students imagined and did not imagine the surveys would be distributed to—changed and were always changing. Thus, the classroom space of relations that Jade was creating through the project was not stable, and the usual space of relations tended to dominate students' imaginations for social practice. Kylene, for instance, lived in the classroom as a set of relations concretely represented as work to be done "just to see" how it is done; ideas did not get distributed into a world beyond the teacher. That space of distribution was ontological. Kylene could not believe she would do work to truly find out what her community wanted in a new school. That was unfathomable, until she could imagine the school day and her body being used to deliver the surveys to the whole school. The object, re-represented as a survey, typed up on paper, seemed to help students believe their ideas would be distributed to the people Jade and I presumed they believed they'd be surveying when they wrote the surveys.

Students' docility, or relationships to the objects of their studies, also played in students' perception of time. When I asked JoAnne about how the class did worksheets, she said, "It's just like, get one sheet at a time, and then we do it, and then we go up and get our other sheet, and we do that." This bodily practice was the daily rhythm of the literacy economy: "Get one sheet, …do it, and then…get our other sheet, …do that." Time and space of the classroom was so valued in known social practice around objects of study that students reproduced that value when they worked, whether or not they were interested. The exchange of information created a rhythm. Until the Building Project created its own rhythm, the space of the classroom continued to fluctuate, as ideas moved in and out of imagined possibilities, belief and disbelief. Without rhythm, whereby students could determine their use of time and determine meanings around objects of study, Jade thought about returning to her usual curricular studies. The in-between space had no discernible rhythm, and spatial practice was not predictable.

The uneven rhythms of engagement that occurred during the project were merely signs of old space's undoing. It took time for students to develop relationships to their practices. Space changed when students wrote speeches in the final two weeks. As they wrote speeches, they did not need sets of worksheets to measure their time, and they did not wait for a teacher to initiate a question to which they could respond (or not, as long as they were asleep or quiet). On the contrary, the students moved around the classroom, read books, took notes, looked through their portfolios, and talked with their writing groups as they drafted speeches. New space was not made by virtue of writing the speech; students had been making this space, from the beginning of the project, with the space of past practice.

The ninety seventh graders voted for Paco and his group to give their speech to the school board. The speech was suppressed, however. The vice principal told Audrie that Sanders could not be represented at the school board twice in a year, and it had already been represented once. This announcement came at the end of the project, right after the city superintendent had been invited to visit Jade's classroom, where a change in engagement had been occurring. In the hallway, the survey results hung on pie graphs. An important result of the survey was that the community didn't want a new school. Upon learning this, John stated, "That's going to be big," and Kylene's response was, "It was kind of shocking.... I hear a lot of kids walking around and saying, 'Well, I hope they tear the school down' and all kinds of other stuff, but when it really comes down to it, they really don't want to tear the school down, they just want to remodel it. Fix it up." The school board, however, had voted to close the school, based on a Crayton-wide community study. It is very likely the superintendent did not want the issue opened up again. When I asked Paco why he thought the speech was suppressed, he said, "There's no why, there's no nothing. It happened." I took the seventh graders to the school board at the end of the year. They went as citizens instead of representatives of SMS.

Right after the project, the space that Jade (with the help of Audrie) changed returned to the usual space. The IRE, textbooks, vocabulary, the parade of worksheets, and disembodied practices took up where the project left off. "Social reality is...ontologically spatial" (Soja, 1996, p. 46): Kylene didn't believe the students would "actually *give* the surveys"; JoAnn explained worksheet literacy—getting one sheet, doing it, getting another, doing that—as though that practice were natural; Paco believed that the speech suppression "just happened." The seventh graders' classroom, a thick place, was an instrument of power. While the new space was also a powerful instrument, its reproduction did not have the support of materials, curriculum, and practices. When the project ended and the seventh graders resumed the practices of old space, they took up those practices without question. They had experienced a thin place but they expected a thick one.

Discussion

In literacy practices, objects are constantly valued, in exchange. Maintaining value, by exchanging ideas, maintains distribution: a flow is established. Revaluing old space, through the Building Project, was a process of redistribution; ideas moved into different relations. For the seventh graders, redistribution was the imagined and real relations between the object and their bodies, as extensions of ideas into networks of relations. In the thick place of their usual classroom studies, ideas moved in narrow channels, directing bodies inward, toward the idea itself. When the classroom became a thin place, ideas moved outward, making divergent relational paths. Probably no one would argue that a thick place is a good thing and probably everyone would agree that a thin place is desirable. Getting there is not easy, however, because, simply put, living between a thick and a thin place is stressful. I will devote the rest of this discussion to that problem, focusing on the place of the object in classroom literacy practices.

People who meet the Sanders study want something different for the Sanders students. They think the right kinds of conversation can be inserted, like a CD, into space, a container. Even I, who worked with Jade in the classroom, thought that the space of students walking around and sharing ideas as they wrote would reproduce itself. I thought that, once this kind of conversation was rolling, it would keep rolling. But it didn't. The classroom had to get on with the things of the curriculum.

Lefebvre (1991) wrote,

> ...merely to note the existence of things, whether specific objects or 'the object' in general, is to ignore what things at once embody and dissimulate, namely social relations and the forms of those relations. When no heed is paid to the relations that inhere in social facts, knowledge misses its target. (p. 81)

The Building Project did not become consistently valuable to the seventh graders until the seventh week of the project. Seven weeks is a long time to live in in-between space. Most teachers don't have that amount of time because of the things of their curricula—the many objects they are to value and make valuable through studies with their students. Jade saw the project through to its end, but she was anxious to return to the usual curriculum because she felt responsible for its content, since all seventh graders in Ohio would be tested on it, in eighth grade.

The objects of school embody and disseminate relations. The seventh graders' curriculum was a spate of concepts that they studied in a manner that created a thick place. These odd objects of study, like first-class levers, had import because of their appearance on the statewide test. And they had supporting material—worksheets and the social practices around them. The things of school, which had the effect of dissociating many student bodies from the networks of relations they lived in, were more believable, in school, than the things of students' real lives—their neighborhood, their soon-to-be-closed school. Students expected to study benign objects, and they were so used to that study that when more objects of study landed, by virtue of being the next chapter in a book or the next set of worksheets, students took them up.

The power/knowledge inherent in things—abstract ideas as well as concrete things, like worksheets—is always tied to social networks. The thick place network happened to narrow participation into a channel between Jade and her students, even though the objects of study were tied to more complex relations. Objects of study were tied to textbook companies, a testing industry, and rhetoric about schooling—especially about school failure. Jade, for instance, was under extreme pressure to support her students' study of science and social studies objects because SMS students scored worse on their standardized exams than all the middle school youth in Crayton. Invisible forces maintained objects such as "structure and design" as well as their textual supports. Jade had difficulty making the objects of study in textbooks and worksheets matter to her students; yet, when her attempts to do projects failed, she returned to what her students knew: old space.

It is not so difficult to understand why changing space fails, if one considers what it takes to survive the in-between place. When students (as in the example of Kylene) do not believe that they are really doing the work that they are really doing, and when, additionally, their old routines of exchanging information have been undone, how does any object, firstly, circulate and, secondly, stay in circulation? Consider the place of the object. If an object is already represented, in a textbook and worksheets, it has monument status. Furthermore, the manner in which a classroom goes about looking at the object already has a history, and it is a history that is not peculiar to SMS. Several classroom studies have revealed that the IRE is a major means of exchanging information across schools (Cazden, 1988; Mehan, 1979) and especially in middle (Alvermann, 1996) and high schools (Wells, 1993). This frequent literacy practice must, then, be tied to the objects of knowledge themselves, which, in public schools, come hitched to texts and an invisible gaze. Teachers are supported with texts, and objects circulate via literacy practices. The manner in which these literacy practices measure time and engage in the production of space cannot be treated lightly. When the rug—objects of study and their textual support—is pulled out from under practice, how do new objects take their place?

The Building Project revealed that inserting new objects and new practices into school could not simply replace old practices. Students themselves required old space to make new space. They could not begin a new practice absent of past practice. They had to use the familiar to build the new. Yet, in university classrooms, we often do not speak about space. We treat objects as though they were neutral, as though any object can be inserted into any space. It took seven weeks for the seventh graders to believe in the space they were making. I provided examples of in-between space that do not begin to demonstrate the numerous kinds of relationships the seventh graders became engaged in when the object of study was unhitched from texts. Early and midway into the project, if Jade didn't lead classroom discussions, students' own discussions moved into racial, gender, and sexual self/other relations that were often very hurtful. The objects of their discussions were their own stories or sometimes just well-chosen quips, meant to make a girl feel sexually harassed or another girl or boy feel the effects of racism. Because the path of student-centered objects often led students into networks of relations that were hurtful, Jade opted to direct discussion because she could control both the object of study and its distribution. Without the aid of textbooks and worksheets, Jade was responsible for keeping objects of study in circulation.

As Jade pressed on, largely through the IRE, actual content started to be built. The constant discussions about what students wanted in a new school, disparity of school funding in Ohio, and thoughts about what the survey results meant to the Sanders community—over time these discussions and literacy practices started to have value: students began to see their ideas distributed beyond the classroom. They saw themselves in relation to others. By the time the students wrote their speech in the final two weeks of the project, they had compiled a lot of data: they had analyzed census data; they had conducted and analyzed surveys; they had read about Sanders history and written and shared their own stories about life in Sanders; and they had built model buildings. Only when the space of the classroom was re-represented with students' own objects (as ideas and concrete things) did they have the material from which to draw to write a speech. It took seven weeks to build up material support for their speeches.

Material support is necessary if teachers want to change space, but it is not simply availability of material that matters. Materials have to be part of the logic of space. They have to make sense as objects in the classroom, and students have to trust their circulation. Hence, when the Building Project had ended and no new ideas for a new project were available, the return to textbooks and the old literacy economy made sense. Students had experienced new space, but they had not come to expect it.

This research revealed the kinds of space made through a circulating exchange of objects. The in-between space revealed in this research causes me to believe that, contrary to popular belief, when classrooms continue to reproduce practices that dissociate student bodies from lived, passionate relations, it isn't necessarily because teachers aren't trying or haven't tried better practices. I believe it is very possible that, when teachers do try to change literacy practices, the space between thick and thin is difficult to survive. In-between space does not reproduce itself, which leaves the teacher with too much responsibility for object circulation and students with no ground at all. This research suggests that reproduction research is still needed and that agency and structure would be better theorized in the relations of space (which include the circulation and distribution of objects) that make them possible.

References

Alvermann, D. (1996). Peer-led discussions: Whose interests are served? *Journal of Adolescent and Adult Literacy, 39*(4), 282–289.

Anyon, J. (1980). Social class and the hidden curriculum of work. *Journal of Education, 162*(1), 67–92.

Appadurai, A. (1986). Introduction: Commodities and the politics of value. In A. Appadurai (Ed.), *The social life of things: Commodities in cultural perspective* (pp. 3–63). New York: Cambridge University Press.

Cazden, C. B. (1988). *Classroom discourse: The language of teaching and learning.* Portsmouth, NH: Heinemann.

Eisenhart, M. (1995). The fax, the jazz player, the self-story teller: How do people organize culture? *Anthropology and Education Quarterly, 26*(1), 3–26.

Foucault, M. (1984). Docile bodies. In P. Rabinow (Ed.), *The Foucault reader* (pp. 179–187). New York: Pantheon.

Giroux, H. A. (1983). Theories of reproduction and resistance in the new sociology of education. *Harvard Educational Review, 53*(3), 257–293.

Giroux, H. A. (1997). *Pedagogy and the politics of hope: Theory, culture, and schooling.* Boulder, CO: Westview Press.

Giroux, H. A., & McLaren, P. (1992). Writing from the margins: Geographies of identity, pedagogy, and power. *Journal of Education, 174*(1), 7–30.

Gutiérrez, K. D. (1995). Unpackaging academic discourse. *Discourse Processes, 19*(1), 21–37.

Harvey, D. (1996). *Justice, nature and the geography of difference.* Malden, MA: Blackwell.

Lave, J., & Wenger, E. (1991). *Situated learning: Legitimate peripheral participation.* Cambridge: Cambridge University Press.

Lefebvre, H. (1991). *The production of space.* Cambridge, MA: Blackwell.

Luke, A. & Freebody, P. (1997). The social practices of reading. In S. Muspratt, A. Luke, & P. Freebody (Eds.), *Constructing critical literacies. Teaching and learning textual practice* (pp. 185–225). Cresskil, NJ: Hampton Press.

Mehan, Hugh. (1979). *Learning lessons: Social organization in the classroom.* Cambridge, MA: Harvard University Press.

Rogoff, B. (1990). *Apprenticeship in thinking: Cognitive development in social context.* New York: Oxford University Press.

Sack, R. D. (1997). *Homo geographicus: A framework for action, awareness, and moral concern.* Baltimore, MD: The Johns Hopkins University Press.

Sheehy, M. (1999). *Un/making place: A topological analysis of time and space representation in an urban Appalachian seventh grade civics project.* Ph.D. diss., The Ohio State University.

Shuman, A. (1986). *Storytelling rights: The uses of oral and written texts by urban adolescents.* New York: Cambridge University Press.

Soja, E. W. (1996). *Thirdspace: Journeys to Los Angeles and other real-and-imagined places.* Cambridge, MA: Blackwell.

Wells, G. (1993). Reevaluating the IRF sequence: A proposal for the articulation of theories of activity and discourse for the analysis of teaching and learning in the classroom. *Linguistics and Education, 5,* 1–37.

Willis, P. E. (1977). *Learning to labour: How working class kids get working class jobs.* Hampshire, UK: Gower.

6

Reading the Spatial Histories of Positioning in a Classroom Literacy Event

Kevin M. Leander

A whole history remains to be written of spaces—which would at the same time be the history of powers—from the great strategies of geopolitics to the little tactics of the habitat.

(Foucault, 1980, p. 149)

Every history that is not merely a chronicle or fable must presume to be intrinsically spatial, to be about spatiality, in much the same way that history is presumed to be intrinsically social, about the sociality of human life.

(Soja, 1996, p. 171)

This chapter considers a large group discussion of texts, a common event in literacy classrooms. Such discussions are produced within and productive of social space. The analysis of social space shifts the focus away from considering context as a backdrop upon which a given classroom interaction is played out. Rather, classroom discussion is considered to be shot through with the production of social space; a few moments of interaction are a nexus of diverse space-producing processes and resources.

In the main, researchers of classroom interaction have bracketed the spaces and times of classroom interactions very tightly, in favor of giving close readings of very short episodes—three minutes of a large group discussion microanalyzed across thirty-five pages of academic text. Some researchers have moved outside of the tight space-time constraints of conversation analysis and critical discourse as methods by offering histories of the voices or discursive practices in literacy classrooms (Kamberelis & Scott, 1992; Rex & McEachen, 1999). Others have considered how interactions are not singular, but involve simultaneous and fractured social spaces with diverse practices and ideologies (Gutiérrez, Rymes, & Larson, 1995; Leander, 2002b). Yet, for the most part, the field of literacy studies has offered a relatively small number of historical and spatial accounts of classroom interaction and has not moved very far in thinking about how classroom interactions produce and are produced by historical and spatial processes.

With what purposes might we interpret classroom interactions in relation to diverse spatial-historical processes? What insights might such interpretation provide? In this chapter, I posit that spatial histories illuminate how identities are produced in social practice. I consider how identity practices or instances of positioning seemingly "within" a given stretch of interaction involve relations among multiple social spaces and their histories. Borrowing Soja's (1996) terms, I am concerned with the trialectical relationship of sociality, historicality, and spatiality as a means of interpreting positioning.

This chapter revolves around eleven lines of a focal literacy event, considering how the historical production of social spaces becomes visible through this event. The first question concerns institutional positioning, or how a particular classroom of individuals comes to be composed as a social configuration. Who gets in the door? I illustrate in this section how, in the case of schooling, individuals are organized and recruited by social spaces being constructed, and then, through their appropriations of these spaces, help in turn to transform them. Secondly, I turn to pedagogy as a form of identity work. What type of pedagogy is taking place, and what social positions are available through it? For a pedagogy to "take place" it is not only enacted in a field of social and power relations, but engages in shaping such a field. Thirdly, I turn the analysis to how participant identities are being constructed within interaction. What social identities are enacted and recognized? Social and critical theorists have considered how particular Discourses are recruited in identity construction (e.g., Gee, 2000). Building on this work, I consider in this section how identity enactment or positioning not only is evident in the immediate space-time, but also has an ongoing spatial history.

Theoretical Orientations

Positioning

By "positioning" I intend to indicate activity and artifacts that contribute to the production of another's identity, one's own identity, or to self-other relations. Positions are offered, accepted, rejected, and otherwise continuously negotiated. From an interactional or "immanentist's" perspective, all positioning is evident in on-the-ground, jointly produced interactions and story lines (Davies & Harré, 1990). In such a perspective, approaches to positioning that draw upon data outside of immediately traceable interactions tend toward the "transcendent" and are likely to be caught up in moving toward static concepts such as "role." While this focus upon interaction and the moment-by-moment production of identity is valuable, to interpret social practices of identity it seems critically important to move outward from focal data to practices stretched out over broader expanses of space and time. Holland and Lave (2001) discuss such a perspective and theorize how identities are practiced through artifacts and interactions participating in "locally contentious practices," which themselves are related to "enduring struggles." A single event will perhaps not make evident the enduring struggles that resonate through it, nor will such an interpretation allow us to consider how disparate temporal practices congeal within an identity-in-the-making. While drawing on Holland and Lave's (2001) perspective on identity-in-practice, I relate their historical perspective to spatiality, asserting a trialectical relation of social identity, spatiality, and historicality (Soja, 1996). In addition to "history in persons" (Holland & Lave, 2001), persons are produced at the interstices of multiple social spaces.

Historicality-Spatiality

In order to illustrate space-producing processes—an account that registers something of the diverse networks of power and agency active within the moment—I offer in this chapter a spatial history of a focal segment of interaction. By "spatial history" I do not mean to indicate that space merely modifies the type of history being offered, nor that I am somehow merely considering the historical aspects of social space. Rather, I consider time and space as intimately and dynamically related (Harvey, 1996; Lefebvre, 1991) and offer a partial and imaginative documentation of the development and coordination of diverse space-times. As in the tradition of microanalysis critiqued above, I have tightly bracketed my focal interaction data. However, rather than focusing upon this moment of classroom life as an object per se, my purposes are to use the interaction as a window into space-time processes. By looking *through* a focal interaction, I interpret the spatial histories that traverse it and that are coordinated and conflict within it.

I begin with the premise that classroom interaction, involving literacy practices such as reading, interpretation, writing, image production, and talk, continually produces social space. Thus, I begin with the belief that expanding the interpretation of interaction across larger scales of space-time will prove productive for analysis. Different spatial histories are evident when we think and research across macro and micro scales of space and time. When we interpret such diverse processes, we will be more acutely aware of the ways in which diverse social spaces are articulated (or fail to be). Finally, I also begin with the premise that "lived space" (Lefebvre, 1991) is coordinated and produced, in trialectic relation, by perceived, conceived, and lived forms of space (see Chapter 5, this volume). This trialectical relationship means, among other things, that I do not consider any single set of resources or processes as primary in interpreting how social space is made. Rather, I interpret across and juxtapose material, social, and discursive practices. I resist the common impulse in social science, critiqued by Massey (1997), to analyze the macro level as discursive and the micro level as material. I find it more useful to dispense with the language of "levels," and its related image of social activity as a set of nested boxes or Chinese dolls, and speak instead of spatial histories that are more or less stretched out, that interact at particular spatial-historical junctures, that are coordinated in particular interpretive processes, and that may be illustrated and analyzed through particular windows of activity. Prior to engaging the analysis through the focal interaction, in the following I offer a brief introduction to the focal interaction, followed by a transcript.

Introduction to the Focal Interaction

It is typical in the study of classroom interaction to offer contextual background. Such background functions as information that is more or less useful for interpreting the given interaction at hand. In this chapter, I reverse the relative foregrounding of the interaction and backgrounding of the context. While my hope is to build a rich interpretation of the interaction, I also want to press the issue that the focal interaction—this bit of lived space-time—is but a nexus in the ongoing production of space-time. It is not merely located in a "background," but participates in producing its own space-time grounding as an ongoing process. Therefore, I only briefly introduce the focal interaction, in order to make it more comprehensible.

The focal interaction of this chapter is eleven lines of classroom discussion taken from a junior-level (eleventh grade) American Studies classroom, taught by two teachers, both white European American, who I have given the pseudonyms "Maureen" and "Sid." These lines of discussion were part of a "Derogatory Terms Activity," which I have analyzed in greater detail elsewhere (Leander, 2002a). The activity was connected thematically with the reading and study of *The Adventures of Huckleberry Finn*, which was being approached as a problematic text. Maureen and Sid used the text to engage students in discussions of race, language, and cultural identity. Maureen's purpose in the activity was for the students to investigate language/power issues by listing, categorizing, and critically reflecting upon derogatory terms associated with particular groups. In the first period of a double class session, students were directed to meet with a small group and to list out all of the derogatory terms they knew that could be used to "put down" a particular group. At the end of this class period and the beginning of the next, students were directed into room 251 (a barn-like room often used for large group activity) and were told to take their group lists and to copy them onto a large (approximately 18 by 3 foot) banner. The banner would serve as a master list for the classroom discussion. After the banner was completed, several students posted it on the wall of room 251, as directed by the teachers. Next, after a few minutes of everyone reading the banner in a noticeably excited atmosphere, the teachers moved the group into a discussion of the banner.

The emotional pitch of the larger discussion rose significantly with Ian's (white European American) response to an earlier utterance by Latanya (African American). This earlier utterance, which was not clearly transcribable, involved Latanya's use of the word "honky" in the classroom. Ian compared Latanya's use of "honky" with what would happen were he to use the racial slur "nigger." The following transcript segment of the focal interaction picks up the interaction at this moment. I focus upon this segment not only because it rekeyed the emotion of the entire following interaction following, but also because it initiated a significant instance of negatively positioning Latanya.

Transcript[1]

1. IAN: I just want to know,   Latanya said, like those honky, I mean, but like if I said, yeah, those nigger—huh! *((aspirated tone, hand over mouth))* that would be like a whole different story I was wondering how that was.

2. LATANYA: No, see   *((rotating body in chair to face Ian, leaning toward him))*   I wasn't saying it like that, I mean, we was usin' the words, *((extending hand out in front of her in direction of banner, palm up))* and I was just—I wasn't tryin' to say it like that.

3. IAN: I'm just saying that when a black person makes fun of a white   *((Sam slams hand down on desk and turns his head toward Ian))*—like the white person's race— *((Ian facing toward teacher while speaking))*

4. LATANYA: It wasn't that, I was talking about the words.

---

[1] Transcription Conventions

( )	inaudible speech, relative to length of space
<(.)	pause of one second for each period>
<((laughs) additional detail>	
<//	overlapping speech of two or more speakers>
<(talk)	questionable transcription>
<u>because</u>	stressed word
NOW	emphatic stress
°sorry°	deemphasized speech, spoken softly
<ha::rd	lengthened sound or syllable>
<—	short break or interruption in speech>

5. IAN: No no no—not now *((turns head toward Latanya))*. I'm just // saying

6. TONY: //CALM DOWN THERE//

7. IAN: that// when a black person makes fun of a white person's race—not in this case, I'm just saying white people don't get mad, but if I just said, like, "nigger," HUH! *((flicks pencil upwards))*

8. LATANYA: *((orienting head and trunk more directly to Ian))* NO, I'm not //
   (   )//

9. MAUREEN: //Let me ask// you someth-

10. ROBERT: *((turning head toward Ian, body facing forward))* That's because you don't have to take it the way we do.

11. MAUREEN: OK, let me interject something, then Sam. Do you really <u>think</u>, it seems to me, and I'll throw this out as an idea for you to think about before Sam goes, like, certain—certain groups have been more historically repressed than others, right? It seems to me that there is *no* word that you can use to describe a white person that is as powerful as °nigger.° Like, you can call me a cracker, you can call me a honky, I'm not even gonna <u>blink</u>. I mean, it would be weird, it would be very <u>weird</u>, but it wouldn't really (.) *hurt* me. I think if I called somebody a nigger it would be very painful. Did you notice? *((starting to point back toward banner))*

Institutional Positioning: Who Gets in the Door?

In the following, I provide a sketch of how the Kempton Technological Academy (KTA) comes to be organized as a space, a process of formation that engages a range of material and semiotic resources and contributes to state and national agendas. I am particularly concerned with how the KTA (as a conceived space) and a particular kind of person were coproduced. This process involved conceiving of the KTA purposes and participants in particular ways, although these ways were clearly not without conflict and contradiction. As an emerging space, the KTA also evolved by how it was perceived and lived by insiders and outsiders. For example, in this brief spatial history I make evident how bounding the KTA space became a resource for defining it as a space of privilege. This association with privilege was not merely an effect of the design of the space, but was also produced and maintained by the responses and recruitment of teachers, students, and parents. Thus, the spatial history of institutional positioning as I am rendering it here concerns the power relations between the KTA's founders and state and national agendas, but also the ongoing, on-the-ground production of the institution by its participants. In brief, "who gets in the door" is not merely a question of initial structuring, but an ongoing process of conceiving (imagining, organizing, symbolically structuring) the KTA and the students identified with it.

Co-constructing the KTA Space and the Middle-Level Student

The KTA, a school-within-a-school at Kempton High, was first planned during the school year 1993–94, and the first class of (freshmen-level) students were admitted during the school year 1994–95. The KTA was funded, in part, through the Illinois State Board of Education as a Career Academy. The goals of the Careers Academies included the integration of "workplace competencies" with core academic subjects, business-education partnerships, block-scheduled classes, and "state of the art technology" (Illinois State Board of Education, 1997, p. 2). Career Academies in the state of Illinois were authorized for funding in 1990 through the reauthorization of the Carl D. Perkins Act, which provided large-scale funding for vocational education and dated back to 1963 (reauthorized and amended in 1968, 1976, 1984, and 1990) (Lehr, 1997). While the KTA was funded as a Career Academy, since its outset it had a somewhat loose relationship to the state vision. In particular, vocational preparation was moved to the background of the program while academic learning was shifted to the fore, as several of the faculty believed that vocational preparation was too limiting a vision for the students. Embedded in this assessment was the desire not to resemble vocational programs and their historical construction as "dumping grounds" for students unsuccessful in schooling. While KTA staff found themselves needing to articulate a sense of difference from the rest of the school in order to create and maintain the KTA as a separate space, they struggled to forge the difference they had in mind without it being absorbed by preconceived categories of school programs. At the end of its fourth year, for example, state pressure was beginning to mount to make the KTA more like other Career Academies, with a more expressed career focus. New courses were being developed and requirements added to enrich the business focus of the KTA.

A partial but troubled solution to shaping the identity of the KTA as a separate social space was its construction of a middle-level student population. While there were specific programs targeted to high- and low-achieving students in the state and in the school, the program director and early group of founding teachers argued in state documents, program funding documents, and brochures for program applicants that middle-level students had special needs that were not well served. It is important to note that the middle level was already identified as a category in Kempton High through tracking, as courses were heavily tracked for "low," "middle," and "high" students, and there appeared to be little movement among tracks for individuals. However, middle students in the school were defined more by default (as neither low nor high) than they were by particular characteristics. In other words, while there were material classroom spaces for middle-level students in the school, where they could be regularly perceived, this type of student was relatively weakly conceived. A critical development in the spatial history of the KTA was the definition of the middle-level student as a particular kind of person.

Early documents about the Career Academies defined "middle-levels students" as those whose standardized achievement test scores ranged from the 25th to the 75th percentile (nationally) and whose "academic records reflect underachievement" (Stern, Raby, & Dayton, 1992, p. 24). The middle, however, also included students who were "educationally unmotivated and socioeconomically disadvantaged" (Raby, 1995, p. 83) or otherwise "at risk." Indicators of at-risk status recognized by the Career Academy model (and highly resonant with the language in the original proposal to the state for funding the KTA) were widely various and included "patterns of irregular attendance," limited English proficiency, and "serious personal problems, such as pregnancy, dysfunctional families, or drug abuse" (Stern, Raby, & Dayton, 1992, pp. 23–24). Thus, early discourses of the middle level were unstable, linked, on the one hand, to middle standardized test scores (25th to the 75th percentile) and, on the other hand, to constructions of "at risk." While the definition by standardized test scores provided a generic and very broad window of who might be included in the group, "at risk" helped to provide some language of need for the middle-level student—language that was accompanied by funding. The KTA was partially funded (one-sixth of its operating budget), in its first three years, by the Job Training Partnership Act (JTPA). In exchange for funding, and also for some limited summer and school-year work opportunities for low-income students, the KTA had to document that at least one-third of its students were at-risk students. While in theory there were supposed to be many different ways of qualifying students as at risk through the JTPA, in practice, according to the director of the KTA, the "bottom line" ended up being low family economic status.

Over time, there was a good deal of discussion in the KTA about what students it should and could serve. While the program director and teachers wanted to avoid its construction as a dumping ground, they also defined the program as related to specific needs. Jean, one academy teacher, characterized "middle-level" students as "gray area" students and remarked about their relation to the school:

> They just sorta stopped there in the middle. And they had needs, but the school didn't do anything special for those students. They also usually were slotted into bigger classes, and usually with more inexperienced teachers.

Many different reports from faculty concerning the characterization of the middle level were offered; characterization included students who were often "off task," students who liked to socialize, students who were more prone to learn in a "hands-on" environment, students who needed extra encouragement and help, and students who lacked adequate parental support and come from "dysfunctional families." Through arguments and negotiations among the teachers and director, the standardized test scores of the middle rose over time. Over the first four years of its existence the KTA gradually increased its definition of the bottom of the middle level from the 25th to the 40th percentile. This rise in test scores paralleled the dropping away of JTPA funding for at-risk students, funding that was part of the KTA budget. During the KTA's fourth year, only about half of the juniors surveyed (sixteen of thirty-three students) self-identified as middle-level students, nearly always citing as a reason that they received middle grades, such as Bs and Cs. Many of the remaining students considered themselves to be high-level students.

The spatial history discussed thus far offers some sense of how a group of youth (and their families) became identified with the KTA. In particular, the history suggests the tension between creating a category of students with special needs, as is most clearly indexed in the at-risk label, and yet the staff's desire to help the KTA avoid identified as an undesirable dumping ground for low-level students. Unique material, symbolic, and social privileges of the KTA helped to produce it as a desirable space for the students and staff and also helped to define the needs of the middle-level students over time. Unlike most of the school space, the KTA space was carpeted and, at least originally, had more up-to-date computer technology than the rest of the school. Some students and faculty outside of the KTA criticized the KTA as being unfairly funded with respect to the rest of the school, and carpeting was commonly used as an example.

Student and Parent Appropriations of the KTA Space

Of course, students were not merely identified and slotted into the KTA space; rather, they (and their parents) elected to *go in the door* of the KTA. In assuming agency with respect to the state and institutional structuring of the space, they appropriated the space, shaping it for their diverse desires and goals. Generally speaking, KTA students considered its programmatic and physical separation from the rest of the school to be a positive quality, interpreting the increased opportunity to get to know others and to access material privileges as a positive difference. In open-ended format, I asked students to sketch pictures and write descriptions representing how they thought the KTA was related to Kempton High. Student responses included the integration of classes, having "nice teachers" and guest speakers, taking field trips, frequent discussion in class, celebrating birthdays with birthday cake, and "learning by doing." The most frequent responses revolved around issues of student-teacher and student-student relationships. Access to teachers for help was especially noted by a number of students as a chief contrast between the KTA space and larger school spaces. Ian sketched the KTA as an umbrella (Figure 1), protecting "Academy Students" from the "rain" of the school. The large droplets are labeled "school rules (some)," "mild violence," "bad teachers," "hard floors," and "mild profanity." This list is a striking mix of material contrasts (hard floors versus carpeting), student-student and student-teacher relations, and institutional power. The academy is a shield against some of the numerous (but seemingly "mild") problems of life in school.

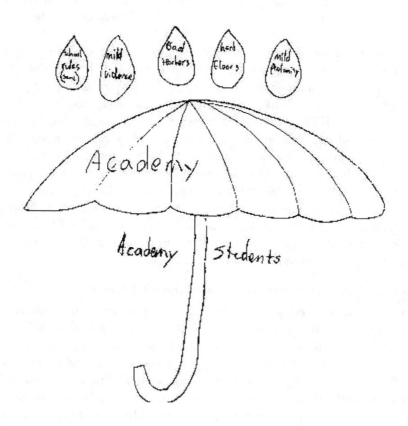

Figure 1. Ian's drawing

Chelle (white European American) described the sense of privilege in the KTA as follows:

> We have advantages from the rest of the school. We have a lot of computers, graphing calculators, and carpet. Inside, the teachers are lenient. When the holidays come around, everyone really gets involved. The Academy acts like a family. The teachers inside the Academy really show that they care by calling your house, every student's house, to talk to them about their grades, and they always express to us that they are always here to help. We have been together for freshmen, sophomore, and junior years. One of these years, we will be totally complete when we actually have a senior class in the Academy.

Chelle's description indexes a high degree of personal identification, as suggested by the continual use of the first-person plural "we" and by Chelle's vision that "one of these years, we will be totally complete." Chelle created perhaps the most striking portrait of quality in her picture of the academy as a set of castle-like doors, the elaborate large handles of which suggest a space accessed by the privileged.

Student and parent decisions to choose the KTA were directly related to how they conceived of and appropriated the particular kinds of privileges it afforded them. How did early conceptions of the social space and student (and parent) appropriations of privileges come together for shaping a particular institutional shaping of space? While space does not permit me to trace many of the geographical-historical movements of this group of students, focusing upon Ian and Latanya, two key participants in the focal interaction, draws out important contrasts that were evident across the KTA student population and purposes at the junior level.

The KTA reorganized familiar geographies of the city that were repeated in the heavily tracked school program, which channeled middle- and upper-middle-class white European-American students in the middle and high tracks, and African-American and working-class white European-American students into the lower tracks. Ian had attended a parochial school ("Father Ryan") and was from an upper-middle-class neighborhood in the south central part of town. On a visit to Father Ryan while Ian was in middle school, the KTA director (Donna) worked to recruit him, along with seven other Father Ryan students, into the program. When Ian enrolled in the KTA as a freshman, approximately one of every five students in the KTA (eight of forty-two) had been at Father Ryan together for middle school and, in some cases, for elementary school as well. As a newly conceived and perceived space, the KTA seemed to capture the imagination and desire of the Father Ryan students and parents in at least two key ways, ways that would secure some of the benefits of a private education for students within a public school program. First, the KTA promised teacher-student relationships that were more akin to what students and parents had come to expect at Father Ryan, including lower student-teacher ratios, and more teacher time available for extra help. Secondly, the KTA was materially furnished with technology and classroom spaces that were distinguished from the larger school. Yet, Ian, along with some of the other students in the program, never considered his own position in the school to be strongly identified with the KTA. While he began as a student in the KTA his freshman year, his social networks in Kempton High at large involved many students who were in the high-tracked classes—middle- and upper-class white European-American students who were socially organized by the school program to prepare for college.

In contrast, Latanya's admission to the KTA was based in part upon her qualification as a low-income and at-risk student. Latanya, an African American, lived in a small home with her mother, sister, and baby brother on the northwest side of town. Because she struggled as a reader, Latanya was also enrolled in the school in a special program that gave her additional study and reading help for one hour per day. Yet, it seems most significant to relate that Latanya was a newcomer to the KTA among a group of African-American newcomers. Latanya was one of eight new students who entered the KTA in their junior year, seven of whom were African American. What drew Latanya to the KTA were reports of specific caring teachers within it that would give extra help (in particular, Sid and Maureen), and the group of African American friends she had who were either enrolled in it or were also joining their junior year. The racial demographics of the junior class during the fourth year (the year of the focal interaction) were thus 50 percent European American (eighteen students), 47 percent African American (seventeen students), and 3 percent Pacific Islander (one student). This racial composition of the group contrasts sharply with its racial composition when the students were freshmen. Of the fifty-one original students, 69 percent were European American (thirty-five students), 29 percent were African American (fifteen students), and 2 percent were Pacific Islander (one student). Twenty out of twenty-four (83 percent) of the students who left the junior class in the Academy during their freshman and sophomore years were white European American. Thus, the spatial history of Latanya's institutional positioning was tied up with the developing trialectic of sociality, spatiality, and historicality comprising the KTA.

In the absence of producing the KTA, it is unlikely that Ian and Latanya would have shared the same classroom space, even less likely that they would have interacted across more than one class per day. Although they would have been students the same school, they would not have been institutionally afforded possibilities of interaction. As an institutional construction of social space, and from the perspective of its founders, the KTA recruited highly diverse students, worked to define them as sharing some common needs, and offered privileged resources to address these needs. At the same time, the KTA was appropriated—taken up and struggled over by diverse students and parents with particular desires of what it could be and who might best comprise it as a social space.

Pedagogical Positioning:
What Spaces are Being Made *for* Interaction?

The spatial history of the KTA as discussed thus far offers some sense of the heterogeneous resources, desires, and networks that were recruited and assembled in producing it as a social space. It allows us to consider the focal interaction as stretched into an institutional past when recruitment gears for the KTA began turning and when former wood and metal shop spaces were refitted with new technologies to meet the needs of middle-level students. This history of a complex institutional set of positions—the KTA—involves diverse participants with contrasting and sometimes conflicting goals. The following discussion interprets the spatial-historical-social trialectic of Maureen's and Sid's pedagogy by looking through the focal interaction. I offer a brief sense of how their pedagogy involved routinely critically engaging the students, and then focus upon the particular pedagogy of the Derogatory Terms Activity evidenced in this episode. In the discussion of the teachers' routines and the focal interaction, I purpose to highlight how pedagogy makes space, how this space-making produces social relations and identities, and how these processes are shaped by history. As a living out of curriculum (conceived pedagogical space), pedagogy is a set of discursive and material practices and resources that actively engages in the production of power relations and ideology. The teachers' pedagogy enters into dialogue with the institutional social space of the KTA but cannot be described by it and is not subsumed by it. Similarly, pedagogical positioning cannot be described merely by the interactional positioning produced by participants in the literacy event, which is discussed in the next section.

The Academy Moms, Civil Disobedience, and Room 251

The spatial history of pedagogy interpreted here involves Maureen's and Sid's counterpositioning to a dominant ideological construction of the KTA by the "Academy Moms." The Academy Moms (a name sometimes used by Sid and Maureen as well) were charter teachers in the academy (unlike Sid and Maureen) and had worked on the original institutional plans for it. The Academy Moms had an average of eighteen years of teaching experience, while Sid was in his fifth year of teaching and Maureen in her seventh during the fourth year of the KTA's history. Maureen had begun to work in the KTA during the second year of its development, while Sid had elected to move into the KTA during its third year, largely motivated by the opportunity to collaborate with Maureen. The Academy Moms were considered by Sid and Maureen to be politically and pedagogically conservative, more given to controlling rather than freeing students for exploration, more oriented to business and technology and less to academics, and more oriented toward thinking about the academy students as individual "children" needing close shepherding rather than as politically and socially engaged young adults in power-laden social relationships. In contrast, Sid, Maureen, and also Sharon (a sophomore English teacher who shared an office with them) were at times considered by the Academy Moms to be not enough associated with building the academy as an institution, somewhat irresponsible in terms of student discipline, more given to arts and humanities than business and technology, and overly political in their curriculum and teaching. Donna joked on more than one occasion to Maureen, who drew upon readings from Thoreau as a central piece in her English/American Studies curriculum, "So, you're teaching civil disobedience, eh? Don't we have enough of that already?"

An important difference between the groups of teachers was their faith in schooling in general and its relation to the academy as a space of difference. The originators of the academy generally expressed a faith in the kind of students that schooling produced when it was practiced with the best tools, best methods, best teachers, etc. In contrast, Maureen, Sid, and Sharon were highly critical of the type of students that even the best schooling produced, and they imagined and discussed the academy as an opportunity to more radically restructure schooling. Sid and Maureen routinely developed curriculum and worked on a pedagogy that engaged students in critical interpretations and productions. Early in the school year the two teachers transformed the Kempton-wide yearly task of reading the school rule booklet into a unit that involved presentations on legal issues and student discipline by administrators, school security, and a school law professor and student presentations of Supreme Court case studies involving education and rights (e.g., *Brown vs. the Board of Education*). Students were tasked to challenge their rights and to write cases arguing for and against state and local positions with respect to schools and students. In history class, which sometimes met separately from American Studies, Sid's students led discussions on how the Constitution guaranteed (or not) the rights of various groups (e.g., women), and how constitutional rights affected daily social life (or not). For English class, Maureen structured discussions and writing throughout the year that critically assessed representations of identity and culture in popular texts, including films such as Disney's *Pocahontas*.

The Derogatory Terms Activity (discussed below) took place in the middle of the school year and followed a routine of critically interpreting texts across Maureen's and Sid's classes and their team-teaching in American Studies. The structure of the activity as large group discussion also indexed the kind of pedagogical position that Maureen and Sid were attempting to create for the students. The teachers emphasized student-student interactions, in contrast to constantly prompting and assessing student contributions, as in IRE (Initiation-Response-Evaluation) sequences (Mehan, 1979). Maureen and Sid also routinely pushed for personal and social stances by inserting into the discussions intertextual references to the students' lives and beliefs within and outside of the school. By their own reports, student had participated in relatively few discussions in nonacademy courses. They also seemed to participate in few discussions within KTA courses outside of those taught by Maureen, Sid, and Sharon. This history did not become evident to me until after observing and interviewing the students after a substitute teacher (Jan) filled in for Maureen for several weeks while she was away on maternity leave. Jan never held classroom discussions, and the students reported that her seat-work-style classes were like most of their other classes within and outside of the academy. Many students became restless and missed the discussions, while others seemed to thrive in the (reproduced) seat-work environment, in particular a group of five or six "white girls" (as labeled by other students) who were often critical of "open" discussion practices.

Maureen's and Sid's pedagogical production of space, within the KTA but also a critical response to the Academy Moms, was also materially produced through divisions in classroom space. The focal interaction instantiates relations of spatiality, historicality, and sociality by its material location in room 251; pedagogical positioning is indexed not just in the curriculum and practices of the teachers but also in the ways in which they materially locate themselves and their students. As the academy expanded and new classrooms were needed for the junior-level courses, these spaces were found at the periphery of the physical space that originally comprised the academy. This original physical space consisted of a large lecture hall with stadium seating, three classrooms, an open computer area flowing into an informal seating area, an area adjacent to the computer area equipped with science tables and equipment, and a fourth classroom across the main hallway (Figure 3). During the fourth year of the academy's history, Maureen appropriated room 251 as her classroom, which was down the hall and nearby the fourth classroom. Sid and Maureen often jointly taught the entire group of juniors in this room. The production of room 251 as the key junior KTA space seemed a temporary compromise to several concurrent dilemmas: the growth of the

KTA, the ideological differences between Maureen and Sid and the Academy Moms, the possibility offered Maureen (by Donna, the KTA director and also an Academy Mom) to teach in a classroom more distant to the KTA, Maureen's and Sid's desire to associate with the KTA and use it for their own purposes, and Maureen becoming pregnant and not wanting to have to walk large distances during the school day.

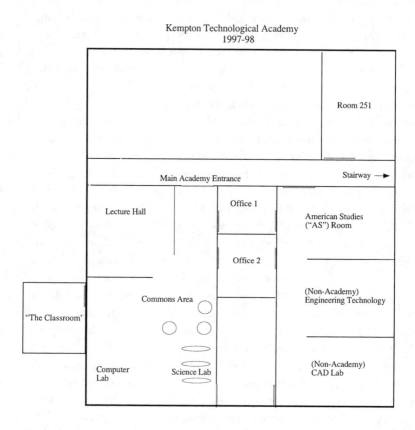

Figure 2. KTA map

Room 251 did not only address institutional and pragmatic matters, but was also the production of a critical social space, distanced but connected to a more dominant production of the academy space. Room 251, in many ways, indexed the ideological differences between these teacher groups and demonstrated how the academy itself was a confluence of multiple social spaces. This ideological and material boundary-making was perhaps even more evident in office space use. The "Moms" primarily used the front office space (Office 1, Figure 2), while Maureen, Sid, Sharon, and few other teachers used the back office (Office 2, Figure 2). These separate architectural spaces appeared to help powerfully structure the sense of different KTA purposes and ideologies. Faculty spoke of these material spaces as representing pedagogical differences and teacher identities, and the spaces also limited the amount of dialogue across the groups of teachers. Donna spoke with me about this division. She intentionally moved the microwave oven from the front office to the back office during the fourth year of the KTA's history in order to create more interaction among the groups. I was more habitually located in the back office due to my focus upon Sid and Maureen's classes, and only noticed a few fleeting microwave visits during that school year.

The Derogatory Terms Activity as a Production of Thirdspace

The Derogatory Terms Activity was imported by Maureen into the KTA from her past experiences teaching in a private school. It was part of a suite of alternative learning activities that Maureen had borrowed and developed in a school that was relatively open to experimentation, and where critical literacy was more commonly practiced than at Kempton. Maureen valued and produced the KTA as an alternative social space in which such experimentation could continue to occur, supported by a programmatic goal to engage students who were otherwise "lost" or underserved in the regular program. Maureen noted that the students she taught in private school, although not homogeneous, were not nearly as culturally and socially diverse as those in the junior-level KTA. She and Sid imagined the activity as drawing upon this resource of student diversity and potentially producing rich critical interaction around the use of identity labels and specific power relations among identity groups. For example, Maureen purposed to use the occasion (and attempted to during the interaction) to discuss how women are sexualized through derogatory language in more oppressive ways than men.

As a set of curricular positions, the Derogatory Terms Activity constructed a liminal space or thirdspace (Gutiérrez, Rymes, & Larson, 1995; Soja, 1996); it was a highly unstable hybridization of the institutional classroom, media spaces, taboo spaces of imagined and observed racists, sexists, and classists, and youth cultural spaces. The banner imported language into the classroom that would typically be disciplined out of it. Prior to discussing the terms on the banner, Maureen and Sid took turns reading the terms aloud for the class. The reading of derogatory language for a school lesson indexed the unstable, laminated (Goffman, 1981) quality of the activity as exiting within and extending well beyond school spaces. Several students remarked in the ensuing discussion the shock of having their teachers ventriloquize (Bakhtin, 1981) words such as "trick-ass bitches" and "motha fucka," even though the teachers seemed to deliberately read the words as objects, facing the list and emotionlessly rattling off the terms.

While social spaces in which students (and teachers) use derogatory language are not entirely bounded from schooling, the present was designed to disrupt the ways in which, in public performance, classrooms are pretended to be removed from the everyday derogation and social divisions that operate within them at a subaltern level. In this manner, the activity itself destabilized social spaces (and therefore, identities) as it foregrounded social relations that are always present (yet often hidden) in the classroom as a heterogeneous space. Destabilization was accomplished through many aspects of the activity, including how it materially produced the classroom space. The banner materially translated the school wall into a graffiti space. Moreover, the material-semiotic production of this graffiti space was linked, as a sanctioned school activity, to all of the students in the classroom. Secondly, students were encouraged in the activity to use the derogatory language but at the same time to objectify it and speak about it at a meta-level, hybridizing it with an academic analytic discourse and social space.

Interactional Positioning: What Spaces are Being Made *by* Interaction?

A pivotal movement in the focal interaction, initiated by Ian, is a shift from discussing practices and identities more distant to those that were copresent in the classroom to using a participant example (Wortham, 1994) from the classroom itself. Ian carefully built a relation between the banner as a world of derogatory language and the here-and-now world of the classroom. He made his question appear academic ("I was wondering how that was," line 1) and, even while positioning Latanya as a user of derogatory language against whites, he suggested that he was not intending to negatively position her ("No no no—not now"). Concurrently, Ian positioned himself as being "[made] fun of" (line 7) and as outside of such immoral action himself, situating himself only imaginatively and conditionally in relation to the use of "nigger" (e.g., "if I said," line 1). Tony (African American) provided some assistance to Ian in positioning Latanya as someone needing correction ("CALM DOWN THERE," line 6). Maureen's interjection (line 11) appears directed at re-grounding the interaction away from the participant example of Latanya and back toward language and race relations in history. She points back toward the banner and also uses herself as participant example ("You can call me a cracker," line 11) in what may be an effort to direct attention away from the Ian-Latanya interaction.

To further interpret Ian's regrounding of the interaction in the here-and-now the classroom—the copresent identities and interactions—I posit that we need to trace his discourse indexed in this brief segment through the spatial history of interaction in this group. Reasserting the trialectic of spatiality, historicality, and sociality, I consider how the interaction provides a window to enduring struggles of enacting and recognizing identity and, in particular, racial identities. While in the previous section I emphasized how, pedagogically, the activity produced a thirdspace that was ripe in its potential for opening up identities and restructuring power, in this section I consider how the interaction was used to reproduce oppressive race relations. However, rather than developing a microanalysis of how the interaction was both indeterminate and socially reproductive (e.g., Leander, 2002a) here, reading through the interaction I focus upon the racial-spatial history that I interpret it to be indexing and extending. This spatial history of interaction and identity positioning emphasizes two claims that are directly or indirectly indexed by Ian in lines 1, 3, and 7. The first claim is that "white people" are distinct groups that are clearly represented by their individual members. Ian positioned Latanya as a "black person" (line 3) using derogatory language, just as he positioned himself and other "white people" as those who "don't get mad" (line 7). The second claim is that black people interact inappropriately. While white people "don't get mad" (line 7) at offenses, with black people it "would be like a whole different story" (line 1). These claims about separate group identities and inappropriate interaction, I posit, are important ways of producing the junior KTA class, in the white imagination, as a shrinking space. In the following, I follow the perspective of the white European-American students who imagined the KTA as a shrinking space and relate this perspective to Ian's positioning of Latanya.

A Spatial History of Interaction and the KTA as a Shrinking Space

A number of white European-American students in the junior class expressed a heightened sense of anxiety about a growing "community of black people" in the KTA. The new group of seven African-American students who entered as juniors, many of whom were close friends with other African Americans in the academy, caused a good deal of anxiety on the part of many white European-American students. This anxiety and anger was often coded and not indexed as about culture or race; rather, it was often linked to the level of noise during interaction or simply to the number of students in the class.

The racialization of (shrinking) space was not constructed through simple numbers of people, however, but by constructing the African-American students as a group or community (e.g., Ian, lines 1, 5, and 7; Robert, line

10). In some cases, this interpretation was shaped as a nostalgic loss of a unified community with unmarked racial identity, and at other times the "black community" was constructed as an active agent, attempting to destroy the (racially unmarked) classroom community (e.g., Mike, following). In both cases, the black community was constructed as shrinking the space for (unmarked) others. In making this argument, students often pointed to how the African-American students sat together. Figure 3 provides a map of student-embodied positions during the focal literacy event.

Notes and Name Key for Figure 3. In the F-formation (Kendon, 1990) diagram, the oval figures represent individuals, with pointed segments representing direction of body orientation. As much of this analysis considers the "marking" of racial identity as a social achievement, bolded ovals are used to represent African-American participants, and non-bolded ovals represent white European-American participants (except for Stephen, who is Pacific Islander).

A group of ten of the African-American students begins on the left side of the classroom and extends to a cluster of students in the back. Of these ten, six of the students were newly admitted their junior year. This sitting together was sometimes interpreted as a coordinated, even strategic effort against white identity. While no one (including African-American students) ever commented that the white European-American students grouped together (although Figure 3 can be read in this manner), such complaints about the African-American students were commonplace. In general terms, such identity marking can be described as a cultural practice of privilege, in which a dominant cultural identity is considered unmarked (e.g., Howard, 1999). I would also like to situate this marking more directly in the ongoing production of social space. This racialization (Smith, 1993) of classroom space was shaped as a response to a perceived loss of space and privilege.

Anth: Anthony	Joe: Joeline	Rod: Rod
Ashl: Ashley	Kare: Kareena	Sam: Sam
Ben: Benjamin	Kev: Kevin (Researcher)	Sha: Shameen
Bre: Brett	Lat: Latanya	Sid: Sid (Teacher)
Cath: Catherine	Lesl: Leslie	Step: Stephen
Chel: Chelle	Mau: Maureen (Teacher)	Terr: Terreyal
Chri: Chris	Mari: Marie	Ton: Tony
Darr: Darrijah	May: Mayoosha	Tren: Trent
Doug: Doug	Mik: Mike	Trac: Tracey
Heid: Heidi	Nico: Nicole	Wil: Willie
Hoo: Hooper	Prec: Precious	
Ian: Ian	Rob: Robert	

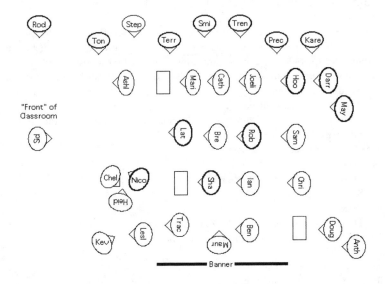

Figure 3. Student positions at the outset of focal interaction

Joeline, a white European American, sketched her interpretation of how the black students segregated themselves from white students in the seating arrangement within the junior class (Figure 4). Joeline described that one side of the classroom represented black students, while the other side represented white students, with a gulf (sketched with wavy lines) separating them. Exceptionally, she described how two black circles represented Tony and Rod, both African American, seated among the white students.

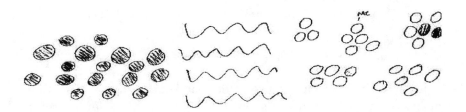

Figure 4. Joeline's drawing

The following interview segment indexes Joeline's interpretation of racial division and strife within the classroom:

Joeline: They always get offended with everything that somebody says to them. I mean everything, whether it be just a little thing, they always start yelling about something. And they're always complaining, always, I mean just everything.

Kevin: Are you thinking mostly the black students are complaining or the white students are complaining?

Joeline: Well, I mean basically yeah.

Kevin: Uh huh. So the white students aren't complaining as much but they're feeling the tension from the black students?

Joeline: Also, we're still giving it back, also.

Kevin: You're giving tension back?

Joeline: But just not a, we're just doing it on a, just under self-defense.

Kevin: Self-defense?

Joeline: Yeah.

Kevin: Do you have any idea where the, what was your sense of where it like comes from? Does it seem—you've been in since the beginning?

Joeline: Yeah.

Kevin: Since the freshman year?

Joeline: Yeah, and it's definitely changed.

Kevin: Has it changed?

Joeline: Yeah.

Kevin: Did it seem to be less tense before?

Joeline: Yea, because there was no (   ).

Kevin: Huh?

Joeline: I mean I'm talking about the dark-skinned students.

Kevin: Uh huh.

Joeline: But they have changed it and I'm totally sick of it. I totally want to get out of the academy now.

Kevin: Really?

Joeline: Yeah.

Kevin: They added more black students and because of that, it's added more tension?

Joeline: Yea, and more grouping off too.

Kevin: More grouping off? That's interesting. In your feeling is it's changed the nature of the group quite a bit?

Joeline: Yea, because we all used to be like, uh, the people used to be in one group basically.

Kevin: Right.

Joeline: And now they've all grouped off into one big one.

Joeline offered an interpretation that one large group of "dark-skinned students" segregated themselves and thus were ruining a former sense of community. A number of white European-American students voiced such anxieties on different occasions, blaming the African-American students for grouping and claiming that such exclusive grouping was morally wrong, while also a threat to the community of the classroom. Joeline's account that the African-American students were "complaining" and "yelling" and that "they always get offended with everything" resonates with Ian's claim that if he were to use an offensive word against a "black person" it "would be a whole different story" (line 1, focal interaction). The notions of segregation and inappropriate behavior are woven together discursively to produce a separatist black group identity that is being inappropriate by nature of its group segregation *and* by the quality of its interaction with whites. Moreover, Joeline's response indicated that the KTA, for her, was a shrinking space—she positioned herself acting in "self-defense" with other white students and indicated that she wanted to "get out of the academy now."

Along with using embodied spaces to argue that the African Americans acted as a unified group, a number of white European-American students complained that the African Americans essentially co-opted the sound space of the class:

Mike: It's two separate groups, it's the white people and the black people, the quiet people and the loud people.
Kevin: Pretty much two?
Mike: They separate themselves and they try to annoy the living crap out of us.

Many of the European-American students critiqued the loudness and associated it with the undisciplined interaction of the African-American students as a group. In particular, several European-American girls criticized not just volume but the sense of being overrun or criticized in trying to speak by Shameen, an African-American male. (Shameen was often used to metonymically represent all African Americans by some white European-American students, even though Shameen's strong participation, joking, and unpredictable behavior was also critiqued by many African-American students). In interview, several white European Americans, and especially males, interpreted the activity of the African Americans in the classroom, as a group, with fear and anger over the loss of a culture war between white and black culture. As Mike put it, "We switched sides.... It's almost like we're the slaves."

The interview material, Joeline's sketch, and the historical overview offers some sense of how, among the multiple social spaces composing the junior-level KTA, it was becoming over time a space where African-American racial identity was marked. Moreover, this recognition work was associated with a shrinking of space in the perspective of many of the white European-American students. Arguments for the racialized shrinking of space were drawn from the perceived, embodied spaces of racial group divisions (Figures 3 and 4), from claims about how interactions ought proceed, and from assumptions linking individual to group identities. Students and teachers interacting in this social arrangement, as considered in the focal interaction, acted into and extended the spatial-historical-social relations that had been produced in myriad previous interactions.

Further Discussion

Soja discusses how an emphasis upon spatiality, following Lefebvre (1991) and others, is "an attempt to restore the ontological trialectic of sociality-historicality-spatiality, with all three operating at full throttle at every level of knowledge formation" (Soja, 1996, p. 171). That is, the turn to analyzing social-spatial dialectical relations does not dispense with history, but rather (trialectically) engages it. At the same time, Soja (1996) and others recognize how engagement with the historical is fraught with problems. Among them, a historical perspective, imagination, and method have so infused social science—have taken up so much space and time—that one is always at risk of an analysis being overrun with the historical. In Soja's terms, there are plenty of available ways to become yet another "quasi-spatializer of history" (1996, p. 181). In writing this chapter, I have been aware of the risks in writing a spatial history in which "space" simply modifies an historical method, with its impulse to homogenize human activity and to offer simple trajectories of development. In closing, I make a few methodological observations concerning the composing of a spatial history of positioning in a literacy event. In particular, I consider how I have come to think about writing about space with the monkey of history on my back.

First, I have considered positioning through two trialectical relationships, drawn from Lefebvre (1991) and Soja (1989, 1996). The first of these trialectical relationships involves the dynamics of conceived, perceived, and lived spaces. The positioning metaphor is useful, I would maintain, as long as it is not left to function entirely as metaphor (without material grounding) nor entirely as readily perceived location (lacking the complexity of the conceived production of space) (Smith & Katz, 1993). Rather, lived social spaces, such as the KTA, or the space of pedagogy produced by the Derogatory Terms Activity, are much more complex, vibrant, and indeterminate than their readily perceived or discursively conceived realizations. The second trialectic, sociality-spatiality-historicality, allows us to consider the ways in which positioning is stretched out across space-time. While a historical perspective on identity might feature the trajectory or the "line" of "development," the trialectical move toward the spatial permits a more fully social account of positioning. Identities are geographical and temporal; individuals and groups are shaped and spread across space and time.

Second, I have attempted to offer at least an opening account of how entirely an interaction is situated or *"emplaced"* in a particular space, which I have described primarily as the junior-level KTA. The analysis has worked not toward understanding general social processes that are applicable in other contexts, but toward the ongoing spatial constitution of a particular "where." Since disclaimers about the generalizability of interpretive work are commonplace, I want to be careful to indicate that I do not mean that my "findings" are simply "situated" and that others must determine their relative broader application. Rather, the interpretive analysis is about the production of situation itself—spatiality and sociality in dialectical relationship. The particularities of spatial processes constituting the junior-level KTA and literacy practices within it, including the definition of middle-level students, changes in racial makeup of the class and discourse about this, and certain practices of pedagogy, are read as space-producing processes that dynamically shift over time.

Third, the spatial history offered here is not a single history, but the shifting relations among multiple, simultaneous spaces (Yaeger, 1996). My intention is to document how multiple space-time processes are copresent and not simple stories of development. The focal interaction, therefore, is not merely the accumulation of endpoints in a spatial history, but is rather a window or nexus through which spatialization may be interpreted. These processes are both heterotopic and heterochronic. For example, the racialization of the classroom discussed in the fourth section of the paper may be read in relation to the KTA as a privileged and bounded space. The privilege and boundedness were not lost in a developmental cycle or narrative toward becoming something else across the four-year span of its initial development. Rather, the discursive-material constitution of a particular kind of privileged KTA space, given in history, is interpreted against its perceived space-time realizations, its activity, and racial demographics four years later. History is collapsed, spaced are folded onto one another. In other places, social spaces which may be produced through relatively distinct processes are interpreted as coherent and driven by the same set of social forces by participants. For example, I illustrated how some of the white European-American students used the material positions of bodies to as perceived evidence in the production of a particular type of (perceived and lived) black community. Writing space does not permit the analysis here, but the associated spatialities of (1) the loss of KTA privilege and (2) a racialized, shrinking space were also co-interpreted with (3) the move to room 251, a transformation enacted by various social-spatial processes discussed above.

Fourth, the spatial history given here leaves open the contradictions and tensions among social spaces as a productive process. The durable repetition of certain kinds of interactional positioning does not provide, in my estimation, a single argument about why the social spaces enacted by Maureen and Sid in their pedagogy were not effective (in their estimation) for opening up critical discussion and new identity possibilities. Likewise, a focus upon the ongoing spatial history of the KTA as an institution fails to provide a single resource for interpreting how or why this interaction, at the margins of this institution, became shaped the way it was. Rather than consider institutional, pedagogical, and interactional forms of positioning as either subsuming one another in space-time or as entirely separate processes, I consider them as concurrent and interwoven. Institutions, pedagogies, group and individual identities are coproduced and articulated in ongoing processes of production. While spaces may be stitched together for the particular ideological purposes of participants and researchers alike, the tensions and conflicts within and among social spaces also produce unpredictable movement and shifts, openings for new possible spaces. For example, Maureen and Sid did not simply enact a pregiven critical pedagogy, but enacted it through a spatial struggle over control of the KTA with the Academy Moms. Additionally, the emplacement of the Derogatory Terms Activity from a distant space-time of graffiti spaces and Maureen's private school teaching into the KTA was a coordination of multiple social spaces that "fired" or "sparked" a critical transformation of social space that brought to the fore new forms of interaction and processes of identification.

Fifth, in collecting a spatial history of a literacy event, I recognize the involvement of participants and myself in the interpretation of a broad range of semiotic texts. These texts, including the focal interaction as a linguistic and nonverbal text and the pictures students drew of KTA-Kempton High relations, are central to my own interpretive processes. Collected *in* history, they are reassembled not simply in historical order, but across the surface of my own text for building particular relationships. These texts are material and discursive and travel in macro material forms of circulation (e.g., academy funding documents) and local discursive practices (claims about race). I believe that this particular trialectic of sociality, historicality, and spatiality enacted in my writing of the chapter mirrors, in many ways, the practices of participants. Ian's claim about Latanya's use of "honky" and Maureen's statement that "certain groups have been more historically repressed than others" (line 11) are not just textual constructions of social space that enfold in (real) time, but statements that also reconfigure space-time. Intertextual relations thus involve the imaginative reconstitution of social space, a form of agency within and against lived boundaries.

References

Bakhtin, M. M. (1981). *The dialogic imagination.* Austin: University of Texas Press.

Davies, B., & Harré, R. (1990). Positioning: The discursive production of selves. *Journal for the Theory of Social Behavior, 20*(1), 43–63.

Foucault, M. (1980). Questions on geography. In C. Gordon (Ed.), *Power/knowledge: Selected interviews and other writings 1972–1977* (C. Gordon, L. Marshall, J. Mepham, & K. Soper, Trans.) (pp. 63–77.) New York: Pantheon.

Gee, J. P. (2000). The new literacy studies: From 'socially situated' to the work of the social. In D. Barton, M. Hamilton, & R. Ivanic (Eds.), *Situated literacies: Reading and writing in context* (pp. 180–196). New York: Routledge.

Goffman, E. (1981). *Forms of talk.* Philadelphia: University of Pennsylvania Press.

Gutiérrez, K., Rymes, B., & Larson, J. (1995). Script, counterscript, and underlife: James Brown versus Brown v. Board of Education. *Harvard Educational Review, 65*(3), 445-471.

Harvey, D. (1996). *Justice, nature and the geography of difference.* Cambridge, MA: Blackwell Publishers.

Holland, D., & Lave, J. (2001). Introduction. In D. Holland & J. Lave (Eds.), *History in person: Enduring struggles and the practice of identity* (pp. 3–33). Albuquerque, NM: School of American Research Press.

Howard, G. R. (1999). *We can't teach what we don't know: White teachers, multiracial schools.* New York: Teachers College Press.

Illinois State Board of Education. (1997, September). *Illinois Partnership Academies: Summative Evaluation 1993–1997.* Springfield: Illinois State Board of Education.

Kamberelis, G. & Scott, K. D. (1992). Other people's voices: The coarticulation of texts and subjectivities. *Linguistics and Education, 4*, 359–403.

Kendon, A. (1990). *Conducting interaction: Patterns of behavior in focused encounters.* Cambridge, UK: Cambridge University Press.

Leander, K. M. (2002a). Locating Latanya: The situated production of identity artifacts in classroom interaction. *Research in the Teaching of English, 37*, 198–250.

Leander, K. M. (2002b). Silencing in classroom interaction: Producing and relating social spaces. *Discourse Processes, 34*(2), 193–235.

Lefebvre, H. (1991). *The production of space.* Cambridge, MA: Blackwell.

Lehr, A. (1997). Public values in school programs: The Carl Perkins Act and the Career Academy. Unpublished manuscript.

Massey, D. (1997). The political place of locality studies. In L. McDowell (Ed.), *Undoing place? A geographical reader* (pp. 317–331). New York: Arnold.

Mehan, H. (1979). *Learning lessons.* Cambridge, MA: Harvard University Press.

Raby, M. (1995). The career academies. In W. N. Grubb (Ed.), *Education through occupation in American high schools: Approaches to integrating academic and vocational education* (Vol. 1, pp. 59–81). New York: Teachers College Press.

Rex, L. A., & McEachen, D. (1999). "If anything is odd, inappropriate, confusing, or boring, it's probably important": The emergence of inclusive academic literacy through English classroom discussion practices. *Research in the Teaching of English, 34*(1), 65–129.

Smith, N., & Katz, C. (1993). Grounding metaphor: Toward a spatialized politics. In M. Keith & S. Pile (Eds.), *Place and the politics of identity* (pp. 67–83). New York: Routledge.

Smith, S. (1993). Residential segregation and the politics of racialization. In M. Cross & M. Keith (Eds.), *Racism, the city, and the state* (pp. 128–143). New York: Routledge.

Soja, E. W. (1989). *Postmodern geographies: The reassertion of space in critical social theory.* London: Verso.

Soja, E. W. (1996). *Thirdspace: Journeys to Los Angeles and other real-and-imagined places.* Malden, MA: Blackwell.

Stern, D., Raby, M., & Dayton, C. (1992). *Career academies: Partnership for reconstructing American high schools.* San Francisco: Jossey-Bass.

Wortham, S. (1994). *Acting out participant examples in the classroom.* Philadelphia, PA. John Benjamins.

Yaeger, P. (Ed.). (1996). *The geography of identity.* Ann Arbor: The University of Michigan Press.

7

A Rhizomatic Cartography of Adolescents, Popular Culture, and Constructions of Self

Margaret Carmody Hagood

I used to think I knew what popular culture was. But, then again, I used to think I understood adolescents and what they were are all about, too, and how and for what purposes they use popular culture in their lives. As a thirty-something European-American woman, I assumed too much. Like many adults, my assumptions were based upon my age, practical experiences, readings about the life period of adolescence, and my understanding of adolescents' pop culture. By this I mean that I've experienced the period of time known as adolescence, and as an adult I've worked with adolescents and read a lot about them and their pop culture interests. Actually, as I came to learn over time, enormous gaps and discrepancies exist between how others identify adolescents as particular kinds of people with particular popular culture interests and how adolescents perceive themselves as users of what they deem popular culture.

These assumptions about adolescents, their literacy lives, and popular culture shifted and changed when I hung out with and became friends with seven twelve- and thirteen-year-olds and studied how they use popular culture in their own lives. It was only after I spent approximately eight to twelve hours a day during two ten-week periods in Australia and the United States with teenagers, listening to their conversations with pals, going to school with them, emailing them daily, chatting with them through notes and online, observing how they actually define and use popular culture in their lives both in and out of school, analyzing photo documentaries they created, and interviewing them, their parents, and their teachers that I began to rethink what adolescents do with pop culture as part of their literacy lives.

Popular culture is most often associated with images and lifestyles that media produce for adolescents' pleasures. Conceived of in negative terms, images of sex, drugs, bodies, violence, and alcohol portrayed in movies, television shows, fashion magazines, or on the Internet usually come to mind when thinking of adolescents' popular culture interests. Though often left unrecognized and unaddressed, popular culture and pleasures also include a world of images and lifestyles associated with religious lives. And just as adolescents use and affiliate themselves with popular culture of the secular world, similar goods and services are available for adolescents in the spiritual world.

During a six-month, cross-continental study I examined how adolescents used popular culture to renegotiate identity for themselves while they were simultaneously categorized with particular age-defined identities according to their uses of popular culture. Using rhizomatic cartography, a form of spatial analysis, I attended to the ways that adolescents use popular culture to accept identities and to push against being categorized with these very same identities they attempt to take on. The remainder of this chapter focuses on the literacy lives and identities of two girls—Tee and Rosa—who constructed notions of themselves from their popular culture interests related to their religious predilections.

Rhizomatic Cartography: A Spatial Methodology

In an effort to rethink identities associated with adolescents, Lesko (2001) explained the need to attend to recursive views of adolescents' growth and change and to examine "local contexts and specific actions of young people, without the inherent evaluations of steps, stages, and socialization" (p. 195). Keeping this statement in mind, I began to question, like others (e.g., Finders, 1999; Sibley, 1995), the period of adolescence as a time of "storm and stress" (Hall, 1904).

Working from theories of identity production and subjectivity construction, I analyzed data about Tee and Rosa according to Deleuze and Guattari's (1987) rhizomatic cartography or rhizoanalysis (also nicknamed "pop analysis"). Pop analysis refers to the ephemeral and temporal nature of rhizoanalysis—being only an analysis of short-term memory. Jackson (in press) used the figuration of a rhizome to rethink the concept of *voice* in a new figuration of *rhizovocality* and to look differently at the excessive and transgressive interconnections of voice. Alvermann (2000) used rhizoanalysis a bit differently to reanalyze data from three studies in an effort to conceptualize the connections and ruptures between and among texts. And Grosz (1994) connected the rhizome to her conceptions of feminism to rethink the interconnections between gender and subjectivity.

According to Deleuze and Guattari (1987), the rhizome has certain characteristics, which include six principles included in rhizomatic cartography (see also Chapter 8):

1. Points on a rhizome need to connect to something else.
2. Rhizomes are heterogeneous not dichotomous.
3. Rhizomes are made up of a multiplicity of lines that extend in all directions.
4. Rhizomes break off, but then they begin again, either where they were before or on a new line.
5. Rhizomes are not models; they have no deep structure.
6. Rhizomes are maps with multiple entryways.

Built off the concept of a rhizome, rhizomatic cartography works as a figuration of a rhizome, which differs from using a rhizome as a metaphor. A figuration is an analytic tool used in work influenced by poststructural theory to move beyond coding and categorizing data in order to redescribe and to represent concepts differently. It is similar to a metaphor in that both are implemented to improve understandings of a concept; yet, unlike a metaphor, a figuration attempts to provide freeing ways to think about a concept by attending to the complexity inherent within it. St. Pierre (1997) discussed the differences between the two, noting, "Figurations are not whimsical flights of fancy imagined to distract us from the day-to-day but carefully considered trajectories that send us headlong into the complexity of living realities" (p. 281). The complexities included in a rhizome should illustrate "relational images" as Braidotti (1994) explained, in order to form new representations of living realities. The relational images highlighted for Tee and Rosa involved the ways in which the girls used religious paraphernalia in efforts to assume identities created for them and to construct their own niches involving subjectivities related to their popular culture interests.

Rhizomatic cartography is an analysis perhaps best described as one of coming and going, of offshoots and new directions. By definition, rhizomes constantly shift and change, growing simultaneously in all directions. Thus, the rhizome maps illustrate the ever-changing multiplicities involved in adolescents' uses of popular culture where tensions arise between identity and subjectivity in adolescents' text uses. By using the rhizome to connect identity and subjectivity, I could examine contradictory data and map how adolescents simultaneously take on identities produced for them and push against those identities. Because rhizomatic cartography picks up in the middle and focuses upon what is already going on when it is happening, this analytical method allowed me to jump into the middle of the diverse lives of a group of adolescents.

Adolescents' Pop Culture: Identity and Subjectivity at Work

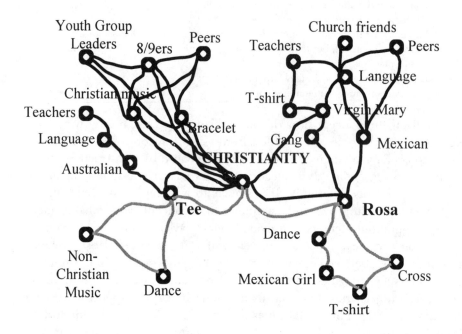

Figure 1. Rhizome of Tee and Rosa's identities and subjectivities

Tee and Rosa demonstrated how adolescents use religious texts as pop culture in contradictory ways: as a form of affiliation within a group and to push against and to counter assumptions about their identities within the group. This rhizomatic map illustrates (1) how Tee and Rosa are produced with identities based upon assumptions made by teachers, peers, and church-related personnel (represented by black lines that connect data points on the rhizome) and (2) how Tee and Rosa both accepted and pushed against these identities while trying to maintain parts of those identities related to their beliefs in Christianity (depicted with light gray lines connecting data points). In the remainder of the paper, I examine these two perspectives of identity production and subjectivity construction of the girls' uses of popular culture. First, I looked at the ways that the girls employed religious paraphernalia to be recognized with a particular religious identity and to associate themselves within a larger religiously affiliated group. In this sense, the girls assume identities using pop culture icons produced for them. With this in mind, in the first phase of data analysis, structures that produced adolescents as particular sorts of people according to identity categories that included race, class, gender, age, ability, appearance/body, and ethnicity (including culture, language, nationality, and religion) were identified. These data became the nodes of the rhizome delineated with dark lines.

Second, I examined how Rosa and Tee use those same religious texts in order to differentiate themselves from others, while trying to maintain their identities within their religious groups. In this phase of data analysis, I attended to the ways that the girls used popular culture to push against the identities that sought to define them as particular sorts of people. As data were gathered I compared the adolescents' own uses of popular culture with the societal categories that named them and produced particular identities for them, locating tensions between how texts defined the girls in particular ways and how the adolescents employed popular culture to push against these identities. This second phase of analysis became the rhizomatic data points denoted in light gray.

And, finally, to examine the relations between the texts that produced the girls with identities and the girls' own uses of texts that often challenged those very identities, I created the rhizomatic drawing featured above. It was only in thinking about and examining the relation between the girls' identity and subjectivity—neither as opposite sides that form a dichotomy nor as entities by themselves—that identity and subjectivity become apparent as inseparable components of the system of production and consumption as adolescents use texts, as those texts are defined for them, and as they define their own uses of texts.

Rhizomes of Identity

Rosa and Tee, though having never met, were both young adolescents whose uses of popular culture affiliated them with particular Christian identities in their in- and out-of-school lives as young adolescents. Both girls were part of religious families, and both had immigrated to new countries when they were five years old. Tee's maternal grandparents were Christian missionaries on the Solomon Islands before moving their family to New Zealand, where Tee was born. When she was five, her family (including an older sister and younger brother) moved to a small town in Queensland, Australia, so that her parents could attend a two-year Bible college. Tee's family liked Australia so much that they decided to stay upon completing their schooling.

Tee's transition to Australia was relatively easy. She explained that Australia was just like New Zealand "except Australia's hotter and it doesn't get any snow, and Australians talk a bit differently than Kiwis." According to Tee, her life hadn't changed much as a result of the move. Tee's teachers at Kehara State High School (KSHS) perceived no differences between Tee's life as an Aussie or a Kiwi, either. In fact, they didn't even realize that she wasn't Australian. Teachers described her "as the typical Australian teen-ager" and "into all the Australian trends" with her stylish shoulder-length haircut that accented her strawberry blonde hair. Tee fit in so effortlessly that it wasn't until three weeks into the study that I learned that Tee had moved to Australia from New Zealand. When she told me that while sitting with a group of friends during morning tea, several girls said that they didn't believe her!

Tee and her family were actively involved in Kehara Baptist Church, which was located near KSHS. She coached and played on church-sponsored netball teams on Mondays, Tuesdays, and Thursdays, attended 8/9ers (the church youth group) on Fridays, played in and umpired netball games and tournaments on Saturdays, and went to church on Sundays. On Wednesdays, Tee regularly attended Student Focus during lunch break. This program was sponsored by the church and was held in an empty classroom on the school campus. When she described the program, Tee said, "It's really fun. You play games and stuff, and then they talk about God."

Rosa was also the middle child of a family of three. When she was five and her older brother, Mario, was seven, her parents moved them, along with their infant brother, Jesus, from Mexico City to the southern United States "to live a better life," her father explained. Over eight years, Rosa's family had to learn a new way of living, a new language, and a different culture. Besides their children's educations, Juan and Helena felt that raising their children as "Mexican Catholic" in the United States was crucial. For them, this process included membership at Santa Maria Catholic Church. This church was in a neighboring city and about a thirty-five-minute com-mute from their home. Juan and Helena thought it important to join that particular community because the church catered to the needs of a growing Spanish-speaking group of Catholics. Rosa liked Santa Maria, but because it was so far away from the family apartment she was only involved on Sun-days. "I have a couple of friends there and stuff," she said. "My mom and my brothers have friends there, too. We go to mass, and then we eat together and come home."

A comparable religiously affiliated program like Student Focus didn't exist at Hancock for Rosa to attend. Actually, though religion was central to Rosa's life, it was more an aspect of her life as a Mexican, which didn't relate well to her experiences at school. Actually, although Tee's and Rosa's interests in popular culture as Christianity seemed similar, I learned over time that the religious texts that produced them with identities as Christians were perceived quite differently in their in- and out-of-school lives.

Tee was a thin, athletic, and outspoken thirteen-year-old. She was quite well liked by other students at Kehara, which surprised her and her parents. Tee described herself "as a loner" when she was in primary school because many of her beliefs and interests involving Christianity clashed with what seemed acceptable with her peers. In the previous year, she often arrived home from school in tears because the other children ostracized her. She didn't think much would change once she began high school. But things did change. In fact, Tee's matriculation into high school afforded her access to a larger circle of friends who shared similar interests in Christianity. In an essay on group identity written in English class, Tee described her group of friends as Christians. She wrote, "Something that make our group different are well all of us are Christians and we communicate with all the groups not just our own."

Tee used her interests in Christianity to be part of this group identity. And aspects of what Tee deemed popular culture, such as religious paraphernalia and music, became a part of group affiliation. For instance, one morning Tee ran up to me at 8:15 as I was walking up the stairs into the eighth-grade wing. "Margaret! I've been looking for you this morning!" She squealed and thrust her left hand up into my face. "Look what Trina bought for me from America!" She steered my point of reference away from her newly polished neon-green fingernails to a royal blue canvas band snugly fastened with a silver buckle around her freckled wrist. On it was stamped W.S.F.J. in large, white letters.

"It stands for 'We shine for Jesus.' All of my friends have these bracelets. Wasn't that nice of Trina to bring it to me? And it's a new one. It's not like the other ones—W.W.J.D. [What would Jesus do?] or F.R.O.G. [Fully relying on God] or even P.U.S.H. [Pray until something happens]," she noted.

"I've only seen the W.W.J.D. bracelets," I replied.

"This one is brand new, and no one has it! I've got to go and show it to Nick before form!" she exclaimed and ran off in search of her friend.

Students used accessories to personalize what seemed like a homogeneous sea of green and black school skirts and pants and matching green-flecked Kehara golf-style shirts. Often this meant searching for ways to stand out or to blend in. Kids' affiliations in groups included wearing funky hair clips or certain joggers, decorating the cover of notebooks with well-liked movie stars, or carrying particular satchels, backpacks, or pencil cases, which in some way signaled membership with a group of peers. And having something new like a hard-to-find Christian bracelet was always exciting.

Among Tee's group of friends, incorporating paraphernalia like Tee's W.S.F.J. bracelet or other Christian jewelry such as crosses or silver rings with fish on them into their attire was a way to identify themselves as a Christian group. Tee and her friends also used stationery adorned with Christian logos such as a Christian fish when they wrote notes to one another. And Tee had even figured out a way to sign her name on school assignments and notes such that she intertwined "the Jesus fish" symbol in her letter formation.

School was certainly a place where Tee felt comfortable sharing her Christian faith, both in the clothing she wore and the discussions she had. The Christian group of fifteen or so boys and girls that she hung out with during morning tea and lunch spent a lot of time discussing aspects of Christianity. Exploring how their lives as Christians fit into other areas of their teenage life was the most central topic. Not only did Tee and her friends attend Student Focus at Kehara, but they also attended 8/9ers together, the Friday afternoon youth group at Kehara Baptist Church. Grade 8 and 9 students from all over the city came to this weekly activity.

Like Tee, Rosa felt Christianity—and specifically Catholicism—centrally in her life. However, her interests in Catholicism, interests that related to her group affiliation with three other Mexican girls at Hancock, didn't seem to fit in at all with school, and she had more difficulty than Tee did to work her religiously tinged popular culture interests into school. One afternoon in October I picked her up at her apartment complex after school because she wanted to go to the mall. Seeing my car pull into the parking lot, she came bounding down the black steel stairs from the second-story apartment balcony. She wore the same pair of khaki bell-bottom *Pipes* jeans she had on that day at school. But she had changed from a red T-shirt with an Old Navy logo into a white T-shirt with the Virgin Mary in a blue, flowing robe silk-screened on the front.

"Hey, I like your shirt!" I remarked when she hopped into my car.

"Thanks! I got it at church. All the kids who were there got the shirt because it was a special day for Maria." She wove her hair into a thick, long braid as she talked. "I like it. I think she looks like an angel with these stars around her head. It's for when she goes to heaven," Rosa explained.

"Oh! Did you get it on the Feast of the Assumption of Mary in August?" I asked.

She rummaged through her backpack. "Yeah. How'd ya know that?" she asked and then pulled out a brown rubber band from her pack and quickly wound it around the end of her braid.

"I'm Catholic, too."

"Oh! You know what?" she said, looking at me, "I wore it to school, and the teacher made me turn it inside out because we aren't supposed to wear religious stuff to school."

"Really? When did that happen?" I asked.

"Sometime in September." She affixed the clip back onto one of the straps of her bag.

"But can't kids wear religious clothing to school?" I asked.

"I don't know. I had to go to the office, and they just made me turn it the other way. Like [the teachers] think that the T-shirt has to do with being in a gang. I still wear it to school. Well, sometimes I wear it, but I'll just wear it under—you know my gray jacket? I'll just wear it under that, and then I'll zip it up."

Both Kehara and Hancock were public schools, so a separation of church and state prevailed. And though religion was not something that was taught or discussed in either school within the curriculum or by classroom teachers, it was more obvious and readily accepted at Kehara than at Hancock. Perhaps this is why Rosa felt that her own interests in Christianity and in Catholicism were squelched at school, while Tee openly used school as a place to express her religious beliefs. Whereas Tee used Christianity to connect with her peers and was seen by her teachers as "into all the trends," Rosa's popular culture interests kept her feeling like an outsider at school. Because she had to turn the T-shirt inside out, she surmised that the teachers thought that her T-shirt was in some way gang related.

This incident at school affected how Rosa viewed wearing other religious articles of clothing that she owned. At her apartment one afternoon, Rosa pulled out a T-shirt from her bureau. On the front was a depiction of the crucifixion of Christ. She said that her mother bought it for her at a church fund-raiser. I asked her if she ever wore it to school. "No, I don't want the teachers to tell me that people might feel bad about it or they might not like it because there was blood on him. Maybe it just looks too violent. I don't know." Protecting her own feelings and assuming that she knew how teachers would read her shirt and react at school, Rosa decided not to wear it to school.

Actually, all sorts of Catholic paraphernalia adorned the tidy, four-room apartment that Rosa shared with her mother and brothers. A well-worn maroon-colored Bible always sat on the table in the living room. Rosa said that it belonged to her mother, but Rosa never read it. And framed on the wall were Rosa's and Mario's first communion certificates from Santa Maria Catholic Church. In Rosa's bedroom, which was covered with stuffed animals and teddy bears and hats, was a framed picture of the Virgin Mary that hung over her bed. Surrounding the picture were photographs of her and her brothers.

Rosa proudly showed the picture to me one afternoon after school. She took me to her room and jumped onto her bed, pointed to the picture, and sat quietly for a moment. As I studied it, she related it to her life as a Mexican and to her Catholic beliefs. "Most people who are Mexican that I know have one of those hanging somewhere in their house," she said. "And, most people keep them in their house because Mother Mary takes care of them so that nothing happens to them."

"Oh, I see," I said. "I really like this picture."

"And that is why there are pictures of me and Mario and Jesus, too. She is watching us."

The T-shirt Rosa wore resembled the image of the Madonna that she kept in her room. Without directly relating the two, Rosa pointed out how the Virgin Mary was important in her life. Her interest in the Virgin Mary had nothing at all to do with gang-related activity as she said her teachers suspected. Instead, for Rosa, the T-shirt had more to do with a Mexican identity that related to her interest in Catholicism.

To Rosa, school wasn't a welcoming place where she felt comfortable sharing her popular culture interests that related to her Mexican and Catholic beliefs. She became protective of what was important to her, keeping her faith away from school or actively seeking to keep it under wraps, as when she wore her T-shirt with the Virgin Mary on the chest covered by her gray jacket. Though not made to wear uniforms at Hancock, she thought that her own interests in popular culture relating to her Mexican identity and to Catholicism weren't accepted by those who were not Spanish speakers. On numerous occasions, Rosa commented about the injustices she perceived at school that were directed toward her group affiliation as a Mexican and Catholic. She talked at length about it when we were at her apartment or at the mall, her two favorite places to go as soon as the school day was over.

"I think that school is worn down," she said about Hancock one early evening as we sat in her living room on the sofa. "It is old, cold, and boring. I don't like what we learn either because it isn't very important to my life."

"Like why isn't it important to your life?" I asked.

Raising her voice a bit, she said, "[Hancock] is racist, and Spanish-speaking kids aren't treated as good as the other kids.... People don't give the

Spanish kids much chance because they don't think that we understand or like we can't speak good English.... Some kids are always telling Spanish kids to go back to Mexico."

Rosa hung out with three other Spanish-speaking eighth-grade girls at Hancock. Other students who weren't part of Rosa's circle of friends often asked her questions about "being Mexican." For example, in the lunch line one day, an African-American boy who was standing next to her told her that she was beautiful and then asked if she was Indian. Rosa laughed and said, "No way, boy! I am Mexican!" To which he replied, "Stop kiddin' me!" And on another day, during art class, Felicity, a white girl whom Rosa didn't know well and who sat across from Rosa at a worktable, said, "You are too white to be Mexican. What did you do?"

Rosa was outlining the phrase "Te Amo" in blue paint on the roof of a birdhouse she had built and had painted yellow. She didn't answer.

"Seriously, what did you do?" Felicity persisted.

Rosa didn't look up, but said, "I am what I am. I don't have to explain anything to you." She spent the last twenty minutes of class painting, and she didn't talk to anyone.

No doubt categorical assumptions about Mexican culture produced Rosa with a particular Mexican identity at school. These assumptions—based upon aspects of Rosa's popular culture interests—produced a Mexican identity that marked Rosa in ways that didn't at all match up with her own uses of popular culture to construct her own understanding of herself as a Mexican girl. Perhaps her feelings of being misunderstood at school kept her from engaging with other students.

Unlike Tee, whose move to another country didn't seem to affect her lifestyle or her popular culture interests, Rosa felt her life was different. She was reserved in school. She did what she had to do to get along in her classes, and despite the fact that she had strong critiques of the school and of many of the people, she did what adults asked of her. Her language arts teacher described her as "the typical Latina girl. She's smarter than she lets on," she said. "I know that she knows the answers to questions, but she won't talk in front of a group." Speaking later about these perceptions, Rosa replied, "Yeah, in classes I am quiet. Even if I know the answer to the question that the teacher asks, I say I don't know, or I answer the question with a low voice and the teacher can't hear me. But outside of classes, like when I am with my friends or I am at home, I just talk all the time! I can't stop talking! See, I love to talk!"

Sure enough, Rosa had much to say outside of school, but she remained reserved in classes. Usually she only spoke up when asked by a teacher to translate information into Spanish for a male student with limited English proficiency who had recently transferred to Hancock from South America. When Sergio arrived, Rosa's class schedule changed. The teachers told her the change occurred so that she could help Sergio with his English. Rosa resented having to change her schedule and to do this work. She felt that the only time being Mexican was appreciated was when she could help out a teacher with language issues. As soon as she could get into the hallway or off school property, she openly vented her frustrations. "Ooooh," she declared one day when we left her reading class, where she had obediently spent the entire period translating for Sergio the teacher's directions and an excerpt from *A Midsummer Night's Dream*. "[The teachers] just get on my nerves. It bothers me because they tell me what I can say, and then they are telling you what you can wear and can't wear to school, and it's like they're telling me that I can't think what I want to think."

Rosa was proud of her Spanish language, of Catholicism, and of her Mexican culture, but she felt that people at Hancock defined her according to these categories in ways that she didn't like. To Rosa, it seemed that language and clothing and religious beliefs were all tied up together. And across all three of these areas, she felt ostracized at school by people who were not like herself. Although students at Hancock seemed to have more freedom than the students at Kehara to "bring their individuality to school," Rosa nevertheless felt that her popular culture interests were not valued. Unlike Tee, Rosa thought that the teachers and non-Mexican students didn't understand or attempt to understand her.

Rhizomes of Subjectivity

But just as these girls were produced as particular kinds of people based upon group affiliations and identities that involved Christianity, they also pushed against their respective group identities that produced them as certain sorts of people. For Rosa, this renegotiation of a Mexican and Catholic identity had to do with expectations of being a Mexican girl, her understandings of Christian icons, and her uses of clothing. Tee's push against a group identity involved music and dancing.

Rosa prided herself on being a Mexican girl, and she often reasoned that she did certain things because she was Mexican. For example, sometimes we would take Jesus with us to the mall because Rosa said that she looked after her baby brother while her older brother did other things because she was a girl and should baby-sit. She also enjoyed cooking with her mother, and she didn't want her brothers involved in their forays because she said that it was what Mexican girls do together. And, on the Feast of Our Lady of Guadalupe (December 9), Rosa went with her family to mass at 5:00 a.m. "to sing to Maria because that is what Mexican Catholics do." Rosa, however, wasn't always content with the identity of a Mexican girl that produced her as a particular kind of person. Rather than just accept that identity, she used other aspects of popular culture to construct new ways of being that changed how she saw herself as a Mexican girl and as a Catholic.

In the fall, Hancock hosted a Halloween dance at school. Rosa's parents didn't want her to go to the dance, but she argued with them about it. After this discussion, Rosa was allowed to go to the dance, and she felt like she had made some progress as a twelve-year-old. "Culturally, as a Mexican girl," she said, "I am not supposed to date until I am fifteen, and I am not supposed to go to dances until then either. But I talked with my mom and dad about it, and so because I act right, I get a lot of privileges." In exchange for these privileges to go to dances, she said, "I just can't skip school; I can't sneak boys into the house; I can't sneak out; and I can't do drugs. If I do any of those things my mom will throw me out of the house. And I *can't* have sex until I am married."

Though Rosa often said that certain aspects of her life indicated that she was "Mexican Catholic," she also pushed against particular icons defining her with a Catholic identity. One afternoon, while hanging out at her house, she showed me a crystal, heart-shaped box with a cross on the lid. Seeing the cross, I asked her if it was something religious.

She seemed a bit annoyed when she responded. "Not everything that has a cross has to be religious." Then she said that she didn't use it religiously; she kept her notes in the box. "Well sometimes people just like something because other people like it, and sometimes I like it because other people like it, but that doesn't mean that it tells me what to do." She went onto say, "Like a cross and those kinds of things. It's important for lots of people, but it's not the same to all of them. So, sometimes it just depends."

Rosa's uses of the box with the cross on it had nothing at all to do with any religious affiliation of being Catholic. To her, a cross meant only what people made of it—just like her T-shirt with the Virgin Mary or the crucifix on the front. She didn't want me to assume that just because she was a Mexican Catholic that all religious icons or symbols defined her as being a particular kind of person or defined her uses of items. She wanted to show me where she kept her notes, not a religious aspect of her life. And when I misunderstood her uses of texts, she became annoyed and let me know as much.

Tee also pushed against the Christian identity that produced her as a particular person. One such incident occurred during a discussion between Tee and Beth and Laudy, two youth leaders of the Christian youth group called 8/9ers. Like Tee and her friends, these youth leaders wore W.W.J.D. bracelets.

"I just bought the newest DC Talk album," said Beth.

"Oh yeah," said Laudy. "I like them. They're like Jars of Clay."

Tee said, "Yeah, I have that one—'Supernatural.' I also have M2M and Britney Spears. You know her, Margaret. She's big in America!"

Beth looked over at Tee and asked, "Do you like her?"

"Yeah, I like her music. She's good to dance to, but I don't like how she dresses and acts."

"Oh," said Beth. "Tee, what radio station do you listen to?"

"Mostly B105," Tee answered.

"Do you?" asked Beth. "You *really* like that station?"

Tee's legs hung off of the table where she sat. She swung them around and thought for a bit. Then she said, "Yeah, I like B105, but I don't like the crappy talkers. They like to swear a lot, and they talk about sex, and I don't really like that. When they do that, I change the station and listen to 96.5 [the Christian Family station]."

"Yeah, 96.5 is the *best* station. You should start there!" Beth replied.

Tee said, "But I like the music on B105."

At this point, Laudy chimed in and said, "If you don't like the trashy talk, then listen to 96.5."

"I do listen to it, but I like the music on B105," Tee reiterated, and then she jumped off the table and went to play air hockey.

Tee didn't mention this episode again. But several weeks later a discussion ensued about music between Tee and her friends at school during morning tea. As they ate their snacks, a dispute arose among them about what kinds of music they could or should listen to as Christians.

"I am Christian, but I like non-Christian music," Tee said.

Mary looked over at Tee and asked, "What if you only listen to Christian music?"

"Then you miss out on a whole heap of good stuff," Tee said. "I like the Vengaboys, and I used to like S2S, but they use baby voices and that bothers me now."

"Well, I'm a Christian so I might as well listen to Christian music." Mary said.

Tee didn't answer. She turned to Adeline and said, "I just made up this really cool dance yesterday. It took me about all day."

"Yeah, what to?" Adeline asked.

"The Vengaboys. I used 'Skinny Dipping.' It is a really good song, it is. It says, 'Take your clothes off. That's what we love!'"

"Oh, I know that song!" yelled Brianna, and she and Tee and Adeline began to sing the lyrics.

An argument then followed about the lyrics of "Skinny Dipping" that Tee wanted to use to create a dance to do for assembly, and several of her friends protested, saying that she couldn't do that because she was Christian.

Finally, I interjected and asked, "Does being Christian matter to like different kinds of music?"

"No!" Tee said adamantly. "I listen to more non-Christian music than Christian music. Most Christian music is like 'All-e-lu-yah! All-e-lu-yah! All-e-lu-yah! All-e-lu-uuuu-yahhhh!' And it's not that good."

"Nah-uh," argued Mary. "Lots of Christian music is not like that!"

"Yeah... but I think non-Christian music is better because there are better beats to dance to," replied Tee.

"But some Christian music is like rock music," Mary shot back.

"Yeah, that's true," said Tee. "You're right."

"We have a Christian dance group at our church. It's like a dance school, and we use Christian music, and it has a good beat," Mary continued.

"That's like 'Directions' at [Kehara Baptist Church]. I am going to join that next year when I'm old enough in grade 9," added Brianna.

"Yeah, they're really good," agreed Tee. "Mary, I just mean to say that I do both. I really like to make dances, and I like Christian music, but sometimes I think it's better to do dances with non-Christian music because the music part, like the beat part, is better."

To Tee, being a Christian was important, but so was music. In the context of 8/9ers, the youth group leaders tried to get Tee to listen primarily to the Christian station, and Mary argued that because she was Christian, she listened solely to Christian music. But Tee saw things differently. She especially loved dancing, and in the afternoons after school, she often spent an hour or two listening to music and choreographing dances. As Tee saw it, she could still be a Christian and listen to radio stations and to CDs that weren't specifically categorized as Christian. She didn't want the group identity to override her own uses of popular culture, uses that extended beyond it. By opening herself up to what she called "non-Christian" music, she reasoned that she had more listening options and better dancing music.

Both Rosa and Tee understood how others produced them with particular identities through their uses of texts they deemed popular culture and how the groups used particular kinds of texts. These girls realized that popular culture was produced for them, and they used that popular culture in ways that perpetuated categorical understandings of membership within a

group identity. Yet at the same time, these girls pushed against those categories that defined them with particular group identities with the assistance of
pop culture.

When Tee and Rosa explained that they used texts differently than defined by others, they didn't mindlessly consume popular culture. Their
constructions of selves might be seen as a matter of using texts strategically to
destabilize the identities that sought to constrain them and to name them as
particular people. It wasn't that they didn't want to have particular identities
or to be recognized with identities at all. Instead, they sought to alter and
reshape identities offered to them through structures and popular culture
texts when they used texts inclusive of their interests in clothing, music,
dance, or religious icons. This idea of readers constructing their own senses
of self, their own uses of texts, and their own identities from those uses is an
enactment of *subjectivity*. The girls' subjectivities illustrate the adolescents' uses
of popular culture text to avoid being named, sorted, and defined according
to larger structures that produced them with stabilized and particular identities.

Spatial Analyses, Adolescents, and Popular Culture

Within local and across global contexts, people categorized Tee's and Rosa's
popular culture based on structures of religion and race. Yet Tee and Rosa
pushed against those structures that produced identities for them in efforts to
redefine themselves without losing their Christian affiliations. Looking holis-
tically at the girls' uses of texts within the rhizome, it becomes more apparent
that they used popular culture to destabilize identities that limited their
options and constricted them from being recognized as someone else, someone different, someone contradictory to another identity they held. They
each attached their popular culture uses to their attempts to push against
structures and to reshape identity.

As an adult, I often thought I understood adolescents' uses of popular
culture, but as I learned over and over again, my takes and understandings of
their literacy lives involving popular culture were not always the same as
theirs. Ultimately, by creating rhizomatic drawings of identities and subjectivities I could attend to what I would have otherwise assumed to be irrelevant from my adult perspective of adolescence and popular culture. This
visual representation of identity and subjectivity illustrated how adolescents'
subjectivity in their uses of popular culture often remains unrecognized
because of the multiplicitous and ostensibly stabilized categories that name
them as incompetent and inexperienced, popular culture as mindless and

unproductive, and literacy as solely the ability to read and write print-based texts.

But examining adolescents' text uses as producing identity through structures and constructing subjectivity as a means to unsettle the structure shows a different picture of adolescents, their popular culture, and their literacies. I found that I needed to push against identities that produced me as more knowledgeable about the period of adolescence and about the ins and outs of adolescents' popular culture because I'd experienced both of them as an adolescent myself and as an adult. In short, it now seems only feasible in a world where adolescents' knowledge of new literacies abounds to push against the common construction of adolescence as bound by age parameters and sandwiched between children who know little and adults who know all. Others have echoed this sentiment (Cook, 2000; Hagood, Stevens, & Reinking, 2002; Katz, 1996; Rushkoff, 1996). I had to take seriously Lesko's (2001) charge "to look at local contexts and specific actions of young people, without the inherent evaluations of steps, stages, and socialization" (p. 195), in order to analyze data in a way that could potentially open up the structure of adolescence and of adolescents' uses of popular culture.

If adults don't attend to adolescents' subjectivities and to adolescents' uses and constructions of texts, then adults remain bound by structural categories that produce them with particular identities. Adolescents' subjectivity doesn't only act in a subterranean fashion as something subversive and underground. If subjectivity is only seen as something that is dark and seditious, then adolescents' text uses can't be recognized as an attempt to push against and to reshape the structures and identities that define them. In short, if adolescents' uses of texts to create new subject positions aren't recognized as efforts of subjectivity enactment, then their uses of pop culture may continue to be defined in ways that reify a staid notion of adolescence as a rebellious time period.

The recognition of adolescents' subjectivities that attempt to construct alternative ways of being and to open up revised identities has forced me to change the ways that I view popular culture texts in their lives. I see now the need to think about ways to learn from adolescents and from their uses of texts, ways that might differ from my own understandings of and assumptions about their usage of texts. In short, rethinking assumptions about adolescents' uses of texts—not as forms of rebellion or subversion in an age period marked by instability, but as a means to create active constructions of naturally occurring contradictions of self—has potential for assisting in new development of both adolescence and pop culture. My hope is that using rhizomatic cartography to map popular culture use from various perspectives as adolescents take up identities produced for them while they simultaneously use texts to construct new subjectivities might begin to illustrate some of the complexities that will undo century-old identities depicting adolescence as an unstable time period and popular culture as the culprit of adolescent ills.

References

Alvermann, D. E. (2000). Researching libraries, literacies, and lives: A rhizoanalysis. In E. A. St. Pierre & W. Pillow (Eds.), *Working the ruins: Feminist poststructural theory and methods in education* (pp. 114–129). New York: Routledge.

Braidotti, R. (1994). Toward a new nomadism: Feminist Deleuzian tracts; or metaphysics and metabolism. In C. V. Boundas & D. Olkowski (Eds.), *Gilles Deleuze and the theater of philosophy* (pp. 159–186). New York: Routledge.

Cook, D. T. (2000). The other 'child study': Figuring children as consumers in market research, 1910s–1990s. *Sociological Quarterly, 41*, 487–509.

Deleuze, G., & Guattari, F. (1987). *A thousand plateaus: Capitalism and schizophrenia* (B. Massumi, Trans.). Minneapolis: University of Minnesota Press.

Finders, M. (1999). Raging hormones: Stories of adolescence and implications for teacher education. *Journal of Adolescent and Adult Literacy, 42*, 252–263.

Grosz, E. (1994). A million tiny sexes: Feminism and rhizomatics. In C. V. Boundas & D. Olkowski (Eds.), *Gilles Deleuze and the theatre of philosophy* (pp. 187–210). New York: Routledge.

Hagood, M. C., Stevens, L. P., & Reinking, D. (2002). What do THEY have to teach US? Talkin' 'cross generations! In D. E. Alvermann (Ed.), *Adolescents' literacies in a digital world* (pp. 68–83). New York: Peter Lang.

Hall, G. S. (1904). *Adolescence: Its psychology and its relation to physiology, anthropology, sociology, sex, crime, religion, and education* (2 vols.). New York: D. Appleton.

Jackson, A. (in press). Rhizovocality. *Qualitative Studies in Education.*

Katz, J. (1996, July). The Rights of Kids in the Digital Age. *Wired* 4.07. Retrieved May 2, 2001, from http://www.wired.com/wired/archive/4.07/kids_pr.html.

Lesko, N. (2001). *Act your age! A cultural construction of adolescence.* New York: Routledge.

Rushkoff, D. (1996). *Playing the future: How kids' culture can teach us to thrive in an age of chaos.* New York: HarperCollins.

St. Pierre, E. A. (1997). An introduction to figurations—a poststructural practice of inquiry. *Qualitative Studies in Education, 10*, 279–284.

Sibley, D. (1995). *Geographies of exclusion: Society and difference in the West.* New York: Routledge.

8

The Rhizome and the Pack: Liminal Literacy Formations with Political Teeth

George Kamberelis

In this chapter, I assemble constructs from critical social theories and spatial theories to discuss specific kinds of literacy formations that have (or have had) considerable political effectivity (i.e., produce or produced significant transformative effects). These formations are ones that are organized and function according to the principles of "rhizomes" and "pack multiplicities" outlined by (Deleuze & Guattari, 1987) and described below. Examples of the work of such formations include but are not limited to the subversive activities of African Americans in the fight for freedom, especially in the antebellum period; the liberation activities of second-wave feminism, especially the writing and circulation of feminist manifestos, consciousness raising guides, and so on; the subversive appropriation of national literacy campaign imperatives by mothers in Third-World countries like Nicaragua; the "unofficial" literacy practices of many adolescents, which often pivot on investments in popular culture and the media and include tagging and the production of grassroots "zines"; the use of citizen band radios and truck stop graffiti to disrupt and invert the policing of mobility on the nation's highways; and many current literacy practices on/of the Internet, especially within radical sites designed to promote public dialogue linked to political work. Importantly, I am not arguing that formations that are organized and function as rhizomes and pack multiplicities are the only or the most politically effective kinds of assemblages. I am simply arguing that, because they have unique histories of effectivity, they are worth attending to more closely and more seriously for the ways in which they might help us reconceptualize collective affiliation and action and political motivations and outcomes.

Because my goals for this chapter are largely theoretical, I begin with a detour through theory. Specifically, I describe and explain Hall's (1986) construct of "articulation," Gramsci's (1971) notion of the "we," and Deleuze and Guattari's (1987) constructs of the "rhizome" and "pack multiplicities." After introducing and describing these constructs, I offer accounts of two very different literacy formations that are (or were) organized as rhizomes and pack multiplicities and that are (or were) quite effective in motivating and/or creating social and political change. I close the chapter with a recapitulation of why literacy formations organized as rhizomes or pack multiplicities seem to have such effectivity.

Articulation

Assembling ideas largely from Gramsci (1971) and Volosinov (1973), Hall (1986) argued that what binds together various practices and effects (which by themselves are not related in any necessary way) into some kind of coherent formation is called an articulation:

> [A]n articulation is thus the form of connection that *can* make a unity out of two different elements, under certain conditions. It is a linkage which is not necessary, determined, absolute and essential for all time. You have to ask, under what conditions *can* a connection be forged or made? So the so-called "unity" of a discourse is really an articulation of different, distinct elements which can be rearticulated in different ways because they have no necessary "belongingness." The unity which matters is a linkage between that articulated discourse and the social forces with which it can, under certain historical conditions, but need not necessarily, be connected. (p. 53)

Articulations are always constituted through a double process of being "enunciated" or "spoken" and "linked with" or "combined." They are thus always produced as discursive and material structures out of historically available conditions of possibility. Additionally, and also quite Gramscian, Hall argued that articulations are constituted as ongoing struggles to position practices within dynamic fields of forces in order to produce spaces in which certain modes of thought and action are (or remain) possible. In other words, articulations involve continuous production of contexts within which certain practices either are or are not available. For example, although there seem to be no necessary relations among blue jeans, country music, Ford trucks, heartbreak, and a host of other objects and practices, they are all held together by/as an historically produced articulation. Similar examples can readily be proliferated.

Articulations, then, involve the production of unity out of dispersion, identity out of difference, coherence out of apparent randomness. Articulations link particular practices with particular effects (e.g., investing in rap music and wearing particular kinds of clothing). And these practice-effect constellations themselves get articulated into larger structures or formations (e.g., particular economic, cultural or political systems or processes). Articulations are ongoing struggles to position practices within dynamic fields of force in particular ways to produce discursive-material geographies within which certain modes of thought and action are possible.

Gramsci's "We"

The notion of the collective, the multiplicity, or the "we" has always been central to most discussions of social action and political activity. For Gramsci (1971), the "we" is always without guarantees. It has to be made and remade, actively articulated in Hall's (1986) double sense of being both "spoken" (discursively positioned) and "linked with" (temporally and spatially produced). Any "collective" is always a structured (and structuring) field and a set of lived relations in which elements and forces from diverse sources are actively combined, dismantled, and bricolaged to form new politically effective alliances between otherwise fractional groupings. Once articulated, these groupings can no longer be returned to static, homogeneous social categories such as race, class, and gender, which are always configured as hierarchies. Recall here Gramsci's insistence on defining hegemony as struggle, as a precarious "moving equilibrium" accomplished through the continual orchestration of conflicting and competing forces by more or less unstable, more or less temporary, more or less contingent, alliances of class fractions (or other relevant social units). From such a perspective, the "we" always favor prescience over science. The "we" is always alert to possibility and emergence. The "we" proceeds knowing/ imagining that there are only competing ideologies, which are themselves unstable constellations that are likely to change. The "we" usually works (and works at) the margins, struggling to make more egalitarian ideologies more visible and more viable. The "we" forms alliances. The alliances sometimes strengthen, sometimes weaken, and sometimes dissolve. When alliances dissolve, the "we" forms new alliances committed to new kinds of transgressive, transformative work.

The Rhizome and Rhizomatics

As I noted earlier, Deleuze and Guattari's (1987) notions of the rhizome and the pack (or pack multiplicities) are particularly useful for understanding Gramsci's "we" as an articulation with considerable potential for political effectivity. For Deleuze and Guattari, the rhizome is an oppositional alternative to what they call arborescent or arboreal ways of thinking, acting, and being, which they claim have defined Western epistemologies at least since the Enlightenment and probably much earlier. As their name suggests, arborescent forms and structures may be imagined metaphorically as trees—linear, hierarchical, sedentary, striated, vertical, stiff, and with deep and permanent roots. They are structures with branches that continue to subdivide into smaller and lesser structures. In their various social and cultural instantiations, arborescent models of thinking, acting, and being amount to restrictive economies of dominance and oppression.

Deleuze and Guattari are clear that they oppose the arborescent model because of its inherent totalizing logic. "We're tired of trees. We should stop believing in trees, roots, and radicles. They've made us suffer too much. All of arborescent culture is founded on them, from biology to linguistics" (Deleuze & Guattari, 1987, p. 15). In the place of the tree, they offer up the rhizome as metaphor for an alternative theoretical model. In contrast to arborescent forms of thinking, acting, and being, rhizomatic forms are non-linear, anarchic, and nomadic. The "rhizome is an acentered, nonhierarchical, nonsignifying system without a General and without an organizing memory or central automaton, defined solely by the circulation of states" (p. 21). Rhizomes are networks. Rhizomes cut across borders. Rhizomes build links between preexisting gaps and between nodes that are separated by categories and orders of segmented thinking, acting, and being.

According to Deleuze and Guattari (1987), rhizomes develop and function according to six fundamental principles (see also Chapter 7). The first two principles are *connection* and *heterogeneity*. "[A]ny point of a rhizome can be connected to anything other, and must be. This is very different from the tree or the root, which plots a point, fixes an order" (p. 7). Rhizomes are thus ever-growing horizontal networks of connections among heterogeneous nodes of discursive and material force. Recall Hall's (1986) definition of articulation as nonnecessary relation.

The third principle of the rhizome is *multiplicity*. A rhizomatic system is comprised of a multiplicity of lines and connections. "There are no points or positions in a rhizome, such as those found in a structure, tree, or root. There are only lines" (p. 8), and these lines are organized as ephemeral horizontal relations that are always proliferating. Multiplicity celebrates plurality and proliferative modes of thinking, acting, and being rather that unitary, binary, and totalizing modes. Rhizomatics "extirpate roots and foundations, to thwart unities and break dichotomies, and to spread out roots and branches, thereby pluralizing and disseminating, producing differences and multiplicities, making new connections. Rhizomatics affirms the principles excluded from Western thought and reinterprets reality as dynamic, heterogeneous, and non-dichotomous" (Best & Kellner, 1991, p. 99).

The fourth principle of the rhizome is the principle of *asignifying rupture*. This principle states that: "A rhizome may be broken, shattered at a given spot, but it will start up again on one of its old lines, or on new lines"

(Deleuze & Guattari, 1987, p. 9). Movements and flows are always rerouted around disruptions in a rhizomatic formation. Additionally, severed sections regenerate themselves and continue to grow, forming new lines, flows, and pathways.

The fifth and sixth principles of rhizomatics are *decalcomania* and *cartography*, which ensure that "a rhizome is not amenable to any structural or generative model. It is a stranger to any idea of genetic axis or deep structure" (Deleuze & Guattari, 1987, p. 12). Because Deleuze and Guattari view genetic axes and deep structures as reproductive rather than productive, they distinguish these from rhizomes by appealing to the metaphors of maps and tracings and the differences between them. A tracing (decalcomania) is a copy and operates according to "genetic" principles, evolving and reproducing from earlier forms. It is a reproduction of the world based on an a priori deep structure and a faith in the discovery and representation of that structure. A tracing is arborescent. "All tree logic is a logic of tracing and reproduction" (p. 12). The tracing replicates existing striated structures. Deleuze and Guattari use psychoanalysis as an example of an historically powerful regime of truth within which tracings are always at work. No matter what an analysand utters, it is read against Oedipus, the phallus, lack, desire for the mother, rage against the father, and so on.

In contrast to tracings, maps (cartography) are open systems—contingent, unpredictable, and productive. Deleuze and Guattari invoke the sense of original cartographic work here and insist that we think of maps as producing spatial articulations with effectivity rather than simply (re)presenting space. From this perspective, a map produces an organization of reality rather than reproducing some prior representation of reality. Like the rhizome itself, the map is contingent and tentative. "The map is open and connectable in all of its dimensions; it is detachable, reversible, susceptible to constant modification. It can be torn, reversed, adapted, to any kind of mounting, reworked by an individual, group, or social formation" (Deleuze & Guattari, 1987, p. 12). The map is oriented to experimentation and adoption. Maps have multiple entryways. Unlike tracings, maps are based on rhizomatic or essentially unpredictable articulations of material reality. In drawing maps, the theorist (like an original cartographer) works at the surface, creating possible realities by producing new articulations of disparate phenomena and connecting the exteriority of objects to whatever forces or directions seem potentially related to them.

Despite their preference for maps over tracings because of the capacity of maps to produce (and not simple reproduce) reality, Deleuze and Guattari do not suggest simply doing away with tracings altogether any more than they suggest that it is possible (or necessary) to totally destroy arborescent structures and to replace them with rhizomatic ones. Instead, they suggest deconstructing arborescent models with rhizomatic ones. Thus, they argue that after constructing maps, we should place tracings back onto them; we should then determine what, if anything, of the tracings contributes to the potential effectivity of the map as an articulation; we should look for breaks and fissures in the tracings; and where we find them, we should interrogate or deconstruct them, which is always also a deconstruction of the arborescent structures they represent. Connecting "the roots or trees back up with the rhizome" (p. 14) discloses lines of flight and also how these lines of flight have been blocked, how they have been articulated to closed and repressive structures, and how they have been forced to take root. Placing tracings back on maps brings into relief the extent to which lines of flight are constantly being intercepted and domesticated by the lines of articulation that hold arborescent structures together. Tracings now function in the service of maps rather than as blinders to new possibilities for how reality might be organized.

Deleuze and Guattari (1987) use Freud's clinical case study of Little Hans to illustrate how lines of flight are created (cartography), as well as how they are captured by and within lines of articulation (decalcomania). Studying the unconscious shows how Little Hans tried to build a rhizome connecting the family house to other buildings, the street, and so on. Freud's decalcomaniac intervention blocked these lines, "BREAKING HIS RHIZOME AND BLOTCHING HIS MAP, setting it straight for him, blocking his every way out, until he began to desire his own shame and guilt, until they rooted shame and guilt in him, PHOBIA...." (p.14). Freud forced Little Hans to take root in the family—traced onto his mother's bed and photographed under his father. Little Hans' only escape route at this point was "becoming-animal perceived as shameful and guilty (the becoming-horse of Little Hans, a truly political option). But these impasses must always be resituated on the map, thereby opening them up to possible lines of flight" (p. 14). "If it is true that it is of the essence of the map or rhizome to have multiple entryways, then it is plausible that one could even enter them through tracings or the root-tree, assuming the necessary precautions are taken (once again, one must avoid any Manichean dualism)" (p. 14).

To summarize these various musings and explanations, rhizomatic formations are "finite networks of automata in which communication runs from any neighbor to any other, the stems or channels do not pre-exist, and all individuals are interchangeable, defined only by their state at a given moment—such that the local operations are coordinated and the final, global result synchronized without central agency" (Deleuze & Guattari, 1987, p. 12).

Although Deleuze and Guattari see rhizomatics as necessary to any radical political work, they reject Utopianism and insist, following Gramsci, that rhizomatic formations are always constructed in the struggle between stabilizing and destabilizing forces. To further explain the nature and functions of rhizomatic formations, Deleuze and Guattari suggest using the linear algebraic metaphors of lines or vectors to think about rhizomes. They posit two basic kinds of lines or vectors: lines of articulation (or consistency) and lines of flight, both of which project their effects across the rhizomatic field. Lines of articulation connect and unify different practices and effects. They establish hierarchies. They define center-periphery relations. They create rules of organization. They encourage stasis. In contrast, lines of flight disarticulate nonnecessary relations between and among practices and effects. They open up contexts to their outsides and the possibilities that dwell there. They disassemble unity and coherence. They decenter centers and disrupt hierarchies.

Finally, every line or vector (of either kind) has its own quality, quantity, and directionality. Thus the effects of any line or vector will vary as a function of these characteristics, as well as the particular densities built up at the intersection of various lines or vectors. From this perspective, rhizomes—as fields or contexts—are produced in the constant struggle between lines of articulation and lines of flight. The coherence and organization of a rhizome are effects or lines of articulation and the instability and dissolution of a rhizome are effects of lines of flight. Lines of articulation make received models of reality eminently visible. Lines of flight expose these models as historically produced and power-laden (rather than natural and power-neutral). Lines of flight also open up new possibilities for seeing, living, and organizing political resistance. Effects are lines or vectors of force. Reality itself is constituted as configurations of these two kinds of lines or vectors. So, deploying or taking up lines of articulation or lines of flight have serious consequences for the production of reality. Taking up lines of articulation ("good student," or "heterosexual parent") helps to keep stable the current organization of a territorialized space and its relations to other territorialized spaces. Taking up lines of flight ("resistant but creative student" or "gay parent") helps open up new configurations of space (i.e., reality) so that new possibilities for thinking, acting, and being may be opened up.

The goal of rhizomatics, then, is not the obliteration of existing strata (or organized, territorialized space) but the discovery of the available lines of flight within that space. Since the strata are inevitable and unavoidable,

Deleuze and Guattari (1987) recommend "diving into the strata," becoming intensely familiar with them, and thus discovering the available lines of flight within them. Following this advice, engaging the strata at the level of the lines of flight that continuously deterritorialize them, can, in some cases, lead to the complete abolition of the strata in question, or, at the very least, the transmogrification of the strata into new formations with new potentialities. Their project thus involves a radical opening up (more than an obliteration) of closed and repressive structures.

Doing rhizomatics thus requires what Deleuze and Guattari call "a commitment to the real," a commitment to experimenting with and intervening in reality and its relations of power. Rhizomatics is a mapping of the real to challenge and perhaps reconfigure the possibilities of reality itself. Rhizomatics goes beyond representation toward reinvention. To the extent that one is redesigning reality and discourse and to the extent that discourse is an intervention into the real, it may be rhizomatic. Attending to the real and rearticulating the real (not simply reproducing or representing it) is the bottom line.

The Belgian surrealist painter, Réné Magritte, is a good example of an artist who attended to and rearticulated the real. He did not use some extant framework or model to "represent" reality. Instead, he produced new ways of seeing and thus new realities. Often integrating imagery and natural language within the same work, Magritte created canvases whose effects were contradiction and paradox. His painting, *Ceçi n'est pas un pipe* (1926), for example, consists of an image of a pipe and the painted words "This is not a pipe." Not only does this painting challenge symbolic representation and destroy conventional equivalence relations between words and things, it also challenges iconic representation since what is painted on canvas is no more a pipe than the words "Ceçi n'est pas un pipe." By knitting together verbal signs and images without affirming their isomorphism, Magritte in effect denies the authenticity of representation and forces us to dwell within unmapped space and to create our own realities.

Deterritorializing/reterritorializing work such as that of Magritte involves using binarisms strategically to avoid naturalized binarisms. Skeptical that we can really ever get rid of binaries, it insists on creating better ones. Deleuze and Guattari insist that we not trace the received. Instead, we should map the real—not intentionally and structurally but strategically and politically. Doing rhizomatics involves reconfiguring an understanding of reality according to strategic political interests. These reconfigurations are readily understandable ex post facto if not predictable. For example, a classic received binary of the Western interpretive tradition is text and meaning. What if we unpack this binary using the clock as an example? A typical interpretation of a clock might run something like this: a device used for measuring the passage of time that is calibrated according to the temporal units of seconds, minutes, hours, days, months, and years. What if we avoided that "representational" model? What if we analyzed this text (in this case, "clock") in terms of its dissolution into lines of flight and its organization into lines of articulation? What if we were to map all the things that this might index or be connected with instead of trying to discover its meaning or predict its reception? What if we regarded this text as a productive force among other productive forces in the continuous production of reality? If we did all these things, then we might connect the clock to our schedules, to food and eating, to the organization of work, to labor, to surplus value, to leisure time, to capitalism, to the calendar, to sundials, to the sun and moon, to the gear and glass making industries, to the fluctuating prices of gold, to the aphorism "time is money," and to a million other things. How might such a way of proceeding (i.e., rhizomatics) help us avoid understandings that received models (e.g., new criticism, psychoanalysis, transformational grammar, educational standards) lead us into? Importantly, the tactics indexed by my speculative but very real questions have their own productive power, their own effectivity because they open up new possibilities for thinking and being, new ways of understanding the world, and thus new ways of organizing political resistance.

Pack Multiplicities

Deleuze and Guattari (1987) argue that "packs" (or "pack multiplicities") are particularly powerful deterritorializing/reterritorializing machines. The construct of the pack, then, holds considerable promise for producing new and effective conceptions of collective affiliation/action and political motivation. In this regard, Canetti (cited in Deleuze & Guattari, 1987, p. 33) distinguished between two kinds of multiplicities: mass multiplicities and pack multiplicities. Even though this is an analytic distinction, even though most multiplicities are probably mass-pack hybrids, and even though mass and pack multiplicities require each other for their existence, comparing Canetti's descriptions of these two kinds of formations is instructive here. Mass multiplicities (e.g., government agencies, labor unions, professional organizations, etc.) are arborescent formations. They are composed of relatively large numbers of members. There is both divisibility and equality among the members. Mass multiplicities are focused around the concentration of form. The aggregate as a whole acts as a unit. There is a one-way hierarchy. Mass multiplicities are predisposed to territorialize. And they work to establish recognizable signs of power and stability.

In contrast, pack multiplicities are rhizomatic formations. They are small or have restricted numbers. They are not centralized but dispersed. They have no fixed territory and are motivated by an impetus to deterritorialize. Pack multiplicities experience qualitative metamorphoses in formation over time and space. They are thus neither totalizing nor finalizable. There are inequalities of membership in pack multiplicities, but these inequalities are impossible to hierarchize because they are often temporary and they shift continuously. Individual and collective action are blurred in the pack. Each member "takes care of himself at the same time as participating in the band" (p. 33). Packs exhibit "a Brownian [random or apparently random] variability in directions" (p. 33) because they are constituted largely by articulated lines of flight or deterritorializations. Unlike mass multiplicities, pack multiplicities matter more in terms of their political motivations and effectivity than in terms of their forms of affiliation.[1]

With pack multiplicities, there is no stable coherent whole to speak of, only assemblages of multiplicity. There is no politics of sublimation in the pack, no notion of transcendent similarity, only a constant becoming of multiply driven ethical and pragmatic singularities. Thompson's (1966) description of the "edge" is useful here. In his ethnography of the Hell's Angels, Thompson described the edge as what projects the biker into the immediate future. It is neither a final destination nor a particular existential state. It is the ever-present possibility of becoming something else. Packness is only attained when there is a change in form, a shift from a group of individuals to an individual group. Packs do not operate with arborescent logics. They come and go, mutate and gestate, gain momentum and change direction. They are unpredictable, but this is exactly their importance and a key reason for their effectivity. There is a need not only for recognizable gains in packs, but also a need for unpredictable disruptions. These kinds of disruptions expose new fissures for differing thought and action. They make apparent the contingency of once stable relationships and alliances. In short, packs enact disruptions that may not be politically pure, politically correct, or particularly pleasant, but they are unquestionably passionate, powerful, and

---

[1] It is worth noting parenthetically here that the activity and effectivity of pack multiplicities are much the same as the guerrilla tactics described by de Certeau (1984). These tactics involve detecting vulnerabilities in the forces of mass multiplicities and attacking these vulnerabilities much like guerrilla forces attack invading armies in multiple directions and in unpredictable ways. Such forces never challenge the dominant order in open warfare, for that would mean sure defeat. Instead, they maintain their own opposition within and against this dominant order. They constantly make guerrilla raids, win small and sometimes fleeting victories, always keep the dominant order guessing, and sometimes gain territory for themselves for good.

often effective. For these reasons, packs often scare institutional authorities, and tragically, these authorities sometimes react swiftly, unjustly, and brutally as in the case of the antiwar student protesters murdered at Kent State University in 1970, the convictions of innocents in the 1989 Central Park jogger case, or the institution of a "No Protest Zone" and the subsequent police crackdown in Seattle during the 1999 World Trade Organization meeting.

Although packs are not top-down structures or organized systems, they have specific sets of tactics. They are dynamic and complex webs of localized mobilizations. There are few, if any, hierarchical chains of command. No networks have a single, specific leader, though at any given time someone may assume a leadership role. "In the changing constellation of the pack, in its dances and expeditions, he will again and again find himself at its edge; at the edge and then back in the center. He may be in the center, and then, immediately afterwards, at the edge again" (Canetti, cited in Deleuze & Guattari, 1987, p. 33). Pack leadership, then, is a continuous mobilization of positions. This mobility through constant repositioning in space means that each pack member is always both responsible for "guarding" a sector while also dependent on the whole pack for its survival. This social fact was brought into relief in the popular film, *Convoy* (Sherman & Peckinpah, 1978), which chronicles the activities of a group of truckers who form a convoy to protest unfair treatment by the police. In this film, the protagonist, Martin Penwald, a.k.a. Rubber Duck (played by Kris Kristofferson) deploys the citizen band radio as a tactic of mobility and subversion, and he organizes media coverage of the convoy to enhance the political effectiveness of their protest. He also claims emphatically, "I'm not the leader. I'm just in front."

As part of a fluid structuring structure, all pack members can mobilize themselves locally much more efficiently and much faster than mass structures such as public schools or national literacy campaigns. With their hierarchical chains of command and plan-driven strategies, these latter structures are quite cumbersome and slow moving. Additionally, pack multiplicities are constituted by lines of flight or deterritorializations that are component parts of their structuring structures and to which they assigned a high positive value. In contrast, mass multiplicities "only integrate these lines in order to segment them, obstruct them, ascribe them a negative sign" (Deleuze & Guattari, 1987, p. 33), usually dismissing deterritorializing and reterritorializing tactics as futile and encouraging or attempting to coerce pack members to join in on mass strategies that operate within proper institutional channels and that consolidate or capitalize on past gains through institutionally supported economic strength, lobbying power, political connections, the law, and so on. In other words, institutionally sanctioned mass multiplicities are always looking for ways to co-opt the activity and negate the effects of pack multiplicities, and they always have state machine on their side.

Now, I am not arguing here that pack multiplicities are necessarily and always more politically effective than mass multiplicities. Indeed, many forms of political affiliation and organization follow the logic of the mass and are effective. Additionally, Miller (1998) and others have shown that at certain times and in certain places, mass multiplicities may be more effective than pack multiplicities because of their ability to mobilize legislative and judicial force. However, what mass multiplicities have never been able to do is to risk past gains in order to establish new lines of flight. They are cumbersome, relatively conservative, and slow. Their effects are often meager and serve centrally located elite; and their political work is readily compromised or co-opted by institutional authorities. In contrast, pack multiplicities can act quickly and with focused intensity. They can create momentous ruptures. They can deterritorialize and reterritorialize space and activity in ways that mass multiplicities cannot. They are not root-bound. They do not depend on myths of origin or representational politics based on authenticity. They do not have to serve higher causes or adhere to particular identity politics. They are grounded in a distrust of those in power and a desire to operate free from debilitating constraints, whether economic or social or ideological or whatever. They do not require the establishment of documentable gains, only unpredictable and not always visible disruptions that create openings for thinking and acting otherwise by exposing the contingency of ostensible, "naturalized" social facts. They emerge and recede; they become powerful and lose power; they choose direction and change direction And, as I already noted, their relative unpredictability is one of the reasons why they are so effective.

A key question relevant to understanding and explaining mass multiplicities is what brings the mass together, and it is usually answered by some appeal to biological or social essentialism (e.g., the identity politics of the civil rights movement or streams of second-wave feminism). Secondary questions thus include the following: Where is the center? Who is the leader? What does the multiplicity represent or stand for? What are its politics? What are its strategies? These questions, however, are all but irrelevant when considering the forms and functions of pack multiplicities. Moreover, answering these questions for themselves would probably lead to co-optation and a weakening (or negation) of the pack's counterhegemonic potential. Instead, the key questions to ask about pack multiplicities include ones like the following: How do packs develop and flourish? How are packs and pack members mobilized? What do they deterritorialize and reterritorialize? What forces do they exert in the world and what real effects does their work accomplish? How do new members learn about and join the pack?

Literacy Formations of the Rhizome and the Pack

As I mentioned in the introduction, one can identify many literacy formations that function (or have functioned historically) as politically effective rhizomatic space/time configurations within which people have organized themselves as pack multiplicities. To show how my detour through theory actually plays out on the politically saturated ground, I will now describe and analyze two of these formations. The choice of these formations was partly arbitrary and partly strategic. I was tempted to choose both an historical and a contemporary formation related to the same basic cause—racial equality or gender equality or labor relations, for example. In the end, however, I decided against such thematic coherence, and I selected two formations, which, despite being different from each other in many ways (e.g., their political aims, the particular oppressor/oppressed dynamics within which they are [or were] situated, and the technologies at their disposal), they seem(ed) to operate according to similar principles, to deploy similar tactics, and to produce similar social and political effects. The historical formation I selected is African-American slave literacies. The contemporary formation is a postcolonial feminist Internet site.

NWH (Niggaz With Hats)

NWH (Niggaz With Hats) is the name of a rap and hip hop band featured in the film, *Fear of a Black Hat* (Scott & Cundieff, 1994). It is also the central rhetorical trope of the film, which is a wonderful parody of both urban ethnographies and rap and hip hop culture. In the film, the band members insist on always wearing hats because their ancestors were deprived of this right while working in the fields as slaves. This deprivation, they argue, left their ancestors exhausted and unable to muster the energy and cunning required to resist their oppression. So hats are both symbolic and real for the band members. They represent their connection to the history of violent and oppressive racism, and they work as discursive-material instruments of political resistance in their own lives as public performers and popular cultural icons.

Historically, resistant literacy practices have always been central forces within rhizomatic formations of African Americans in their efforts to intervene in reality. More specifically, African-American slaves used aural, visual, and written literacies both to elevate their levels of learning and personal understanding and to create spaces for themselves within an otherwise arborescent society—closed, repressive, and racially violent. Ideologically, personal and collective transformation was believed by slaves to result directly from the acquisition of literacies. Pragmatically and ethically, literacies led to increasingly rhizomatic attitudes and actions.

Lines of flight from the lived experience of slavery (and from slavery as an institution) were disclosed in a variety of places and through a variety of means. In the antebellum period, for example, lines of flight populated many language and literacy practices rooted in African cultures and cultural icons, the mobile leadership of literate preachers, the actions and activities of specific African-American slaves, the advocacy practices of slave mothers, and benevolent actions and activities of some slave owners. Many of these lines of flight remained visible and productive after the Civil War, and others came into view as well. These included various programs within the Freedman's Bureau, for example, as well as many makeshift and usually "underground" schools. Because my goal here is not to offer a comprehensive account of historically subversive African-American literacy practices but only to show how the effectivity of such practices was in no trivial way grounded in their organization as rhizomes and pack multiplicities, I will analyze only a subset of relevant practices in this chapter.

According to Joyner (1986), literacy practices such as storytelling, spirituals, and work songs constituted "the most significant form of resistance against the spiritual and psychological, if not the physical effects of slavery" (p. 229). The effectivity of such practices is often attributed to the fact that they were articulated to an African past, which offered more agile and mobile indices of identity compared with those claimed by the slave master (Blassingame, 1972). The historical study of resistant practices on the part of slaves has yielded a quite compelling vision of slave culture as a set of collective cultural practices that amounted to a rhizomatic network that challenged the "absolute control" of the master (Faust, 1980). Slaves were hardly "passive recipients" of the whims and dictates of their masters. Rather, they actively sought out lines of flight from the slave masters' control, often engaging in subversive practices to undermine the intents and dictates of the masters.

Storytelling, a practice that had been integral to social life in Africa, was one of these subversive literate activities. It usually took place in informal settings after the completion of work responsibilities and often followed in the tradition of African Trickster myths (Blassingame, 1972). Importantly, Trickster figures, such as the rabbit and the monkey, were small clever characters, who operated through wit and cunning to outsmart larger more powerful adversaries. These figures held an undeniable attraction for African-

American slaves largely because they were integral to the effectiveness of storytelling as a resistant cultural practice:

> In mythic terms, such slave rituals as story telling functioned to give symbolic form to the validating concepts and beliefs of the slave world view. If the master was able to manipulate certain rituals of interaction between blacks and whites to enhance his authority, the slaves were able to manipulate rituals of interaction among themselves in such a way as to undermine the master's authority and to enhance their self image. (Joyner, 1986, p. 4)

Undermining the master's authority was accomplished largely because signifying practices involve producing double-coded utterances that have both ostensible and hidden meanings. For example, songs such as "Follow the Drinking Gourd," "Wade in the Water," and "Steal Away" seemed innocent enough but actually contained valuable (but hidden) information about how to escape to the north. Additionally, ordinary words seemed to have ordinary meanings but had hidden ones as well. The word "conductors," for example, referred to people who helped slaves to escape. Safe hiding places were referred to as "stations." The words "passengers" and "baggage" were used to denote escaping slaves (e.g., Pathways to Freedom: Maryland & the Underground Railroad, http://www.mpt.org/learningworks /pathwaystofreedom). There is also considerable evidence that the patterns of quilts made by slave women contained secret messages related to escape routes and tactics. According to these histories, quilts were aired out during the day, an innocent enough practice on the surface of things, but also one that allowed slaves to read and respond to the secret messages the quilt patterns contained.[2] Finally, other artifacts such as "lawn jockeys" also func-

---

[2] Important to note here is the lively current debate about the historical veracity of claims about double-coded messages in some African-American quilts created in the antebellum South. Based primarily on oral histories and symbols and knot patterns unique to particular quilts, some scholars argue quite convincingly that these quilts did indeed contain such messages (e.g., Benberry, 2000; Tobin & Dobard, 1998). Other scholars doubt such claims in the absence of written artifacts and material artifacts that would substantiate such claims (e.g., Wright, 2001). Given that many other African-American texts and artifacts have been proven to contain double-coded messages, it seems plausible and even probable that quilts contained them as well (V. J. Harris, personal communication, February 3, 2003; P. L. Richards, personal communication, February 1, 2003). Also worth noting here is the possibility that establishing the absolute historical veracity of double-coding practices in relation to some African-American quilts may itself be testimony to the creativity, ingenuity, flexibility, and nimbleness of the packs who engaged in these practices in the first place. Why leave a trace of any sort that might be picked up by plantation radar. Finally, debates about the veracity of claims about double-coded messages in quilts often play out along relatively predictable race and gender lines. Compared with European-American scholars, more African-American

tioned as double-coded signs. For Whites, they were material and ideological embodiments of slavery as a legitimate social institution. For Blacks, they were markers of "safe havens" along the road to freedom (V. J. Harris, personal communication, February 3, 2003).

Several principles of the rhizome—asignifying rupture, cartography, and decalcomania—are central to the effectivity of all literacy practices rife with double coding. It is neither the ostensible nor the hidden meaning of a double-coded utterance that is important. Instead, it is the effects that are produced as a result of having two meanings in the first place. Some readers will be guided by decalcomania in their meaning construction processes, and others will be guided by new cartographies. In the antebellum South, Whites read these various signs from according to the tracings of racism and white supremacy. Blacks read them according to new and ever-changing maps of freedom. The practice of double coding thus allowed subversive communicative activities to be simultaneously invisible and perfectly visible. A line of flight.

That double coding was an effective line of flight is not at all a trivial claim. The problem with almost all information technologies from hollering to two-way radios to letter writing to the Internet is that they are actually or potentially open systems that anyone may listen in on or look in on, usually legally. Thus, countersurveillance tactics must be developed and deployed. In the case of African-American slaves, their conversations, songs, and storytelling activities often occurred within earshot of their oppressors. Recognizing this, they produced communicative tactics that involved special linguistic codes with both apparent and hidden meanings. Moreover, they continually changed the content and structure of these codes, which made decoding them extraordinarily difficult. In short, the slaves created a politically effective countersurveillance network—an oral-literate map of the plantation system, its instruments of surveillance, and its escape routes. On the surface of things the slaves seemed to have appropriated White norms for communicating with each other, which meant that slave owners no longer had to worry about what they might be saying (and therefore what they might be up to). However, because a second layer of coding was laminated onto these norms, what was really happening is that slaves could engage in subversive

---

scholars seem willing to consider subtle changes in symbols and knot patterns, as well as oral historical data (especially when these data corroborate each other), as reasonable evidence for the possibility that some antebellum quilts contained double-coded messages. Similarly, compared with men, more women seem willing to regard the products of "women's work," as well as oral histories about such work, as possibly being connected with subversive political activity.

practices without anyone ever knowing they were doing so. Information flow remained open within the network yet closed to plantation authorities for whom it was never clear how to connect which messages with which meanings. In a very pragmatic sense, the slaves shined the light of surveillance back upon the surveillance tower, blinding its eye of power and rupturing its effectiveness. The ability to double code information flow made the difference between technical and tactical competence a difference that really made a difference.

One implication of this example is the fact that communicating and monitoring communication is not simply a matter of technological sophistication. It also demands tactical competence, which involve sophisticated and dynamic strategies for interpretation. Plantation authorities, as well as the all other authorities in the South were unable to keep up with the mobility of the double-coded and ever-changing codes of the slaves. They had the technical competence but not the tactical competence requisite for interpreting all levels of meaning encoded in the slaves' talk, songs, and stories.

Importantly, these countersurveillance networks that articulated mobility to polysemy to freedom were typically organized in and by small, mobile, shifting groups. Pack multiplicities. This historical fact brings into high relief some of the key differences between mass multiplicities (in this case, the institution of slavery) and pack multiplicities (in this case, the agile and mobile spatial-discursive activities of the slaves themselves) that I drew attention to earlier. As a technique of governing, mass multiplicities are organized according to the demands, rationality, efficiency, and technical competence. Thus, they function by creating and enforcing uniform modes of conduct. They exert power through normalizing (and thus reifying) the "other" rather than adapting to an always-changing other. Because mass multiplicities operate according to this arborescent logic, they are slow to react and slow to develop effective counter-counter strategies. Although they may have all the latest technologies, they are still unable to understand and thus respond to the agile and mobile spatial practices of the people who are subjected to these technologies. Although they remain technically in contact with the other, in fact, they are interpretively way out of the "contact zone." Oral/aural literacy practices such as talk, song, and story exemplify the effectivity of rhizomatic and pack multiplicity practices and formations. Importantly, this effectivity is grounded not in some inherent technological determinism but in elusive and dynamic popular truths and tactics of resistance.

The double-coded literacies of African-American slaves were even more complex (and more powerful) because of a second way in which they were articulated to European-American literacies and their concomitant ideologies. Although the slaves' aural, visual, and written literacies produced an underground resistance to plantation life, all external interactions and rituals of communication with the larger society reinforced the slaves' status as a lower order of humanity. A bit of history is instructive here. European society, reflecting the cultural prejudices of such thinkers as Hegel, Hume, and Kant, viewed societies without the cultural practice of literacy and written historical records as inferior. This view became the conceptual underpinning of the idea that Africans and subsequently African-American slaves were "childlike" or even "puppetlike" (Gates, 1985). This line of articulation was very powerful and pervasive. To disrupt it and to move their resistance from underground to above ground, slaves had to create lines of flight that reversed their imposed (even self-imposed) subhumanity and re-visioned both public and private images of themselves. Because print-based literacy was a "visible sign of reason" (Gates, 1985, p. 9) in the early to mid 1800s, an obvious way for African Americans to disrupt the line of articulation that reduced them to children or puppets was to become literate. And they did. And when they did, they often escaped or at least attempted escape.

In addition to having to overcome the widely held view of being intellectually incapable of reading or writing, slaves also had to overcome many legal barriers. Following a flurry of slave rebellions led by literate preachers in the 1820s and 1830s, most Southern states passed laws prohibiting slaves from reading and writing and from being instructed in how to read and write (Gilmore, 1978). But rather than stifle the desire to become literate, these laws seemed to produce a desiring machine in relation to print-based literacies, which fueled the subversive orientation of literacy practices among African-American slaves. Yet this desiring machine faced many practical impediments. With a negligible number of literate slaves or free Blacks in positions to teach reading and writing skills, those slaves desiring print-based literacies were forced to procure their initial instruction from within White plantation communities (Genovese, 1974). However, because of the slave-holding society's legal opposition to literate slaves, those determined to become literate had to find what Bullock (1967) termed "hidden passages" of educative opportunity in the midst of official prohibition. Hidden passages were, in effect, lines of flight created by the clergy, sympathetic members of the slave masters' households, and occasionally even slave masters themselves who were either sympathetic to the slaves or in need of a literate slave to perform an important plantation function.

The church was one space within which rhizomatic literacy activities flourished. Religious instruction was perceived by Whites to be a "most efficient police" in terms of quelling the rebellious inclinations of the slaves

(Aptheker, 1943). What the White clergy did not realize, however, was that such instruction, which included instruction in reading and writing, would fuel the articulation of print-based literacies to emancipation among the slaves and allow them to deterritorialize the insidious and oppressive intent of religious instruction and to reterritorialize it as a desiring machine intent on resisting the oppressive practices of slave masters (Rawick, 1978).

Deterritorializing oppression was central virtually to all religious practices within the African-American slave community. Slaves frequently risked corporal punishment, even death, to carry out their religious observances in the ways they preferred. While resistance to oppression was part of the dispersed religious orientation of African-American slaves, much resistance was organized in those communities where there were literate slave preachers. In this regard, Turner (1973) found that, compared with nonliterate preachers, literate Black preachers led their congregations to look for lines of flight and to engage in resistance. Less literate preachers more often encouraged their followers to work within the lines of articulation of the institution of slavery and to wait for the afterlife for freedom and justice. Also worth noting here is the fact that the three most historically prominent and ambitious slave uprisings were led by literate preachers, slave and free, at the top of their leadership cadre (Denmark Vesey, Gabriel Prosser, and Nat Turner). Together, these preachers and their often small, dispersed, and mobile congregations struggled against their own brutalization, exploitation, and treatment as subhumans by becoming literate and struggling to become free (Rawick, 1978).

Importantly for the sake of characterizing resistance in terms of the principles of pack multiplicities, preachers often occupied multiple roles—leaders, father figures, examples, and guides, and their leadership styles were less centralized than mobile and dispersed. Part of what made literate preachers effective was a heightened ability to discriminate between arborescent and rhizomatic formations, what in their minds, were considered to be genuine religious beliefs rather than beliefs designed to articulate slaves to oppression (Boggs, 1972/1863; Cheek, 1970). Literate preachers thus tended to resist whatever the masters or White clergy advocated knowing that it served the interest of a closed and repressive structure. They also mapped out liberation theologies based on their alternative readings of the Bible. In contrast, illiterate or less literate preachers tended to preach what the slave masters told them to preach.

Partially through the influence of literate preachers, the ability to read and write became almost indistinguishable from the ability to see the injustice of one's fate and to struggle for freedom. Connecting reading, writing, and freedom had the effect of making slavery intolerable and of seeking out lines of flight, sometimes by whatever means necessary. In the words of Gates (1987) "the first slave to read was the first to run away" (p. x).

While the literate preacher was sometimes the catalyst for viewing reading and writing mechanisms of transgression and transformation, it was the multiple, dispersed activity of individual slaves and small groups of slaves that really enabled literate values and practices to be marshaled in the interest of asignifying rupture and deterritorialization. In this regard, preachers were not leaders in the traditional sense of the term as much as they were "out in front" of the pack. Pack leadership was more a continuous mobilization of positions than a centralized and centralizing force. As pack members, each and every slave was always both responsible for "guarding" a sector while also dependent on the whole pack for its survival. "Each [took] care of himself at the same time as participating in the band" (Deleuze & Guattari, 1987, p. 33). Such a mode of operation may be read off many narratives written by slaves including that of Hall (1972/1863):

> ... the more I read, the more I fought against slavery. Finally, I thought I would make an attempt to get free, and have liberty or death.... I told one of my brothers that I was going to be free. He was the only one of my mother's fifteen children that I had any confidence in, for all the rest believed everything the white man told them. He had learned to read, as I had, and knew better. (pp. 416–417)

Similarly, Martin (1972/1867) provided an account of other clever practices to which he resorted to in order to obtain reading instruction from the White children who refused to teach him:

> Having nothing to do between meals, I was made an errand-boy of the gamblers who infested Columbus.... [F]rom their conversation I learned that there were coloured people in some far off place called Canada who were free. I learned too, from seeing them reading and writing, that they could make paper and the little black marks on it talk.... For a long time I could not get it out of my head that the readers were talking to the paper.... When, however, it became a reality to me, I made up my mind to accomplish the feat myself. But when I asked the white boys with whom I played marbles to teach me how to read, they told me that the law would not allow it.
>
> But though the white boys would not teach me to read, they could not control or prevent the acquisition of a quick and retentive memory with which I was blessed, and by their bantering one another at spelling.... I learned to spell by sound before I knew by sight a single letter in the alphabet. (p. 709)

This abiding investment in print literacies led slaves to make extreme personal sacrifices to learn to read and write and sometimes to teach other slaves these skills as well (Bellamy, 1971; Douglass, 1987/1845; Genovese,

1974; Martin, 1972/1867). The breadth and intensity of the slaves' investment in print literacies articulated reading and writing to emancipatory
desires in a way that made print literacies almost indistinguishable from the
desire to become free.

That the articulation of print-base literacies and freedom was simultaneously personal and collective was even more evident in accounts by or about
slave women, whose subversive activities were both more private and more
communal that those of slave men. "Black men... excelled in the art of poetic
preaching in the male dominated church, but in the church of the home... it
was black women who preached" (hooks, 1988, p. 5). Whereas individualism
and the assertion of individual rights was always at least a clear subtext in
narratives by and about slave men, narratives by and about slave women
always foregrounded the welfare of family and community. The central
protagonists in these accounts were usually African-American mothers who
devoted their lives to their children's education and freedom through self-
sacrifice and a variety of subversive practices (Gates, 1988). Indeed, many of
the males who learned to read and write during slavery would not have done
so without the subversive and self-sacrificing activities of their mothers. Susan
Boggs (1972/1863), for example, described her efforts on behalf of her son's
(James Curry) education as follows: "I had my son taught to read and write
while I was there in a secret school, but I was always so busy getting money
to pay for it that I never learned to read myself" (p. 420).

For African-American women, then, the articulation of print literacies
and freedom was always also articulated to communal desires and agendas,
and it almost always operated as multiply driven ethical and pragmatic
singularities. Indeed, the fundamental social/familial orientation of slave
mothers precluded the association of print-based literacies with individual
concerns alone. African-American women slaves saw the welfare of their
children as their primary responsibility. They educated their children before
themselves, often secretly and at great risk. They refused to escape without
them, and when they did attempt escape, they did so within local, small,
dispersed, mobile, and temporary formations because formations with such
characteristics were most likely to be effective (Wallace, 1990). Finally, both
literacy learning by individuals and their escape to freedom were viewed by
women as inseparable from general welfare and transformation of the collective (Martin, 1972/1867). This intense articulation of the personal and the
communal coupled with the equally intense articulation of print literacies and
freedom suggests that slave women operated according to an even more fully
developed pack multiplicity orientation than slave men.

To summarize the argument developed in this section of the chapter, African-American slaves utilized the tactics of connection, heterogeneity, multiplicity, asignifying rupture, and cartography to acquire aural, visual, and print literacies (and thus freedom) by thoroughly exploiting the passages of opportunity or lines of flight that became visible to them despite the many ideological, legal, and practical barriers imposed by White society to prevent them from doing so. In their exploitation of these tactics, slaves often assembled as pack multiplicities. As individuals within packs, they seemed almost constantly attuned to possible lines of flight that crisscrossed an otherwise closed, repressive, and violent racial landscape. These lines of flight almost always involved oral and/or written forms of literacy, and these forms of literacy were almost always complexly articulated to European-American ideologies and the slaves desires for freedom and dignity. Most importantly, these articulations often created openings that immediately or eventually contributed to the restructuring of power relations between Whites and Blacks.

She Wolves in Cyberspace

A plethora of websites by, for, and about women has cropped up during the past decade or so. Some sites are separatist spaces, virtual equivalents of second-wave feminist consciousness raising groups such as Riot Grrls (http://www.techsploitation.com/socrates/riot.grrls.html). Others are online journals for women such as *Feminista!* (http://www.feminista.com). Many of these sites are spaces for women to gather to share ideas and advice, to inspire one another, and to celebrate womanhood, but, they are also flooded with advertising and other marketing tools aimed primarily at adolescent girls and young women (e.g., *Cybergrrl*, http://www.cybergrrl.com). Only a handful of sites seem to be spaces specifically set up for engaging in serious (if also fun) social and political work. Importantly for my purposes here, many of these sites seem to function as rhizomes and their participants as pack multiplicities.

For simplicity's sake and given of the space constraints of the chapter, I have chosen to describe and analyze just one of these sites. It is Mimi Nguyen's *exoticize this!* (http://members.aol.com/Critchicks), also known as *exoticize my fist!*. At the risk of exoticizing the site myself, it seems important to note that *exoticize this!* began as an:

> attempt to create a "virtual" community for asian american feminists—as well as act
> as a coalition-building tool to create networks with asian feminists abroad—in light
> of the void. but even more, i'm just one stop-over in a growing chain of awesome

feminists *period* on the web.... So this [site] will *always* be under construction... i'm so proud to be a part of this network. (http://members.aol.com/Critchicks/original.html)

This myth of origins, as well as the following additional snippets from Nguyen's "Original Statement," provide a sense of why I want to argue that this site functions according to principles of the rhizome and the pack:

> I got exceedingly irritated trying to find rad Asian/American women's work on the web and figured everybody else must be sick of it too. So much for the Web's "liberating" p.r.: typing "asian women" into search engines will get you about twelve million porno sites. I want substantive and feminist girlie action, not that kind of white-straight-male... neocolonialist fantasy crap. I want heavy theory mixed in with radical lesbionics, museum art installations and grubby print 'zines, and I want to find them all in one place!... This is an Asian American site. This is an Asian American feminist site. (http://members.aol.com/Critchicks/original.html)

In a side bar note, Nguyen goes on to advise the reader to "eat lots of noodles to nourish the revolutionary in you, then go forth in the world + kick ass, girlfriend!" As it has developed, the site has attracted and connected with many other "amazing women" as evidenced by the huge number of links that proliferate from *exoticize this!* in all directions. As promised, the site is always under construction and includes not only in-your-face, manifesto-like contributions from Nguyen, but also both popular and academic essays, reviews, and commentaries by her and others that are exceptionally smart, pithy, and even sublime. More than promised, the construction process is driven not only by Nguyen herself but also by contributions and suggestions from multiple site visitors and contributors. In fact, virtually anyone with Internet access and the desire to participate in the ongoing formation of the site may do so. And although Nguyen owns and manages the site, she does so with a light touch and in the spirit of dialogue and the celebration of diversity, though there are no links to antigay, misogynistic, or right-to-life sites. What results is an almost endless, intersecting, and transversing network constituted by a profusion to links to links to links, each of which is ever-changing. In other words, the site is "an acentered, nonhierarchical, nonsignifying system without [an overly authoritative] General and without an organizing memory or central automaton, defined [largely] by a circulation of states" (Deleuze & Guattari, 1987, p. 21). The site is "perpetually prolonging itself, breaking off and starting up again" (p. 20). It is "an essentially heterogeneous reality" that "evolves by subterranean stems and flows along river valleys or train tracks; it spreads like a patch of oil" (p. 7), and it does so in at least two ways. First, it is widely accessible on the web—always there, so to speak, with no specified shelf life and no signs of aging (other than lapses in activity and a lack of updates in some regions). Second, the site is constituted by an almost endless chain of connections that proceed unpredictably in all directions and produce seemingly endless configurations or assemblages. The following buttons constitute the homepage, for example: "politics + activists," "articles + essays," "pop culture," "academics," "allies + friends," "bibliographies," "books + authors," "zines- maga + otherwise," "art," "filmic interventions," "grrrls + personal pages." Each of these buttons links to numerous (often seemingly boundless) related sites. For example, "books and authors" links to the "bookshelf" at SAWNET (South Asian Women's NETwork), a comprehensive forum for those interested in South Asian women's issues. It is a well-organized and easy-to-navigate website with eighteen buttons ranging from women's organizations to children's books to academic articles to information on careers, grants, and funding, each of which lead to many links to other sites. One of these linked sites is "Kaya," a not-for-profit independent publisher of Asian and diasporic fiction, poetry, critical essays, art, and culture (http://www.kaya.com). Another linked site is "The Asian American Writers' Workshop," "a nonprofit organization dedicated to the creation, development, publication and dissemination of Asian American literature" (http://www.aaww.org/).

Despite the fact that "hey! this *third world women site* is owned by *mimi nguyen!*" and true to Nguyen's desire to cultivate difference and hybridity, *exoticize this!* is multiplicity multiplied having "neither subject nor object, only determinations, magnitudes, and dimensions that cannot increase in number without the multiplicity changing in nature" (Deleuze & Guattari, 1987, p. 8). Lines of articulation struggle with lines of flight, the organization of power fights against its disorganization to constitute the rhizome. The site is simultaneously an owned and managed entity, an invitation to dispersion, and dispersion itself as I will later show in my descriptions of small sectors of two sites linked to *exoticize this!*: The Feminist Theory Website and GROWL. On its first plane of dispersion, *exoticize this!* is constituted as dozens of links, which may satisfy some people's needs and desires for information, participation, and collective affiliation. Others, however, may want to move into second, third, or fourth planes of dispersion where new and different potentials for knowledge, activity, and pack membership may be found or created.

Asignifying rupture is a common dimension of *exoticize this!* In fact, the site's potential for negation is worn on its sleeve and indexed by the imperative subtext of the site's very title: "X-This, asshole!" (with obvious gestural accompaniment). The site is not so much about constructing coherence, meaning, and community as it is about decentering/disrupting/ deconstructing received traditions, representations, and practices of meaning, coherence, and community. The site is about the expansion proliferation of ideas and political action across space and time. *exoticize this!* thus celebrates constant disruption (both internally and externally) by lines of flight that constantly work against the ossifying potential of lines of articulation. As new links are added and old ones deleted, as contributors create consensus and dissensus, as old pathways are shut down and new ones opened up, the rhizome is broken and shattered in certain spots, but it starts up again, sometimes along old lines and sometimes along new ones. Movements and flows get rerouted around disruptions without a General governing them. Severed sections regenerate themselves and continue to grow, forming new lines, flows, and pathways. "Segmentary lines explode into a line of flight, but the line of flight is part of the rhizome. These lines always tie back to one another" (Deleuze & Guattari, 1987, p. 9). The processes of deterritorialization and reterritorialization are constantly at work. Among the spaces commonly deterritorialized are heterosexuality, traditional gender roles, apolitical orientations, and high culture. Among the spaces commonly reterritorialized are alternative sexualities, nontraditional gender roles, strategic radical politics, and popular culture. This kind of activity/activism thus suggests that it may be the more subversive and not the more egalitarian affordances of the Internet that constitute its greatest potential for rearticulating distributions of power and enacting social change. Importantly, this potential seems constitutively related to unique articulations among social, cultural, political, and technological capabilities and initiatives that are possible only (or at least more readily) in cyberspace.

exoticize this! is conjunctive as well as disjunctive. Because each of the links connected to *exoticize this!* is dynamic, the entire assemblage of links is exponentially dynamic. "[T]he fabric of the rhizome is conjunctive, and. . . and. . . and. . . ." (Deleuze & Guattari, 1987, p. 25). It connects "any point to any other point," operating "by variation, expansion, conquest, capture, offshoots" (Deleuze & Guattari, 1987, p. 21). As "a practical combination of a 'do it yourself' ethic—learned from punk and riot grrl—and years of feminist and leftist activism and theorizing" (http://members.aol.com/Critchicks), *exoticize this!* "ceaselessly establishes connections relative to the arts, sciences, and social struggles. As unlimited semiosis, the site is like a "tuber agglomerating very diverse acts, not only linguistic, but also perceptive, mimetic, gestural, and cognitive: there is no language itself, nor are there linguistic universals, only as a throng of dialects, patois, slangs and specialized languages" (Deleuze & Guattari, 1987, p. 7).

As participants assemble strategically in and across *exoticize this!* and the sites linked to it, they form packs that create new lines of articulation and expose new lines of flight. In relation to this point, Burbules (1998) has argued that Internet linkages are "associative relations that change, redefine, and enhance or restrict access to the information they comprise" (p.103). The possibilities for enhancing or restricting access through articulations are important for understanding how distributed collective action might occur in cyberspace. Bounded by no fixed territory, participants may follow "any particular line of association between distinct textual points" and thus produce "the nature of association this link implies" (p. 104). Like the double-coded language practices of African-American slaves, this process of cultural/collective production creates a temporary and tenuous pack multiplicity with a fictional but strategic identity politics from which to work toward social change. This fictional but strategic coherence may operate in many different ways. Participants may find useful information for academic or political work by navigating various "promising" pathways created by people with kindred interests. They may find camaraderie in difference. Participants may engage in conversations across huge divides of race, class, and sexual orientation. They may find publication outlets for their otherwise marginalized work, and this work may eventually become less marginal as has feminist and postcolonial work in print journals during the last two decades. Finally, participants may coalesce into various social formations around key issues or by constantly running into each other while traversing the same spaces, and these formations may engage in more focused political work. Whatever strategies are enacted toward whatever goals, "each takes care of himself at the same time as participating in the band" (Deleuze & Guattari, 1987, p. 33).

With respect to this point, the throng of heterogeneous discursive activity that constitutes *exoticize this!* is typically not the work of lone individuals but of pack multiplicities, which emerge, solidify, sometimes disband, and re-form in new ways. Although Nguyen may be found preaching to her pack on the site's homepage, the more heterogeneous and contingent nature of leadership within the site becomes unmistakable. In just a few clicks from the homepage, for example, The Feminist Theory Website (http://www.cddc.vt.edu/feminism/enin.htm) comes into view. Here, the voice of Mimi Nguyen is no longer "out in front." It has been replaced by the voice of Kristin Swithala. Later, the voices of Karen Adsit, David C. Jacobs, Christina Lee, and Jeremy Hunsinger mingle with Switala's as these scholars become a pack multiplicity successfully working to build coalitions of feminists the world over. Together and with others, for example, they have showcased 31 fields of feminism, 119 national/ethnic feminisms, and almost 100 individual published feminists. They have also created various collaborative projects within which feminists from many diverse cultures have worked together doing intellectual-political work.

Not surprisingly, some of the most explicit countersurveillance work and grassroots activist work accomplished within *exoticize this!* may be found by in the "politics and activists" section of the site. For example, a link to "The South Asian Women's Organizations" website yields listings from and links to similar sites all over the globe. Most of these sites afford opportunities for joining activist organizations or assisting them in doing their work. For example, through GROWL (Grass Roots Organizing for Welfare, http://www.ctwo.org/growl/), participants are recruited to write letters to senators and congress people in opposition to policies as diverse as the marriage promotion bill, the death penalty, and radio censorship or in support of legislation that would restore federal welfare laws, certain labor laws, and certain indigenous rights. As of January 7, 2003, the organization had effectively recruited 2,564,913 such letters. More importantly, GROWL has an impressive history of coalition building and success in affecting legislation and policy making through its letter-writing campaigns and other lobbying efforts.

That Internet communication figures importantly in these efforts is not a trivial matter. Information technologies literally reconfigure space and movement within and across space in ways that allow authorities to increasingly govern from a distance. Governing at a distance implies acting at a distance, which depends upon communicating at a distance. Conversely, those who are governed at a distance can also act (and react) at a distance through mobile information technologies such as the Internet. The notion that the Internet is a superhighway, then, is more than metaphorical. It is an exceedingly supple, fast, and efficient means for transporting and enacting culture and politics. Whereas double coding was a signature tactic of African-American slave packs, mastery over information flow, speed, agility, and mobility are signature tactics of the cyber packs that form on GROWL (and similar assemblages). They articulate these tactics to heterogeneous, multiply-driven ethical and pragmatic singularities to adapt and respond to new threats quickly and with intensity—recruiting thousands of petition signatures, for example, in a remarkably short span of time. They deterritorialize and reterritorialize both virtual and real space in ways and at speeds that the mass multiplicities of the state that "govern" them simply cannot keep up with. Although they may not have political pedigrees or be especially "pretty," these packs are passionate and powerful, and they often produce the political effects they desire. Theoretically, their effectivity suggests that information technologies like the Internet ultimately function in productive rather than repressive ways. Depending on how mass multiplicities are articulated to pack multiplicities, and depending on their use and their users, information technologies may work as steroids of state power or as technologies of freedom for everyday citizens or both.

Like all rhizomes, *exoticize this!* embodies ever present tensions between the forces of cartography and decalcomania. Cartography is most readily apparent in the sites more horizontal and transverse pathways of dispersion, and decalcomania is most readily apparent in its more vertical ones. Decalcomania may also be read off the ways in which Nguyen, herself, organizes links and provides commentary on various nodes and spaces within the site.

Moving more or less horizontally within the site, political activist spaces connect with spaces containing academic articles on a wide range of topics, which connect with spaces containing homegrown "zines" on both popular and esoteric subjects, which connect with spaces where skateboarder to share experiences and folklore:

> bryan and i met up with **alleyoop** (aka jenny kim) at her main hangout of old town **pasadena**. we were duly impressed that she knew **every kid** on the street that we pointed out... not just the ugly ones either! and during dinner she wowed me even more! not only is alley a cute skater, but she knows all about the **brady bunch** and **three's co**. i started whispering "**i need air! give me air!**" and she actually got the marcia brady ghost reference! and to top off her tv literacy, she was able to do the lines of **terry** from my favorite episode of three's company! i was literally dumbfounded. (http://www.blairmag.com/blair3/alleyoop/alley.html)

In this particular space, the "slacker" image of skate culture has been ruptured and replaced with a celebration of skating skill, everyday cognition, and media literacy prowess. Moving more or less vertically in relation to this space, however, one also encounters monologic sets of youth-produced texts representing skate culture, as well as equally monologic sets of academic accounts of skate culture as subculture.

Most pathways leading transversely from these skate culture spaces re-open possibilities for connection and heterogeneity. One may, for example, move into territories and interact with others to celebrate gay and lesbian culture, to join specific political alliances, to read and/or write political manifestos, to view and respond to graphic art or film, to chat with friends made along the way, to read bibliography after bibliography on a wide range of subjects, to contribute material to journals and e-zines, or to build a new site and get it connected to *exoticize this!*

Along the way however, one may choose to move more vertically for a while, in which case the forces of decalcomania within the site become more obvious again. Spaces devoted to feminist theory, for example, seem to have been constructed from within and to operate according to roughly the same cultural logic. Similarly, the popular "zines" accessible within and across linked sites are remarkably similar in genre and style if not in content. Additionally, if one attends closely to the "road signs" and "travelogue" provided by Nguyen, one's travels are more like an organized tour than an expedition into uncharted territory. As such, one gets to see and experience not all that may be seen and experienced but only that which Nguyen believes is most worthwhile. Of course, one may choose to leave the tour and go off on one's own at any time.

To summarize much of what I have said about *exoticize this!*, the site is a proliferating flow of text and activity that is continually reconstituted through tensions and transactions between the lines of flight and the lines of articulation that make it up. Importantly, these tensions and transactions articulate present realities to transgressive, liberatory politics. Thus, the site is rhetorical and pragmatic action, which, with its constant political subtexts and explicit disruptions, often succeeds at reconfiguring the politics and reality of gender, sexuality, ethnicity, literacy, and community. As an ever-expansive network of generative texts and practices that negotiate the interplay of fixity and fluidity, coherence and its loss, the site suggests both the possibility of coherent political community and the ultimate inadequacy of coherence as a signifying principle. Constituted partly as/by asignifying rupture, *exoticize this!* foregrounds the transformative power of the subversive (rather than the egalitarian) affordances of cyberspace. In place of "Can't we all just get along [and be a community]" it substitutes "Lets hook up, go out there, and 'kick some ass' rather than just worrying about who we are!" Disruption becomes a source of agency for participants/contributors on the site because agency on the site is construed not only as a matter of "finding one's own voice but also about intervening in discourses of the everyday and cultivating rhetorical tactics that make interruption and resistance an important part of any conversation" (Reynolds, 1998, p. 59). By interrupting and talking back (hooks, 1988), those who work/work on *exoticize this!* draw attention to their own marginalization as sensual-sexual-intellectual-literate-political beings, thus indexing a more pervasive politics of exclusion. They "use online literacy practices to transgress against conventional. . . boundaries, to achieve multiple goals, and to construct cyborgian, hybrid identities in the process of practicing online literacies" (Hawisher & Selfe, 2000, p. 281). One salient example of this potential realized is a journal entry in which Nguyen, herself, announces that she is not simply lesbian but bisexual and that she has a boyfriend. Over time, she celebrates this relationship in other journal entries. Importantly, however, this celebration does not eclipse or negate other kinds of sexualities and relationships, which are also validated in myriad ways and in myriad places on the site. Among other things, this becomes one small sign of the social fact that heterogeneity, multiplicity, transmogrification, the reconfiguration of binarisms, a refusal to abide by laws of the negative, and pragmatically utopian visions are all constitutive of the site.

In addition to drawing attention to the politics and practices of exclusion and its discontents, *exoticize this!* exhibits and promotes a multimedia, consumer-oriented awareness that is common to many Internet literacies. Importantly, these literacies often function as elusive and temporary textual politics. Clicking through the site requires participants to face this explicit textual politics (and its concomitant politics of explicitness) and urges them to adopt an in-your-face responsiveness toward them. In relation to this point, many spaces accessible on/through the site display the actions and effects of collaborative or collective political and pragmatic work. This work is often local. It is typically motivated by a sense of urgency. Its goals are not necessarily to produce long-lasting effects, even though this sometimes happens. And its leadership is supple, agile, mobile, and sometimes not even visible. *exoticize this!* is thus a kind of networked collective of political activists (and activist allies) who work individually and collectively through their (mostly) textual practices. They make full use of many information technologies to enact a kind of agency that fictionalizes stability and celebrates the kind of temporary positionality that Miller (1989) has argued seems requisite for effective political writing, resistance, and action from the margins. *exoticize this!* and the packs that form on it are Gramsci's "we" without guarantees. Their enactment of local situated literacy practices and literate subjectivities, along with the rupturing of hierarchical information flow, function as "collaborative interruptions" of the sort that have always been central to radical feminist work that has been effective at reconfiguring the politics and realities of gender, sexuality, ethnicity, and family in the public sphere. As with all pack multiplicities, the public identities and the particular kinds of identity politics of these cyber packs remains ambiguous.

This ambiguity is maintained largely because their textual practices and representations always invite reader (re)construction both through different articulations of links and through the extensive use of guest books, email contacts, webrings, commentaries, and the indexing of similar pages. Importantly, this ambiguity is a key reason why *exoticize this!* and similar radical feminist websites (as well as the specific packs that form on these sites) are politically important (and effective). Deterritorialization is a signature feature of all rhizomes and mobility and shifting identities are signature features of all packs. But their effectivity is also constitutively related to the fact that, like

African-American slaves with their double-coded speech, these rhizomes and packs work in the broad daylight of the public sphere. Their ambiguous and ambiguously networked texts and practices function as open challenges to the apparent hegemony of the Internet. Reading and writing become subversive practices, even though they may conform (at least in part) to the textual conventions of the public spaces of which they are a part. Web mistresses and web participants are social and political cyborgs. They are both insiders and outsiders. Moving across these positions allows them both to adopt and to subvert political strategies developed within the more arborescent social and political formations that largely constitute the public sphere. Other paradoxical deterritorializations and reterritorializations are relevant here as well. Web mistresses and participants sometimes generate fixed texts within fluid networks or fluid texts within fixed networks. In doing so, they create "third spaces" (Bhabha, 1994) by paradoxically articulating particular kinds of "identity politics" with an ideological resistance against any logic of essentialism or coherence. Like all rhizomes, *exoticize this!* and similar Internet formations are continually constituted both as responses and challenges to the networks of discourse and power that inform them. As such, they can function to rupture and redirect flows of cultural capital and control. And although increased commodification (e.g., pop-up advertising) and regulation (e.g., copyright legislation, anticontent laws, censorship) suggest that social and political activism on the Internet may become more difficult, radical feminist pack multiplicities may still engage in localized resistance by reading and writing open texts, creating open networks of information flow, acting strategically and with speed and intensity, and exploiting existing networks and structures in order to remain publicly visible and accessible.

Finally, if you multiply the transformative power of the many heterogeneous and connected spaces that constitute *exoticize this!*, then it becomes very clear that the site affords ways of thinking, acting, and being that have enormous potential for transformative and transgressive politics. The site is a complex articulation of diverse resources drawn from a wide array of domains, linked in multiple and complex ways, made accessible to the public, and constantly recreated through dialogue among its participants and technological innovation. It is a rhizomatic formation where arborescent boundaries are pushed, expanded, dismantled, and reassembled in ways that allow (even demand) political, social, and cultural recognition and response. Navigating the site affords access to lines of flight that are often invisible or inaccessible to most people through most common or popular information networks. The effects of addressing and being addressed by "others" within *exoticize this!* and of witnessing the local political work accomplished in and through the site are powerful testimony to the transformative potential of the rhizome and the pack.

Concluding Remarks

In various ways and to various degrees, social formations such as the ones I have described (or mentioned in passing) are rhizomatic pack multiplicities. Among other things, they deterritorialize systems of authority by disrupting, circumventing, or subverting instruments of surveillance and regulation, and they reterritorialize the spaces in which these instruments operate. Importantly for my purposes in this chapter, they also deploy literacy technologies to affiliate with and to communicate with others to form or join emerging packs. Without such technologies, would be members would not be able to assemble as packs, and packs would therefore never come into existence. These technologies are thus essential to the tactics of pack activity. Because these formations are engines of deterritorializing effects, they are marked as dangerous by institutional authorities, who continually (but usually with only limited success) try to find better ways to monitor and control them. This is why, in the title of this chapter, I refer to such formations as liminal literacy formations with political teeth.

Liminal literacy formations with political teeth are local, mobile, and agile. They involve transmogrification, multiple codings, utopian visions, and a commitment to intervening in reality and its relations of power to enact those visions. They also involve mapping the real to challenge and perhaps reconfigure the possibilities of reality. These formations use binaries strategically to create new and binaries that are more effective for egalitarian and transformative purposes . They reconfigure understandings of reality according to strategic political interests. They are understandable but not predictable. These formations generate action, thought, and desire by proliferation, juxtaposition, and disjunction rather than by subdivision and pyramidal hierarchization. They refuse to subscribe to old categories of the negative (law, limit, lack, repression) that are fundamental to Western thought and hegemony. Instead, they enact and celebrate the positive and multiple, difference over uniformity, flows over unities, mobile arrangements over stable systems. These formations do not engage in political activity to discredit any line of thought on speculative grounds alone. Instead, their political activity functions as an intensifier of thought, and their political analyses multiply the forms and domains available for the intervention of political action. These formations refuse a politics aimed at restoring the rights of individuals because they recognize the individual itself as a product of hegemonic regimes of power. Instead, they strive to "deindividualize" by means of multiplication, displacement, and diverse/diversifying combinations. They do not celebrate power or the will to power. Instead, they function as a constant force of deindividualization because they do not regard the group as an organic unit of hierarchized individuals but as individuals who are always already part of pack multiplicities and likely to join others. These formations operate according to an antimethod or antilogic. They regard discourse in terms of its dissolution into lines of flight and its organization into lines of articulation. In doing so, they open up new ways of understanding the world and therefore new ways of organizing political resistance. In short, their activity/activism is a constant flow of pedagogical politics and political pedagogy.

Among other things, liminal literacy formations with political teeth suggest the need to interrogate and reimagine key tropes of political action and identity politics such as "community." In this regard, Harris (1997) suggested that the construct of a "public" may be more politically useful that the construct of a "community" for understanding how intellectual, social, and political work actually gets done, especially in the current historical epoch. From his perspective, a public:

> refers not to a group of people (like community) but to a kind of space and process, a point of contact that needs both to be created and continuously maintained.... Thinking in terms of public rather than communal life can give us a way of describing the sort of talk that takes place *across* borders and constituencies. It suggests that we speak as public intellectuals when we talk with strangers rather than with the members of our own communities and disciplines (or of our own interdisciplinary cliques). (pp. 108–109)

A public, then, involves the articulation of "points of contact" to create nonessential spaces that spawn both interaction and interruption and that create the kind of fictionalized coherence necessary for loosely coupled collective subjectivities with political effectivity. "Each takes care of himself at the same time as participating in the band" (Deleuze & Guattari, 1987, p. 33). Within such spaces, people work to disarticulate traditional binaries such as identity/difference, public/private, local/global, and center/periphery, and to articulate more complex formations of the sort Gilroy (1993) has called "the changing same," with their polymorphic representations of identification, belonging, and collective effectivity. These formations and their representations are necessarily temporary and contingent because they do not depend upon arborescent structures or principles for their existence. For example, they are not centralized or centralizing but dispersed and dispersing. They are motivated by political goals and effectivity rather than affiliation or a sense of transcendent similarity. And they do not depend upon permanent and recognizable signs of power and stability but on the constant flow and articulation of multiply driven ethical and pragmatic singularities.

This re-visioning of collective or community as a "public" suggests that liminal literacy formations with political teeth have some implications for literacy pedagogy. Among other things, such formations show how people can discover or create possibilities for local resistance and exploit those possibilities by creating provisional, polymorphic texts and practices, by deploying those texts and practices within extant systems and structures, and by making those texts and practices public without really being public. Liminal literacy pedagogies of this sort are a lot like what Giroux and Shannon (1997) called "performative pedagogies." Performative pedagogies open up "spaces that affirm the contextual and specific while simultaneously recognizing the ways in which such spaces are shot through with issues of power" (p. 4). Connection. "At stake here is a notion of the performative that provides diverse theoretical tools for educators and cultural workers to move within and across disciplinary, political, and cultural borders that allow them to address the challenges presented within multiple public spheres, including the academy" (p. 4). Heterogeneity and multiplicity. Performative pedagogies "refuse closure, insist on combining theoretical rigor and social relevance, and embrace commitment as a point of temporary attachment that allows educators and cultural critics to take a position without standing still" (p. 4). Asignifying rupture. Perhaps most important, performative pedagogies "reject any rendering of the pedagogical that conveniently edits out the difficulties and struggles posed by institutional constraints, historical processes, competing social identities, and the expansive reach of transnational capitalism" (p. 4–5). Decalcomania and cartography. Finally, like all rhizomatic social formations, performative pedagogical publics are necessarily contingent, multiple, heterogeneous, and loosely coupled. Their existence and effectivity depend less on a politics of affiliation than on spatial-temporal-discursive coincidence and immediate and often transitory ethical and political goals. People who choose to form of join these "publics" maintain contingent, ambiguous, and often anonymous forms of participation. These "publics" are held together by shifting and mobile points of contact. Whatever stability they have is temporary—created to enact specific political/pedagogical actions and activities and then dispersed. Finally, these "publics" exist primarily to work within hegemonic regimes of power and truth in order to subvert, resist, and change them.

References

Aptheker, H. (1943). *American Negro slave revolts*. New York: International Publisher.

The Asian American Writers' Workshop. Retrieved January 7, 2003, from http://www.aaww.org.

Bellamy, D. D. (1971). The education of Blacks in Missouri prior to 1861. *Journal of Negro History, 56*, 143–155.

Benberry, C. (2000). *A piece of my soul: Quilts by Black Arkansans*. Fayetteville: The University of Arkansas Press.

Best, S., & Kellner, D. (1991). *Postmodern theory: Critical interrogations*. New York: The Guilford Press.

Bhabha, H. K. (1994). *The location of culture*. New York: Routledge.

Blair Magazine, 3. Retrieved January 17, 2003, from http://www.blairmag.com/blair3/alleyoop/alley.html.

Blassingame, J. W. (1972). *The slave community: Plantation life in the antebellum south*. New York: Oxford University Press.

Boggs, S. (1972/1863). [Interview with American Freedmen's Inquiry Commission]. In J. W. Blassingame (Ed.), *Slave testimony: Two centuries of letters, speeches, interviews and autobiographies* (pp. 418–421). Baton Rouge: Louisiana State University Press.

Bullock, H. A. (1967). *History of Negro education in the south from 1619 to the present*. Cambridge, MA: Harvard University Press.

Burbules, N. C. (1998). Rhetorics of the web: Hyperreading and critical literacy. In I. Snyder (Ed.), *Page to screen: Taking literacy into the electronic era* (pp. 102–122). New York: Routledge.

Cheek, W. F. (1970). *Black resistance before the Civil War*. Beverly Hills, CA: Glencoe Press.

Cybergrrl. Retrieved January 7, 2003, from http://www.cybergrrl.com.

de Certeau, M. (1984). *The practice of everyday life*. Berkeley: University of California Press.

Deleuze, G., & Guattari, F. (1987). *A thousand plateaus: Capitalism & schizophrenia* (B. Massumi, Trans.). Minneapolis: University of Minnesota Press.

Douglass, F. (1987/1845). Narrative of the life of Frederick Douglass, an African slave. In H. L. Gates (Ed.), *The classic slave narratives* (pp. 243–332). Chicago: Mentor.

Faust, D. G. (1980). Culture, conflict, and community: The meaning of power on an antebellum plantation. In P. Finkelman (Ed.), *The culture and community of slavery* (pp. 83–97). New York: Garland Publishing.

Feminista! Retrieved November 15, 2002, from http://www.feminista.com.

The Feminist Theory Website. Retrieved November 1, 2002, from http://www.cddc.vt.edu/feminism/enin.htm.

Gates, H. L. (1985). Editor's introduction: Writing race and the difference it makes. *Critical Inquiry, 12*, 1–20.

Gates, H. L. (Ed.). (1987). *The classic slave narratives*. New York: New American Library.

Gates, H. L. (Ed.). (1988). *Six women's slave narratives*. New York: Oxford University Press.

Genovese, E. D. (1974). *Roll Jordan roll: The world the slaves made*. New York: Pantheon Books.

Gilmore, A. T. (1978). *Revisiting Blassingame's the slave community: The scholars respond*. Westport, CT: Greenwood Press.

Gilroy, P. (1993). *The Black Atlantic: Modernity and double consciousness*. Cambridge, MA: Harvard University Press.

Giroux, H. A., & Shannon, P. (1997). Cultural studies and pedagogy as performative practice: Toward an introduction. In H. A. Giroux & P. Shannon (Eds.), *Education and cultural studies: Toward a performative practice* (pp. 1–9). New York: Routledge.

Gramsci, A. (1971). *Selections from the prison notebooks* (Q. Hoare & G. N. Smith, Trans.). New York: International Publishers.

GROWL (Grass Roots Organizing for Welfare). Retrieved November 7, 2002, from http://www.ctwo.org/growl.

Hall, C. H. (1972/1863). [Interviewed by American Freedmen's Inquiry Commission]. In J.W. Blassingame (Ed.), *Slave testimony: Two centuries of letters, speeches, interviews and autobiographies* (pp. 416–417). Baton Rouge: Louisiana State University Press.

Hall, S. (1986). On postmodernism and articulation: An interview. *Journal of Communication Inquiry, 10*, 56–59.

Harris, V. J. (1997). *A teaching subject: Composition since 1966*. Upper Saddle River, NJ: Prentice-Hall.

Hawisher, G. E., & Selfe, C. L. (2000). Inventing postmodern identities: Hybrid and transgressive literacy practices on the web. In G. E. Hawisher & C. L. Selfe (Eds.), *Global literacies and the world-wide web* (pp. 277–289). New York: Routledge.

hooks, b. (1988). *Talking back: Thinking feminist, thinking Black*. Boston: South End Press.

Joyner, C. (1986). History as ritual: Rites of power and resistance on the slave plantation. In P. Finkelman (Ed.), *The culture and community of slavery* (pp. 1–9). New York: Garland Publishing.

Kaya:: A Publisher of Asian/Diasphoric Literature and Culture. Retrieved October 27, 2002, from http://www.kaya.com.

Martin, S. (1972/1867). [Autobiography Written for Good Words]. In J. W. Blassingame (Ed.), *Slave testimony: Two centuries of letters, speeches, interviews, and autobiographies* (pp. 702–735). Baton Rouge: Louisiana State University Press.

Miller, S. (1989). *Rescuing the subject: A critical introduction to rhetoric and the writer*. Carbondale: Southern Illinois University Press.

Miller, T. (1998). *The well-tempered self: Citizenship, culture, and the postmodern subject*. Baltimore, MD: The Johns Hopkins University Press.

Nguyen, M. (2002). *exoticize this!* Retrieved September 1, 2002, from http://members.aol.com/Critchicks/.

Pathways to Freedom: Maryland & The Underground Railroad. Retrieved August 17, 2002, from http://www.mpt.org/learningworks/pathwaystofreedom.

Rawick, G. P. (1978). Some notes on a social analysis of slavery: A critique and assessment of the slave community. In A. L. Gilmore (Ed.), *Revisiting Blassingame's slave community* (pp. 17–26). Westport, CT: Greenwood Press.

Reynolds, N. (1998). Interrupting our way to agency: Feminist cultural studies and composition. In S. C. Jarratt & L. Worsham (Eds.), *Feminism and composition studies: In other words* (pp. 58–73). New York: Modern Language Association.

Riot Grrls. Retrieved December 11, 2002, from http://www.techsploitation.com/socrates/riot.grrls.html.

Scott, D. (Producer) & Cundieff, R. (Director). (1994). *Fear of a black hat* [Motion picture]. United States: Samuel Goldwyn Company.

Sherman, R. E. (Producer) & Peckinpah, S. (Director). (1978). *Convoy* [Motion picture]. United States: EMI/United Artists.

South Asian Women's NETwork. Retrieved November 7, 2002, from http://www.umiacs.umd.edu/users/sawweb/sawnet.

Thompson, H. S. (1966). *Hell's Angels: A strange and terrible saga*. New York: Ballantine Books.

Tobin, J. L., & Dobard, R. G. (1998). *Hidden in plain view: The secret story of quilts and the underground railroad*. New York: Random House.

Turner, R. E. (1973). The Black minister: Uncle Tom or abolitionist? *Phylon, 34,* 86–95.

Volosinov, V. (1973). *Marxism and the philosophy of language* (L. Matejka & I. R. Titunik, Trans.). Cambridge, MA: Harvard University Press.

Wallace, M. (1990). *Invisibility blues: From pop to theory.* New York: Verso.

Wright, G. L. (2001). Critique: *Hidden in plain view: The secret story of quilts and the underground railroad.* Retrieved January 10, 2003, from http://historiccamdencounty.com/ ccnews11_doc_01a.shtml.

CONTRIBUTORS

MARGARET CARMODY HAGOOD is an Assistant Professor of Literacy in the School of Education at the College of Charleston in Charleston, South Carolina.

ELIZABETH HIRST is a Lecturer in Literacy and Language Education in the School of Education and Professional Studies at Griffith University in the Gold Coast, Queensland, Australia.

GEORGE KAMBERELIS is an Associate Professor of Education in the Department of Reading at the University at Albany, State University of New York.

KEVIN M. LEANDER is an Assistant Professor in the Department of Teaching and Learning at Vanderbilt University.

ELIZABETH BIRR MOJE is an Associate Professor of Literacy, Language, and Culture and the Joint Program in English and Education in the Educational Studies Program at the University of Michigan.

MARGARET SHEEHY is an Assistant Professor of Education in the Department of Reading at the University at Albany, State University of New York.

EDWARD W. SOJA is a Professor of Urban Planning at the University of California, Los Angeles.

ANITA WILSON is a Spencer Post-Doctoral Fellow at the Lancaster Literacy Research Centre, Linguistics Department, Lancaster University, UK.

AUTHOR INDEX

SUBJECT INDEX

208

Colin Lankshear, Michele Knobel,
Chris Bigum, & Michael Peters
General Editors

New literacies and new knowledges are being invented "in the streets" as people from all walks of life wrestle with new technologies, shifting values, changing institutions, and new structures of personality and temperament emerging in a global informational age. These new literacies and ways of knowing remain absent from classrooms. Many education administrators, teachers, teacher educators, and academics seem largely unaware of them. Others actively oppose them. Yet, they increasingly shape the engagements and worlds of young people in societies like our own. The *New Literacies and Digital Epistemologies* series will explore this terrain with a view to informing educational theory and practice in constructively critical ways.

For further information about the series and submitting manuscripts, please contact:

Michele Knobel & Colin Lankshear
Montclair State University
Dept of Education
210 Finley Hall
Montclair, NJ 07043
michele@coatepec.net

To order other books in this series, please contact our Customer Service Department at:

(800) 770-LANG (within the U.S.)
(212) 647-7706 (outside the U.S.)
(212) 647-7707 FAX

Or browse online by series at:

www.peterlangusa.com